MOTORCYCLE
FUEL
INJECTION
HANDBOOK

MOTORCYCLE
FUEL INJECTION
HANDBOOK

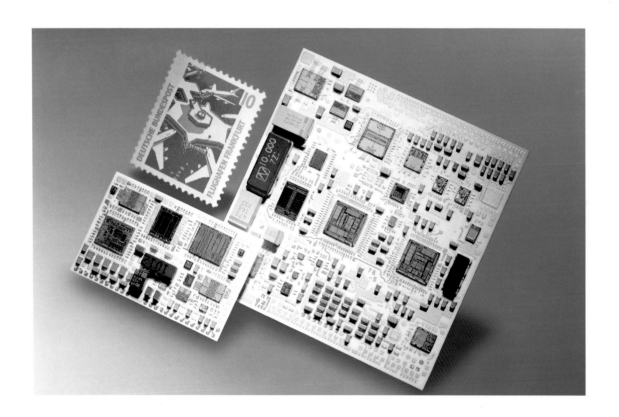

Adam Wade

MOTORBOOKS
INTERNATIONAL

First published in 2004 by Motorbooks International, an imprint of MBI Publishing Company, 380 Jackson Street, Suite 200, St. Paul, MN 55101-3885 USA

MBI Publishing Company books are also available at discounts in bulk quantity for industrial or sales-promotional use. For details write to Special Sales Manager at Motorbooks International Wholesalers & Distributors, 380 Jackson Street, Suite 200, St. Paul, MN 55101-3885 USA

Library of Congress Cataloging-in-Publication DataAvailable
ISBN 0-7603-1635-X

Edited by Peter Schletty
Designed by Chris Fayers

Printed in China

CONTENTS

The Author

Adam Wade spent a number of years as both an automotive mechanic specializing in fuel injection and an automobile restorer before his riding bug pushed his career over to the world of motorcycles. In the 10 years since then, he has worked for dealerships large and small in varying capacities, has been a successful AMA Pro Racing mechanic, and has worked for Emgo, Aprilia, and Factory Pro Tuning. He is currently a tech author and photographer for *Dual Sport News*, and is also a successful freelance motorsports photographer. He hand rolls his own cigarettes, and he prefers riding alone and with no particular destination to group rides. He chose a black-and-white jacket photo to help hide the fact that, at 35, he is noticeably graying. He also fights fibromyalgia daily.

Dedication

To Bevan—the future belongs to you. Grab hold.

To Dave Anker and Eric Leighton, for giving me chances to show I could do it.

To Marc Salvisberg, for teaching me that you can't usually find the right answer in a textbook full of theory.

To Jamie Bowman. I hope you're tearing it up with Joey Dunlop and Barry Sheene somewhere, my friend.

And to Dave, for saying he would buy me dinner if I published the following list of BMW ECU modes: closiepoo loopiepoo, openiepoo loopiepoo, limp home modypooiepie.

PREFACE & ACKNOWLEDGMENTS

Technology. Every year it marches forward, changing everything it touches. Motorcycles are no exception; from the latest in dazzling factory race machines to the most exotic of show bikes, we eagerly await the shape of things to come. From mechanic to racer to regular enthusiast, we go to cycle shows and read the magazines to catch the scoop on the next wave.

Lighter, faster, safer, and more energy efficient—these are the shape of things to come. But magazines and bike shows send us an even bigger message: The future is here today, on showroom floors around the world. While perhaps not the dramatic show bikes draped with covers awaiting their unveiling, each year's production bikes display cutting-edge technology brought to mass production. Linked brakes, ABS, ceramics and high-tech coatings and composites, computer-optimized engine designs, and, of course, fuel injection.

More and more motorcycles are coming from the factory with fuel injection as standard equipment. Fuel-injected mass-market production models now come from manufacturers including Suzuki, Yamaha, Kawasaki, Honda, Harley-Davidson, Ducati, BMW, Aprilia, Laverda, MV Agusta, Cagiva, and Moto Guzzi. In fact, nearly every motorcycle company has at least one model with fuel injection in their dealers' showrooms.

But fuel injection is a world apart from the CV carburetors that have been used, and tuned, for decades. It's a whole new universe for mechanics, racers, tuners and consumers alike—a world of mysterious components, operations, and, occasionally, troubles. A range of sensors gathers information that we don't comprehend, and a black box with dozens of wires processes all of it while hidden under a metal or plastic shell. But, as with carburetors before fuel injection, you turn the throttle and the bike goes. What are the fuel injectors doing? How can we modify or repair something we don't understand? Anyone with interest in diagnosing, altering, or simply understanding these high-tech systems has a whole new field to learn.

The aim of this book is to provide a working knowledge of the concepts and operation of fuel injection: how it works, why it works, and why things are done a particular way with the systems we see today. In addition, you'll find a history of motorcycle EFI from the 1980s onward, along with a make-by-make overview of newer systems and how they function. There is coverage of the range of available aftermarket parts and tuning tools for motorcycle EFI, as well as a peek into the many worlds of motorcycle racing and how this technology has touched them. And last, you will gaze into the future of fuel injection and motorcycles. You will find a glossary and chart of abbreviations in the back, which at times even *I* make reference to.

If you want to understand how motorcycle fuel injection works, why it's designed as it is, or where it came from and where it's going, then this book was written for you.

WHY IS THIS BOOK EVEN HERE?

This book will be read by many different people from many different backgrounds. Each of you reading right now has a different set of ideas about how an engine works, what fuel injection does, and why things are done a certain way, not to mention what that way actually *is*.

My purpose in writing this book is to make you forget as much of that as possible. Because, time and again, I find myself talking to people who base their understanding of engines and EFI on gross misconceptions. You have to be able to let go of all that to understand what is *really* going on while you are busy twisting the throttle.

I don't want a single person reading this book to feel bad about this. It wasn't that long ago that *I* had fundamental misconceptions about some of those things, and I've been doing this for a living for the better part of 10 years now (longer if you include engines with four wheels to keep them off the ground). One should never be afraid to let go of misconceptions and replace them with correct information. That's the hallmark of a true professional.

So don't let your pride (or my pride!) get in your way. Question everything. If it doesn't make sense, then something is wrong with your mental model of how it works. Either a piece of the puzzle is wrong or a piece of the puzzle is missing. Your job as a thinker is to figure out which, and handle it. My job as author is to not only give you the pieces, but also to help you understand the principles that unify them in a coherent whole.

I should also take a moment to comment on the limitations of this book. As nice as it would be to cover every possible facet of every possible area, that's outside the scope of both my knowledge and the space constraints of the book. We won't even discuss the desires of my target audience!

That said, this book is to be largely about four-stroke motorcycles that were factory-equipped with some form of EFI (electronic fuel injection). There will be some discussion of adding EFI to motorcycles that did not originally have it, as well as aftermarket options and racing applications. If you came looking for ideas for a supercharged two-stroke EFI system to compete with Orbital, you'll have to wait for the next book or two to get your answers. This book is mainly for people with modern cruisers and sportbikes (which are the primary machines with factory EFI), people who want to modify or race them, people who need to fix them, and, of course, just plain old people who want to know how and why.

I always wanted to find books like this when I was younger and hungry to learn everything I could. Hopefully, I'll be able to provide someone with the sort of book I could never find when I was 14 years old and dying to know the answers to those two great questions: "How?" and "Why?"

ACKNOWLEDGMENTS

I would be remiss if I did not take some time to mention the many people who contributed information and assistance in the production of this book: John Deakin, for helping me think like a pilot, and for being someone else willing to share information regardless of popular opinion; Matt Walters, who provided me with ideas and tools to create the next book; Carl Toll, who shared ideas and excitement, as well as his GTS1000; Sid Young, Edward Helbling, David Vastag, Tim Marsteiner, and Maya, for sharing their photos and diagrams with me to help bring my words more to life; the fine people of the DIY-EFI mailing list, for sharing their knowledge and making me think; the GTS1000 mailing list and the Turbo Motorcycle International Owner's Association for connecting me with the people and bikes I wanted to see and the manuals I wanted to read; Steve Klose, Colin Goodall, Robert Mitchell, and others from the many turbo motorcycle websites

Most people reading this book will have many questions about fuel injection; that's probably why they picked up this book in the first place. Learning about the inner workings of your machine can spare you from endless trouble and confusion. Much better to prepare yourself in advance by reading this book than to try and diagnose a fuel injection fault in the middle of lane-splitting through rush hour traffic!

who helped with contacts and information; Lorcan Parnell and the good people of 750turbo.com for helping me decipher the cryptic Kawasaki "race mode" instructions on the GPz750 Turbo; Greg Goss, for having the daring to disassemble two vintage fuel injection computers and let me ride a CX500 Turbo (which I had no choice but to purchase, I loved it so much); Matt Keebler, for letting me photograph and then cut up his Power Commander; and my editors (of course) Darwin Holmstrom and Peter Schletty, for their patience, encouragement, and assistance in turning this book from an idea into a reality. Heal that ankle, Darwin!

To the companies and businesses (and the people from them) that generously shared their products, information, and time with me: Don Church of Kawasaki (to whom I will forever be indebted for his generous and rapid responses to my requests for information and images); Phil Warth and Keith from CAPS (for their timely assistance with Kawasaki press images); Ken Cotzin (formerly) of Motul; Shane Tecklenburg and Marc White of MoTeC; Ammar Bazzaz of Bazzaz Performance Design; Russ Collins of RC Engineering; Stuart Hilborn of Hilborn Fuel Injection; Scott Winn of Cagiva USA and Fast by Ferracci; Dale Wells and James Hazen of Optimum Power Technology; Allen Alvarez of Daytona Twin Tec; GP Motorcycles of San Diego, California; Alba Action Sports of Poway, California; Fuzzy and the great mechanics at San Diego Harley-Davidson/Buell; and all the other people and businesses that have done so much to make this book happen.

I also have to thank Johnny Prato and David Vastag for reminding me why I was doing this (and reminding me that I *could*!), and Maya, for spending late nights poring over mysterious graphs in Photoshop. To Tim and Donna Moles, for a place to stay, late-night anime, and being all-around great people; and to Tia, Kym, Bear, Wendy, Eyeball, Spider, and the rest of the Denver contingent of the UTMC, for companionship, cheer, coffee, and something to ride. To Frank Hoppen, for keeping me busy, teaching me a great deal, and getting me started on my future. To Larry Niven, for giving me a much-needed kick in the butt 10 years ago (which he has probably long since forgotten). To Keith Code, for teaching me so much about motorcycles, business operations, and life. And to David M. Bailey, for showing us all how it's done.

And to some of the people who got me (at least some part of the way) this far in life: Mikie Leister (AFM #256), Bradley Maris, Theresa Gonzalez, Laura Bailey, and so many more from past and present.

To Soul Coughing, Steely Dan, The Beta Band, Crystal Method, and Thomas Dolby for providing me with inspiration and keeping me awake on late nights.

And the people who I cannot here name, but who have all contributed to my life and this book in ways they know in their hearts.

Modern motorcycles are required to meet many different requirements on many different levels. Some of those priorities conflict, which requires the engineers and designers to work out the details of how and where they wish to compromise. Even high-dollar exotic motorcycles like the Ducatis pictured here have had design goals plotted out and weighed, just as with workhorse models. Motorcycles courtesy of GP Motorcycles

DOWN TO BUSINESS

I know you're all eager to learn the details of how and why EFI does what it does. But before we begin, we're going to have to start with a fundamental understanding of what a four-stroke engine does, and how it does it. Now, now . . . no grumbling! I promise that you need to know at least as much as I tell you here to really understand how fuel injection works.

Those of you who have the time and inclination should take the time to read what is possibly the best and most technically detailed and correct book ever written on the subject of four-stroke motorcycle engines, their ancillaries, and their principles of operation: *Sportbike Performance Handbook* by Kevin Cameron. My overview here will be brief and direct, but Cameron's excellent book will give you details that will bring the book you now hold into much sharper focus. And that's not to mention the excellent sections in his book on suspension, chassis, handling and tires, and so much more. I can't recommend it enough to anyone interested in how a motorcycle works, and how to make it work better.

Whether you read Kevin's book or not, it's now time to tackle the purpose and principles of a fuel system. If you're well-read in the principles of four-stroke engine operation, consider this a refresher.

WHAT FUEL DELIVERY DOES

This may seem like a ridiculously simple topic. "Duh, a fuel delivery system takes fuel from the tank and stuffs it into the engine," you may be saying to me. And that is, of course, what happens. But there is a difference between a complex, multi-sensor EFI system, with a sophisticated engine computer controlling injector timing and spark, and the first primitive carburetors. So we continually have to *look deeper* while examining this or any other system or subject.

Even carburetors are very complex when you look at the various pieces and how they all work together to get the job done. In some sense, EFI is much more complicated—but it can be as simple or as complicated as the designer wants it to be. Everything depends on the *goals* of the design. But like the designers, we need to understand the basic principles to formulate our plan for achieving our goals and for determining whether they are realistic or not.

Fuel delivery does a heck of a lot more than just move fuel. Its most important task is to *meter* the fuel—to control when and where fuel is delivered and to determine how much is provided to the engine. There are a variety of approaches we can take and a variety of tools we can utilize, but, ultimately, that's our primary concern.

This may seem like a simple task. But let's consider for a minute that under any given set of engine conditions, there are typically three possible useful mixture peaks: one for best power, one for best fuel economy, and one to best feed a catalytic converter (and that's not to mention the many other factors that go into determining the ultimate expression of any of those things). How do we decide which to pick? Or perhaps we should pick something in between so we end up trading off our benefits in a way that better suits our goals.

As with everything else in this book, and in all areas of motorcycle design and modification, the key word is going to be *compromise*. How we (or the designers) figure out what makes best sense for those compromises, depending on our (or their) goals, is something we will examine and discuss throughout the course of this book. While we go, we will spend a fair amount of our time thinking about why motorcycle manufacturers chose the compromises they have chosen in the stock systems found on motorcycles over the past 25 years.

I want you to look over the next fuel-injected bike you ride and ask yourself, "Why did they do that? What compromises fit their goals? How do my goals differ and why?"

THE TWO IMPORTANT NUMBERS
FROM AN ENGINE

"Wow," you must be saying. "He's starting off this chapter about the boring ol' engine and how it works (which I am sure I already know) with there being just two numbers that are important! Well, I already know all about torque and horsepower, so I guess I can just skip right on to the next chapter."

Wouldn't it be nice if life were that simple? You probably wouldn't need this book, for instance. Every block would have at least one engine tuner on it, and it would be nearly impossible to get bad results. If you've even tried so much as having someone tune a set of motorcycle carburetors for you after installing an exhaust, though, you know better. It seems like the engine is a huge tangle of confusing, mysterious, conflicting bits and pieces that you need a four-gas analyzer and a Ph.D. to understand.

The good news is that it's not some black art that you will never learn without an apprentice hat. The bad news is that you have to start with a few ideas that are rather remote from the final output (torque curve, fuel consumption, etc.), and then draw some lines to interconnect things. But I promise you it's worth the effort. Once you get a handle on these concepts, not only will you understand what EFI is modeling in its maps and calculations,

Tuning a motorcycle for best performance takes knowledge and skill, even with the precise control of EFI. Understanding how each system contributes to the whole is essential for consistent good results. Here, a GSX-R750 is readied for racing on the AMA circuit.

you'll understand how changing the intake or exhaust may affect your machine, why engines idle roughly with big cams, and you'll even be able to diagnose starting and running problems with knowledge and facts, in addition to the experience you now have.

In any case, back to those two important numbers. You did remember we were talking about those, yes? Well, the two numbers that we really care about when we're working to make the best mixture and the best power, economy, or emissions are not horsepower and torque. Not even fuel/air ratio. The real players in this equation are volumetric efficiency (VE) and thermal efficiency.

Volumetric Efficiency

If you have read much about four-stroke engines, you have probably seen reference to VE before. But what is it? Well, it's a reference to how much *air mass* ends up in the cylinder at a given rpm, when compared to a reference value (100 percent) of the cylinder's volume at BDC (bottom dead center) multiplied by the density of atmospheric air.

In other words, if you were to take a single-cylinder engine and turn it over by hand until it was at BDC on the intake stroke, the mass of the air inside the cylinder would be our reference. The *volume* of the cylinder has been filled as full as it can be, based on the "engine" of atmospheric pressure pushing it into our cylinder. And if the engine can trap 100 percent of that air mass at a given engine speed when it is running, it is said to have 100 percent volumetric efficiency under those conditions. With supercharging, ram air, or tuning of the intake and exhaust, it is possible to exceed 100 percent VE, sometimes by a good bit.

A lot of different factors affect VE. Most are in the intake or exhaust system, but the cam timing and the shape of the combustion chamber also play a part. What may not be clear is *why* VE is so important. It's important because VE controls how much power you can make. Volumetric efficiency tells you how many molecules of air end up inside the combustion chamber to be burned, right? Well, think about this: it takes about 10,000 gallons of air to completely burn one gallon of fuel. The stoichiometric (chemically ideal) air/fuel ratio is by mass, not by volume. Fuel is *much* denser in its liquid state than air is. So we are limited in our power delivery not by how much fuel we can deliver, but by how much air we can get into the combustion chamber (and keep there). It's also why some racing fuels are oxygenated, bringing extra oxygen into the cylinder, but in a denser form, so we can make more power.

I'll come back to VE in a moment, when I start talking about the intake and exhaust systems and the important role they play. But first I want to cover thermal efficiency.

Thermal Efficiency

Perhaps even more important than VE is thermal efficiency. What good does it do to cram a lot of air into the combustion chamber if we waste the heat energy we get from burning it? After all, that heat energy is what we turn into useful work with the pistons and crankshaft.

Obviously the gases that come out the tailpipe are warmer than ambient temperature, so there's some of our combustion heat lost. Our cylinder fins (or radiator, if we are water-cooled) also get hot, so there goes some more heat. Now both of those "wastes" of heat have some positive effects, so we can't say they are automatically bad things.

The materials from which the engine is made are generally metals, and one of the properties of many metals is that they start to lose their strength at a certain temperature. If you go past that

temperature, they get soft and eventually melt. That's what causes the holes you might see in piston crowns from engines that have been detonating. So it's important we keep the temperatures in the metal components themselves below a certain temperature to make the engine last a long time. The heat loss helps maintain an optimal temperature.

Also, the combustion chamber walls are the coolest areas in the combustion chamber. Since gasoline needs a lot of heat to burn (which can be provided by increasing either pressure or temperature), a mixture that is right up against cool combustion chamber walls will often not burn. In fact, in a really cold engine, wet fuel can end up on the walls and not evaporate, washing oil off the rings (which dilutes the oil, causes engine wear, and raises hydrocarbon emissions). So we want the combustion chamber surface to be fairly hot, but not *too* hot—we use the cooling system to regulate that.

With exhaust gases, the heat contained in them makes them expand as well. This raises their pressure and helps push them out the tailpipe. This expansion effect is used to our advantage in helping to get more of the exhaust gases out of the cylinder before the exhaust valve closes. This is one of the reasons that some racers use header wrap—it keeps the heat in the exhaust instead of letting it radiate out through the metal in the exhaust system. This increases exhaust velocity, which improves scavenging and enhances pressure pulse tuning.

These things are usually pretty well fixed by design criteria. We can manipulate them with header wrap or a different thermostat, and it is the combustion chamber wall temperature issue that determines the temperature for peak power. Again, we have the compromise between throwing away heat energy and delivering more in the first place from more complete combustion.

What is not fixed for the purposes of this book is burn speed. Ideally, we would like our fuel to burn instantaneously, right at the best crank angle for the peak pressure pulse (PPP)—this would be the point with the best mechanical advantage on the crank. Unfortunately, the pressure rise from burning the fuel that fast would be so severe that it would blow the engine to pieces in just a few seconds. Instead, we ignite the mixture *before* we even get to top dead center (TDC). The burn starts as a small kernel around the spark plug, and it speeds up both its rate of pressure increase and the rate at which it burns (from flame front expansion), and this is how we get our peak pressure at about the right crank angle for best power.

On the one hand, we take away some of the engine's power by forcing the piston to work against the start of the flame front; but if the PPP occurs too late, the volume of the cylinder will be expanding too quickly to develop a lot of pressure to push the piston downward. So we find a compromise between late ignition and late PPP—this compromise is typically at the point of best power.

Spark advance plays a part here, but even more important is burn rate. There are many things that affect burn rate, including mixture and charge density (how dense the mixture is at TDC). We will talk throughout this section about things that affect charge density and burn rate, and how we (or the OEMs [original equipment manufacturers]) strike compromises between these and other factors to achieve our (or their) goals.

THE FOUNDATION IS LAID

Now that we have these abstract concepts floating around, let's see if we can find some concrete systems and effects that we can use as examples. VE and thermal efficiency are ideas that will tie

The various sections of an exhaust system work together to provide the desired power delivery curve. This AMA race bike is equipped with a titanium 4-2-1 exhaust system. You can bet the tuned lengths of each section of piping were chosen very carefully by the manufacturer of the exhaust system and then tested to confirm the design.

together intake and exhaust tuning, mixture, cam timing, and even spark timing. So let's move on to something we can really sink our teeth into: gas flow.

FOLLOW BACKWARDS

The easiest way to get a quick grip on what's important in moving the air (and post-combustion gases) around is to follow it backwards, from the exit of the muffler. I understand this is not a very conventional way of approaching things, but follow with me, and I think it will become clearer as we go along.

The Exhaust System

OK, so we're fighting our way through the hot, expanding exhaust gases as we enter the muffler. And right here is the first important thing for us to notice: Both air and exhaust gases have *mass*. And this means they have *inertia*. It takes a certain amount of energy (and time) to get gases moving, and to get them stopped. Also, if put in a container with a small opening in it (like, say, an exhaust system) and heated, that heat will be turned into motion as the gas expands and increases in volume in the only way it can, by pushing itself out the opening.

Tuned Lengths and Power

We also notice, as we sit at the edge of the muffler tip, that there are pulsations to the exhaust gases. These pulses are caused by the exhaust valves opening and the hot, expanding exhaust gases

moving through the exhaust system. Just like an air bubble rising through water, there is a layer right above the pulse where the standing gases get compressed by the pressure pulse smacking into it. These pressure pulses travel at the speed of sound in the gases they are traveling through. When they reach a division or a joining of the pipes, or the end of a pipe, part of the pulse is reflected back down the pipe, toward the engine. When it gets to the exhaust valve, it bounces off the valve and goes back the other way again.

Each section of the exhaust system has a resonant frequency. This is related to the length and diameter of the section in question. When pulses happen to occur at the same speed as the resonant frequency, that pulse bounces back, goes to the end of its section and heads back to the other end again. It reaches the other end of the section at the exact time a new pulse is entering. This means there is a negative pressure at the start of the tube, helping to pull the exhaust gases down that section. This is called extraction, and at certain engine speeds it helps clear exhaust gases from certain sections of the exhaust, allowing better filling of the combustion chamber (and, thus, more power).

The opposite can happen as well. The pulse can come back to the start of the exhaust section and work against the exhaust pulse exiting the engine. This prevents a full charge of fresh mixture from completely filling the cylinder and slows down combustion (as discussed above). Engine speed, cam timing, and all the various pieces of the exhaust and how their lengths interact will control the behavior of these sound waves.

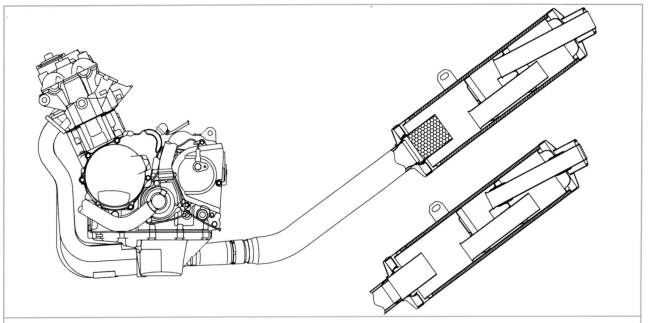

FIGURE 1-1: Original equipment exhaust systems must deliver power smoothly throughout the rev range, make good power, and still meet standards for noise emissions. Here we see a cutaway of the exhaust system of the Kawasaki ZX-6RR, showing the tuned volumes inside the muffler that lower noise emissions without creating significant back-pressure. The cutaway exhaust canister below the full system is shown without the honeycomb catalytic converter, for countries that have less strict emissions requirements. Kawasaki Motor Corporation USA

A well-designed street or road racing exhaust system will have sections that absorb resonant waves as well as creating them, helping to smooth out the torque curve for even power delivery. It will be designed around the rest of the engine to complement, rather than work against, the entire system, just as the separate sections of the exhaust tubing can work for or against smooth power delivery. Four-into-two-into-one systems generally excel in this department, mainly by adjusting the length of the various sections so none really helps exhaust scavenging, but none really hurts it, either.

Some road racing systems are designed for top-end power at the expense of smoothness or low-rpm power. Drag racing exhaust systems often follow a similar pattern. These exhaust designs don't really care if they create dips in the torque curve at lower rpms, since the bike will spend almost all of its time at higher rpms. Instead, they are designed specifically to resonate very near the peak rpm of the engine, so as to help create extra power in the small range of critical rpm where the engine lives on the track. Four-into-one systems are a better way to go when trying to get this effect. (You can still get it if you design a 4-2-1 system the right way, but it costs less and is easier to design than a 4-1.)

So again, we need to be thinking about the compromises. It is possible to design an exhaust system to offer a fairly notable improvement in helping mixture to enter the combustion chamber, which will make more power. But the price for that will be areas in the engine's range where that improvement will be balanced with an equally sized holdup that will work against the mixture entering the combustion chamber. If you have ridden a lot of motorcycles, you probably already know that a smooth power delivery generally makes for a more rideable bike. Balancing an improvement in power against a loss of drivability is one of the keys to designing an exhaust that feels good to have on the bike.

The Combustion Chamber

So we have fought our way up through the pressure pulses in the exhaust, waited for the exhaust valve to open, and dropped through into the combustion chamber. Now we have to take a look at what happens in the two full revolutions of the crank that comprise a complete cycle of combustion.

If you're reading this book, chances are pretty good that you understand the basics of how a four-stroke engine works. *Sportbike Performance Handbook* has such a wonderful treatment of this, I won't even go into detail. If you have any questions, refer to Kevin Cameron's wonderful explanation.

The Effects of Cam Timing

Suffice it to say, there is cam *overlap*, which is the time that both intake and exhaust valves are open. If there is high pressure in the intake and low pressure in the exhaust, as measured at the valves, then the high pressure on the intake side will help push out the exhaust gases, and the inertia of those intake gases will help fill the cylinder—when the exhaust valve closes, that inertia will keep air piling into the combustion chamber, even as the pressure builds. The combustion chamber starts to get crowded by all the molecules of air (and fuel) piling into each other, with suddenly nowhere to go. The intake valve closes, and the mass of air captured is higher than it might otherwise be because of the supercharging effect that has occurred.

We've already talked about how the amount of this effect can be changed, as well as at what engine speeds it occurs, by tuning the lengths in the exhaust system. The same thing can also be done with cam timing, which controls *when* those effects start and end inside the combustion chamber. As with the pressure pulses in the exhaust system, those in the combustion chamber can be tuned to a particular engine rpm through changes in cam lift, duration, and overlap. And as with the exhaust system, these can be tuned to work *with* or *against* those of the exhaust system, thus either flattening the torque curve at various points, or amplifying it at certain places.

The advantage to having a lot of overlap at high engine speeds, where gas flow velocities remain high, is obvious. At low engine speeds, though, the gases in the intake runners and exhaust headers have to start and stop, start and stop, and as we have seen, these gases have mass, and thus inertia. It takes energy and time to get them started again once they have been stopped. So at low engine speeds, there is often very little airflow into the cylinder before the exhaust valve has closed. This leaves exhaust gases in the combustion chamber, which can slow or even prevent combustion if the compression stroke does not produce enough turbulence in the combustion chamber. This is the reason that hot-rodded V-8 car motors have a loping idle—that's a high-overlap cam at work, reducing idle combustion efficiency and working against smooth idle.

The Combustion Chamber's Shape

The other factor to be considered here is combustion chamber shape. Again, I will refer you to *Sportbike Performance Handbook* for the full monty. Suffice it to say that the shape of the piston crown and combustion chamber can act to help or hinder scavenging, and can also be designed to force the mixture into the center of the combustion chamber (this is called squish), which not only mixes the fuel more thoroughly with the air, but also increases compression. The rapid motion of the mixture near TDC that is caused by squish area has a secondary effect of moving the flame front from the spark around the combustion chamber more quickly, thus speeding the burn and making more power (but requiring less ignition advance). The density of the mixture at the point of combustion controls how much of the heat energy held in the fuel will be released as useful work, as well as how quickly it will be released. This is why higher-compression engines make more power *and* are often more fuel efficient in the process.

The enemy of compression, of course, is detonation. Detonation occurs when the fuel burns extremely rapidly, usually through a very rapid rise in pressure, which causes runaway acceleration of combustion. It can happen for one of three reasons: Because there is a red-hot carbon deposit hot spot at some point in the combustion chamber that starts a secondary burn and increases the combustion pressure exponentially over a regular burn; simply from straight compression ignition (which is how a diesel engine works); or by advancing the ignition timing so much that pressure rises rapidly as the piston is still on the compression stroke, thus accelerating the rise in pressure over a normal combustion event (which would be one where the piston is beginning its downward

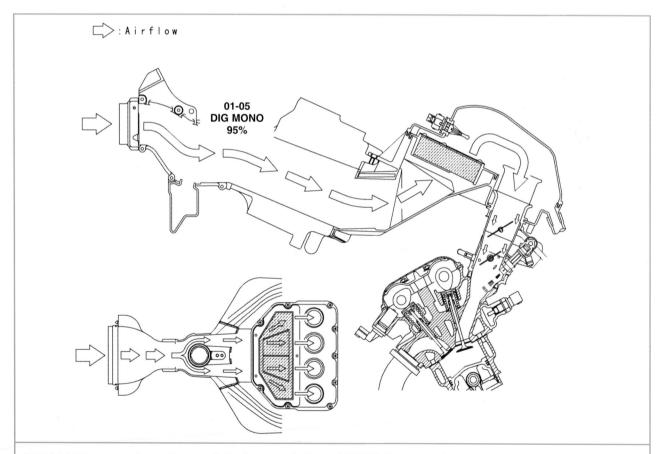

FIGURE 1-2: *This cutaway diagram illustrates the intake system of a Kawasaki ZX-6RR. Generous intake tubes can flow plenty of air for the hungry engine, and you can see that the shape of the airbox helps the air flow smoothly into the throttle bodies. Note the Helmholtz resonator below the mouth of the intake tube (it is shaped a bit like a shark fin); this helps quiet intake noise. Kawasaki Motor Corporation USA*

Most throttles found on motorcycles are of the butterfly type. Here, Stuart Hilborn demonstrates his modular throttle body system that can be set up for any bore spacing at will. This particular setup is for mechanical fuel injection; note the variable pressure regulator attached to the throttle shaft by a tie rod on the far right side of the assembly. Assembly courtesy of Hilborn

motion as the combustion event builds its most rapid gains in combustion chamber pressure).

Ordinarily, we want to increase compression, since it increases the thermal efficiency of the engine (how much of the heat energy in the fuel gets turned into work). However, beyond a certain point, the pressure and heat start to melt or smash holes through pistons, squeeze oil films out of bearing surfaces, overstress head studs and engine gaskets, and generally cause some really bad problems. Increases in heat energy released during combustion also send NO_x (nitrogen oxide) levels skyrocketing, as well as potentially melting actual pieces of the engine and weakening others to the point where they are permanently damaged by the increased pressure and heat. With four-stroke gasoline engines, there is such a thing as too efficient a burn! And, as with all things in designing a system based on internal combustion, we must find a compromise. Here it is between reliability, cost and weight of materials, power delivery, and emissions.

To help prevent secondary ignition, sharp edges are generally avoided as much as possible in the combustion chamber and, insofar as possible, squish areas generally do not open rapidly into an open chamber. This helps smooth out transitions in gas pressure, rather than having them occur suddenly. Compression ignition is avoided by keeping compression ratios within a reasonable level, as well as by preventing deposits from building up inside the combustion chamber.

So now we have explored a little bit about cam timing, combustion chamber shape, and exhaust tuning, and how they can work together, or against each other, and how one has to find a good balance between them to achieve our goals. What's left but the intake system?

THE INTAKE SYSTEM

The sharp reader has probably surmised by now that the same principles that work in the exhaust system also work in the intake

tract, and for the same reasons. In the case of the exhaust system, we have the exhaust gases being the engine that drives the rush of gases toward the atmosphere, and atmospheric pressure at the exhaust tip resisting the push, with resonant effects helping or hindering the push. In the intake system, atmospheric (or ram air) pressure is the engine moving the intake air, and the intake valve and its timing become the restriction on that push.

Again we have resonant effects helping or hindering the push, but there are a few differences that bear discussion (and then, believe it or not, I'll explain how these differences can also be applied to the exhaust system!). Some of them will largely focus on the differences between automobile and motorcycle systems and what impact that has on fueling for motorcycles versus that for cars.

Throttles

The biggest difference between a standard motorcycle exhaust system and a typical motorcycle intake system is, of course, the throttles. Not only do the throttles change the density of the air entering the engine (thus changing the mass ingested by the engine in a given intake cycle), but they also act as a reflector for sound waves, which changes the resonant frequency of the intake section between the airbox and the intake valve. This is why some poorly tuned bikes will run poorly at full throttle at a given rpm, but much better at part throttle.

Most motorcycles use one butterfly-style throttle per intake runner. In some rare cases, racing bikes may have flat-slide throttles or even barrel-type throttles. However, both types are more expensive to manufacture (barrel throttles are typically CNC machined to order), and both require more physical space for installation than butterfly throttles (flat-slides are worse here). Flat-slides also require a very stiff return spring to prevent any chance of sticking throttles.

Butterfly-style throttles are more disruptive to airflow at part-throttle, and they are harder to resonance tune because of the

so it demands very short intake runners with the throttle between the plenum and the cylinder, as well as the packaging consideration of combining the air filter holder with the plenum, which saves space and weight.

The main effect of this difference is that throttle response on a typical car is not so abrupt and rapid as it is on a typical motorcycle, since it takes a little while for the engine to deplete the air mass stored in the plenum. Throttles in a motorcycle application have a much more rapid and dramatic effect on the air mass that can reach the engine. This means substantially improved throttle response, but at low engine speeds especially, it also means there is a huge jump in air mass when the throttle is suddenly opened. This typically results in a huge jolt if it is allowed to occur and fueling matches it. If it is allowed to occur without enough of an increase in fuel, a stumble will result. Both are undesirable.

Damping Down Throttle Response
The answer, as with carbs before, has been to damp down sudden changes in available air mass after a sudden change in throttle opening. Some systems have used smaller throttle bodies than they could, but that improves low-rpm smoothness at the expense of high-rpm power (another compromise). Most systems today use a secondary throttle above the operator-controlled one, this one driven by a servomotor actuated by the ECU. The ECU opens the secondary throttle at a certain speed based on engine speed and operator demand. Although it was pioneered on Suzuki models (where it still predominates), it can also now be found on several Kawasakis, as well as the new Triumph Daytona 600. Yet another strategy (used by Yamaha) has been to employ the very same vacuum-diaphragm-operated slides as found on motorcycle CV carburetors to limit the change in air mass based on the engine's ability to rapidly cope with those changes. This has been the approach that many consider the most successful in terms of providing good drivability and throttle response, but it suffers a penalty in terms of space (since like a CV carburetor, there needs

Even turbocharged motorcycles require a plenum; here we see one for a 1982 Honda CX500 Turbo. The black-painted pressed steel plenum is bolted to the front plate, which contains intake runners, throttle bodies, injector mounts, the fuel rail, and vacuum pull-offs for various sensors. Assembly courtesy of Greg Goss

changing angle of the throttle plate. Furthermore, the response of butterfly throttles is greatest when almost closed, and response reduces steadily as the throttle is opened. While this can be overcome with cam lobe-shaped throttle opening wheels, it tends to make mapping a little more of a challenge. Still, the reliability, low price, efficient use of space, light throttle action, and utter simplicity of the butterfly throttle mean you're unlikely to ever encounter another type of throttle on a motorcycle.

Differences in the Car World
The main difference between many fuel-injected automotive intake tracts and those commonly found on sporting motorcycles is that on cars, the throttle is typically in front of the plenum (I left the components in their physical order on the bike, so if you don't know what a plenum is, read the section below and then come back!), and prevents it from refilling as it is depleted by engine demand. On motorcycles, the plenum is typically in front of the throttles.

Why? Because cars generally have a lot of room under the hood for a large plenum in addition to an air filter, and have more vehicle mass to accelerate (and thus need less throttle response than a motorcycle). A motorcycle needs better throttle response,

To prevent the throttle demanding more from the engine than it can deliver, many motorcycles have throttle bodies containing a second set of butterfly valves above the first that are opened by a stepper motor under the control of the ECU. Here you can see a set of throttle bodies for a Kawasaki ZX-6RR. The large black square is the stepper motor, and the two smaller rounded items flanking it (one black, one gray) are the throttle position sensors. Two sensors are required, one to determine rider-controlled throttle opening, and one to give feedback to the ECU regarding how far the secondary throttles are open. Kawasaki Motor Corporation USA

The base of a Kawasaki ZX-6RR airbox. The isosceles trapezoid at the front is the air filter; air enters from below and flows up through the filter. Note the unequal length velocity stacks (here made of rubber). This is to smooth out peaks in the torque curve and help make the motorcycle respond more smoothly to throttle input. Kawasaki Motor Corporation USA

and sometimes lower engine noise as well. Both items are largely confined to factory systems, and the exhaust throttle plate is best controlled by some kind of mapped electronic controller to give best effect throughout the rev range.

Velocity Stacks

Attached to the airbox end of the throttle bodies on many bikes are velocity stacks. These pieces of aluminum or plastic are used for two reasons: To change the length of the intake manifold at full throttle, thus changing the peaks and valleys in air delivery based on resonance; and to use the curved lip at the airbox end of each stack to help the air to move smoothly through the throttle body and manifold (with what is called laminar flow), which allows more of the kinetic energy of the air to be used in filling the cylinder, and less in fighting against eddies and whorls in the airflow. Not only does turbulence reduce flow, but it also generates heat, which further reduces the density of the ingested air. Many of you have likely noticed that most inline four-cylinder sportbikes have different lengths of velocity stacks on the center two cylinders versus the outside two cylinders. This is so that peaks and valleys in air delivery are more evenly distributed between the cylinders, making for a more even and flatter torque curve.

The Airbox

Beyond the velocity stacks is the airbox. In the early years of motorcycles, no thought was paid to airbox design. It merely held the air filter and kept it out of the weather. This is why older bikes could often benefit from removing the airbox entirely. However, things began to change significantly by the mid-1980s, as manufacturers started paying attention to the details in their quest for more power and less weight.

Not only does a properly designed airbox (which largely means having one with enough internal volume) do nothing to inhibit atmospheric air pressure from pushing itself into the engine when

to be sufficient room between the throat and the cam cover to allow for the vacuum diaphragm and slide).

As I mentioned before, some of these tricks can be (and sometimes are!) used on exhaust systems. The famed Yamaha EXUP valve, and others much like it, have shown up on a variety of motorcycles, and are used largely to alter the resonant length of the exhaust system. Such values operate in a manner very similar to the ECU-controlled secondary butterfly in many intake systems. Also, some exhaust systems use resonator chambers attached to the rest of the exhaust tract to provide the same function as they do on intakes—to help smooth out the torque curve

Factory or aftermarket velocity stacks can offer a performance boost. As with an exhaust system, it is often possible to alter the power delivery curve to one's benefit by changing the tuned length of the intakes (by changing the length of the installed velocity stacks). Here we see a set installed on a Ducati racing homologation Desmoquattro model. Changing the length of the stacks can add more power at particular engine speeds, or smooth out a lumpy torque curve. Note the carbon fiber airbox tray (which uses the underside of the fuel tank as a lid), as well as the shower-type injectors (ringed by yellow bands). The quick-release clip connecting the fuel tank to the fuel rail can be seen on the far left. Motorcycle courtesy of GP Motorcycles

A Kawasaki ZX-6RR with the airbox cover installed. Compare this to the cutaway of the intake system on page 16 to get an idea of just how much volume is available for the engine to draw from, and note how the shape of the lid helps keep the intake flow laminar (straight) as it enters the velocity stacks. Less turbulence in the intake tract means more air in the cylinder when the intake valve closes. Kawasaki Motor Corporation USA

the intake valve opens, but it also works in conjunction with the intake tubes to create a very special, and very useful, device—a Helmholtz resonator. In the late "dark ages", before motorcycles were seen on any roads anywhere, a physicist in Germany named Hermann von Helmholtz (1821–1894) discovered that certain proportions of chamber volume, tube diameter, and tube length would make an enclosure that would absorb certain frequencies. This behavior makes such tuned enclosures perfect for designing airboxes, to help take the peaks off of some of the high spots in intake resonance, or to help fill in some of the dips. Additional Helmholtz resonators are often attached to the bottom of the intake pipes to help eliminate audible intake noise and allow the motorcycles to meet sound emissions standards (see Figure 1-2).

Variable intake geometry is not used a great deal on motorcycles at this point in time, mainly due to weight and space considerations. However, the ability to change the tuned length and tuned volume of parts of the intake system lets you maximize the positive effects of resonance for more of the operating range of the engine.

Suzuki has become fond of using a vacuum actuator to move a plate in the bottom of the airbox on their sportbikes. This allows more smoothly delivered power over a wider operating range. The drawbacks are weight and complexity (even for a system this simple), as well as a slight restriction in maximum airflow. However, its benefits are such that other manufactuters have begun incorporating similar features on their cutting-edge sportbikes as well. More complex systems are becoming commonly available on cars, but they rely on stepper motors and larger adjustable-length chambers, which would interfere a great deal with the space and weight constraints of modern motorcycles.

Ram Air

Motorcycles also often take advantage of the ram effect, wherein the motion of the motorcycle through the air raises intake pressure. The air molecules get pushed into the intake tubing by the forward motion of the motorcycle at a faster rate than the engine can take them in. This effect actually has very little to do with the size of the tubing. Provided it is large enough to flow the air capacity being used by the engine and then some, there is no benefit from additional tubing diameter. The increase in pressure is dictated mainly by the volume of the airbox. The greater the volume, the more air mass the airbox is holding, and the more capacity the airbox has to deliver a lot of molecules to the combustion chamber when the intake valve opens. In other words, the more volume in the airbox, the more slowly the pressure will drop from engine demands. What's more, air intakes are positioned to avoid heating of the intake air by the radiator or engine components, thus further increasing the density of the intake air.

A Suzuki GSX-R1000 being prepared for the racetrack. With the upper cowling removed, you can clearly see the massive intake tubes for the ram air system. Mesh grilles prevent debris from entering the airbox, while the length of the tubes is not only tuned to the rest of the intake tract, but also allows the engine to breathe cool air from far out in front of the bike's radiator.

A cutaway Kawasaki ZX-6RR, revealing most of the intake tract and engine. Note the smooth path for airflow from the throttle bodies into the intake runners as well as the large plenum volume. You can also see the in-tank fuel pump attached inside the floor of the fuel tank, and the crank sensor trigger wheel peeking out from behind its cutaway cover at the bottom of the frame.
Photo courtesy of Nolan TA, Sydney, Australia

The Airbox as Plenum

An airbox in such an intake system can honestly be referred to as a true plenum. From the Latin word meaning "full," a plenum is a chamber that is a sort of reservoir for air demands. Think of it as being like a portable air tank for filling tires—the tank is constantly being refilled by atmospheric pressure (or ram pressure if you are moving fast enough), and each time a valve opens it is like topping off the air in a tire. A plenum with the proper volume will tend to maintain a relatively stable air pressure over a wide range of engine conditions, thus acting as a damper between engine demands and conditions outside the bike. Properly designed (which mostly means having enough volume), it ensures a substantial supply of air for engine demands at all times.

Fitting the Intake Puzzle Together

Again the major point here is that all the different sections of the intake tract work together to make a compromise to best achieve the goals of the designers. In the case of street bikes, those goals are generally smooth power delivery, low noise, and as much power as possible. And again, a balance has to be struck between these goals, since what works to help one in one area often works against another.

TYING IT ALL TOGETHER

Wow. We've now followed the path of air all the way through the system, from outside the motorcycle in the front (where atmospheric pressure is the engine that pushes air through the motor), past the throttles, through the combustion chamber where it is used to release power from the fuel, and then out the exhaust system and back into the atmosphere. And we haven't even gotten to fuel yet! But understanding how gases behave in the various parts of their path through the motor is key to understanding injection and how it works, as we will see.

You'll note that each part of each system for handling gas flow on a four-stroke motorcycle (intake, cams, combustion chamber, exhaust) runs into many of the same choices for compromise—since the speed of intake and exhaust pulses changes with engine speed, each piece of the puzzle will amplify or negate those pulses based on its length. How to combine them so all the little pluses and minuses fit together to achieve the goals one sets in designing them is a huge puzzle, and to make matters worse, what gives you a desired effect at one engine speed could cause problems at another. It's a very intricate and delicate puzzle, where changing one piece affects all the others in a variety of ways, depending on engine speed, road speed, throttle changes, etc. It's one of the reasons that some exhaust systems from great companies are lousy on particular models, and why it's so hard to improve on a stock airbox in most cases.

And manufacturers again have to find a compromise between cost of manufacturing, weight, absolute power, sound emissions, a smooth powerband, and more. It's a great balancing act involving a lot of parameters, a lot of people, and a lot of thought. Keep in mind that manufacturers spend millions of dollars on computers and software to analyze gas flow, fluid dynamics, structural changes, etc. Every little bit of the engine is subjected to intense scrutiny by teams of engineers trying to make those bits lighter, make them work better, and make them from cheaper and more durable materials. All the parts of a motorcycle work together in a complex web of priorities, and it is with a great deal of caution that we attempt to alter that delicate balance. It's as easy to do great harm to this balance as it is to improve it for our own ends.

But beyond the manufacturer's design of the intake, exhaust, and engine, all those pieces (and how they fit together) end up being a big key in the design of a fuel injection system. For that, there is one major reason: it's relatively easy to add more fuel, but your power output is limited based on the amount of available air. As I said at the beginning of the chapter, by volume, an engine needs about 10,000 times *more* air than fuel for regular combustion. (The next time you fill your fuel tank, try envisioning a box big enough to hold all the air it will take to use up those few gallons of gasoline. By comparison, an adult human breathes only 600 gallons of air per *day*.) This is why I started out with a brief explanation of how air gets into the engine and how post-combustion gases get out. Without understanding that, you can't understand how to meter fuel. Because metering fuel is very much about modeling the passage of gases through the engine, most especially air.

And the Key Concept Is . . .

Probably the most important concept that comes out of all these variables is that of *volumetric efficiency*. Now you're starting to understand why I spent time on that abstract concept at the start of the chapter, aren't you? See, I don't include stuff just to confuse you! It's all there for important reasons.

As you can imagine, if you tune the intake system so that at a given rpm, a pressure pulse will reach the intake valve just as it opens on our test cylinder, the air will be at a higher pressure than ambient, and thus have more mass. This is the ram effect as it was used in the old ram intake manifolds that were so popular in the past for muscle car engines. This has the effect of supercharging the cylinder as it fills—the pressure at the intake valve is the pump that fills the cylinder, so the more pressure that's there (from higher than ambient air pressure in the airbox from high vehicle speed, from tuning the length of the intake tract, or perhaps from a turbocharger), the more air mass that ends up in the cylinder once the intake valve has closed. If that mass is more than 100 percent of the mass of an equivalent volume of ambient air, then you have exceeded 100 percent volumetric efficiency. If you close your throttle, much less air is able to move past the throttle plate and push its way into the engine—the pressure in the intake manifold drops, the air becomes less dense, and even though the engine takes in the same volume at the same engine speed as the first case, the air mass entering the cylinder is much smaller. In this case, VE is much lower than 100 percent.

Of course, the tuning of the exhaust system has the same potential effect on VE from *lowering* the pressure in the headers at the exhaust valve as it is opening, which helps the exhaust gases out of the cylinder. This lowers the resistance to the intake charge pushing its way in once the intake valve opens. Cam timing and engine speed are also factors, as is the design of the combustion chamber (if the path from intake to exhaust valve requires a lot of changes in direction for gases, it will restrict flow).

So the two things that can affect VE are the restrictions and tunings of the intake, exhaust, cams and combustion chamber design, and the throttle angle (or alpha). Very shortly, it will become clear why this is so very important to know and understand when thinking about tuning a fuel system (even a carburetor!).

Volumetric efficiency is only the start, though. Then we have to contend with actually getting the heat energy out of the fuel that we deliver with that trapped air. And that's a whole other kettle of fish, consisting of ignition timing, compression ratio, throttle position (it does more than double duty!) and combustion chamber shape.

THE BASICS OF COMBUSTION CHEMISTRY

We've covered VE and how various parts of the motorcycle work together to give us a certain air mass in the combustion chamber. But now we need to explore what it takes to get the best burnable mixture we can, and to burn as much of it as possible. Further,

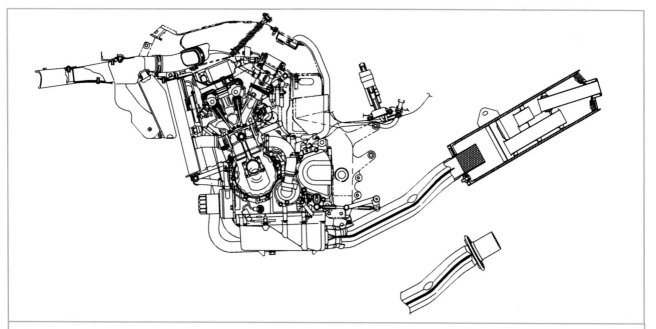

FIGURE 1-3: All the individual components must be tuned properly to work together as one. A cutaway view of a Kawasaki ZX-12R, showing the complete path of gases from the front of the intake tubes to the tailpipe. Note the extremely large plenum gained by using the inside of the frame as an airbox. The air filter cleverly slides into a cutout in the frame itself. Also, note the shallow pent-roof combustion chamber, which lends itself to high compression ratios without detonation. The lower exhaust mid-pipe in the image is for markets that do not require the built-in honeycomb catalytic converter. Kawasaki Motor Corporation USA

we want to turn as much heat energy into work as we possibly can without damaging the engine in the process.

Homogeneous Mixture and Combustion

Under ideal circumstances, the entire delivered fuel mass should be completely evaporated and *evenly distributed* in the combustion chamber so it burns at the proper speed and uses up as much of the available oxygen as possible. If an area in the combustion chamber has a very lean mixture, it may not burn at all, causing misfire or incomplete combustion.

In a conventional four-stroke engine (the kind we are discussing here), this means more hydrocarbons in the exhaust, a drop in both power and gas mileage, and the possibility of damaging the catalytic converter (if there is one on the vehicle). Any oxygen sensors in the exhaust will have their life shortened by this as well.

Conversely, an area with a rich mixture will generally burn more slowly, which means that power is usually lost. Gas mileage drops, and HC (hydrocarbon) emissions skyrocket. Sometimes this is used to the favor of the engine in some ways (like to help prevent detonation in air-cooled engines), but there are better ways, especially given the tools we have with EFI. And if the mixture gets *too* rich, it will misfire as well, and you end up with a very similar outcome to lean misfire (unburned HC in the exhaust, potential catalytic converter damage, and loss of power and economy).

The Range of Mixtures, and What They Mean

The most important part of this equation is the fact that gasoline only burns well in a very, very narrow range of air/fuel ratio (AFR). Lambda (the Greek letter λ) is simply another way of describing an AFR. A lambda of 1.0 is exactly the stoichiometric ratio for a given fuel. It's pretty well known that the stoichiometric ratio for gasoline is 14.7:1 by mass. But depending on the VE of the engine, and more importantly the thermal efficiency at that particular moment, the graphs for best power or economy will shift toward either the rich or the lean side of textbook numbers.

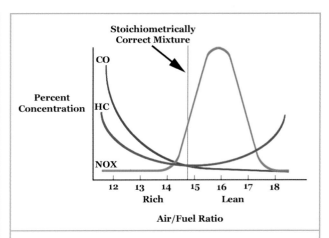

FIGURE 1-5: A graphic illustration of how variations in combustible mixture change exhaust gas composition. More NO_x means a hotter burn; an increase in hydrocarbons could be either rich or lean. Only carbon monoxide is an accurate indicator of the quality of the mixture burned in the combustion chamber. Maya Culbertson

There is no one magic number you can use for ideal AFR, regardless of engine speed, intake and exhaust tuning, throttle position, or any other variable. The VE (and more importantly, mixture density and burn speed) changes at different engine speeds and throttle openings. This means fuel vaporization and optimal spark timing change, as well as exhaust gas composition. Thus the ideal mixture for any given desired outcome (emissions, power, economy) changes based on engine speed, throttle position, spark timing, and all the other factors that go into determining a tune for the engine and its associated systems!

Mixture

Power falls off as you move away from the slightly rich power peak (more so as you go lean, which is why leanness is commonly asso-

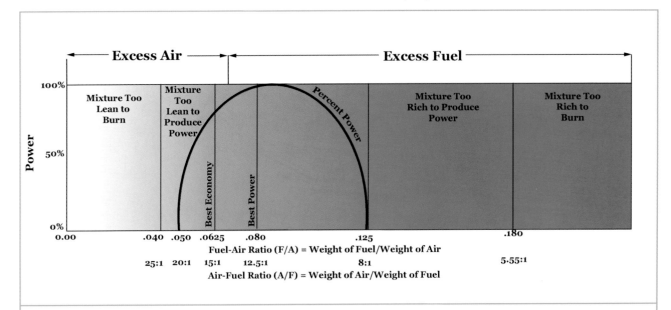

FIGURE 1-4: Gasoline only burns well in a fairly narrow range of AFR, and then only when in a very uniform mixture. This graph demonstrates the small AFR band of combustibility, and the even smaller band of useful work. Maya Culbertson

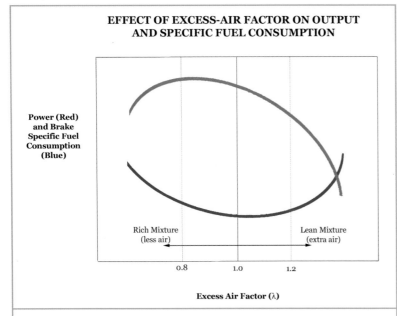

EFFECT OF EXCESS-AIR FACTOR ON OUTPUT AND SPECIFIC FUEL CONSUMPTION

Power (Red) and Brake Specific Fuel Consumption (Blue)

Rich Mixture (less air)

Lean Mixture (extra air)

0.8   1.0   1.2

Excess Air Factor (λ)

FIGURE 1-6: *As shown in this diagram, best power is achieved when nearly all of the available oxygen is used in the combustion process, which requires a slightly rich mixture. Best fuel economy occurs when nearly all of the available fuel is consumed by combustion, which requires a slightly lean mixture.* Maya Culbertson

Because combustion is not ever completed 100 percent inside the combustion chamber, and the mixture is never 100 percent homogeneous (evenly mixed). Combustion in an engine is incomplete for a variety of reasons that can be studied in more detail in one of the wonderful books available on combustion science. For our purposes, all we need to know is that a stoichiometric mixture will mean extra O_2 and extra HC in the exhaust over the levels acheived by perfect combustion. And that is why best power is rich of $\lambda = 1$, and best economy is lean of $\lambda = 1$. If you have a slightly rich mixture, you come much closer to ensuring that every molecule of O_2 has sufficient fuel near it to almost all be used up for generating power, even though that leaves more unburned HC in the exhaust. If you have a slightly lean mixture, you come much closer to ensuring that there is sufficient O_2 adjacent to all the HC in the fuel to use almost all of it up for making power; there will be excess O_2 in the exhaust, but almost all the fuel will be burned in the combustion chamber. Since a catalytic converter burns off excess HC and O_2, a stoichiometric ratio delivered at the intake valve will mean as complete a combustion of both the available HC and O_2 as possible before it all leaves the muffler.

Emissions Controls and How They Work

All of this is important because there are regulations controlling the amount of those gases that a motorcycle can emit. And every year, those restrictions get tighter and tighter. As you can see, running somewhat lean will lower the levels of residual CO and HC, which is a good thing. Sure, power will be lost compared to peak, but this might be a good strategy for idling and running at cruise. But when you run in that range, levels of NO_x go up! What can we do?

Well, the answer used to date (and for a long time, it was good enough to meet emissions standards) has generally been to inject air into the exhaust port right after the exhaust valve when the throttle is closed. This helps burn the extra HC and CO in the exhaust while the exhaust gases are still very hot and reactive and being offered more heat by the cylinder head. It's a good system as far as it goes, but that isn't very far. In fact, it typically only operates in the region of high-rpm, closed-throttle running, where carbureted bikes tend to run very rich. In this way, it helps afterburn the excess hydrocarbons. Some bikes are now using a catalyst and no O_2 sensor, and are relying on this system to provide enough excess oxygen for the catalyst to work while still allowing us a richer mixture to the engine for best power. However, emissions standards are tightening to the point where soon these simple designs will no longer be enough of an answer.

So what to do now? Well, the automotive world developed the answer for us, in the form of the three-way catalytic converter. This device works by using several different kinds of metals that catalyze (help along) chemical reactions when heated to a certain temperature. Heated by exhaust gases, the metal-coated honeycomb inside the converter takes fuel and oxygen that did not fully burn in the engine, and burns it off in the converter, thus heating it further. It breaks apart NO_x, allowing it to return to regular N_2, and allowing the oxygen to turn CO into CO_2. It lowers levels of all the major pollutants in the exhaust gases. So where's the catch?

ciated with a touchy throttle response). Fuel efficiency falls off as you move away from the slightly lean efficiency peak (the lowest BSFC, or brake specific fuel consumption, the amount of fuel used to make a given amount of power). And emissions themselves are even more complex.

As you can see on this graph, changing the mixture changes how the combustion chamber gases combine and what waste products they leave behind. And these waste gases vary greatly depending on how you change the mixture (spark timing also plays a role, but it is typically the factor that is solidly in second place). Notice how the gases change at various different points on the curve. When there is less available oxygen, the mixture burns cooler and slower, and there are fewer oxygen atoms in the burning gas that can attach to the carbon atoms that have broken off from the gasoline molecules, releasing energy. This leads to increased levels of CO (carbon monoxide) and reduced levels of CO_2 (carbon dioxide), as you might imagine. When there is enough available oxygen, the fuel burns fairly well, and CO drops, while CO_2 increases. Because the mixture burns more readily in this state, and releases more of its heat energy, the combustion gases get hotter, which knocks apart an increasing number of nitrogen molecules (N_2), and some of the oxygen atoms combine with them, creating nitrogen oxides (NO_x), which are among the worse pollutants. You can see the levels of these gases spike right near $\lambda = 1$. As you go lean of that point, CO continues to drop (as there is now excess available free oxygen to turn almost all the free carbon into CO_2). Excess hydrocarbons (HC) drop steadily from rich to lean, right to the point of lean misfire (where they again rise).

The "Best" Mixture—Or Is It?

Ultimately, we need to pretty well forget about stoichiometric ratio as a target, except for running a catalytic converter. Why?

The catch is that a catalytic converter needs specific proportions of different combustion byproducts to do its magic. It cannot be allowed to get too hot, as well. Since combustion inside a combustion chamber is never fully complete, and one of the main jobs of the catalytic converter is to complete it, the engine *must* be fed with a correct stoichiometric mixture at λ = 1. More than a very small variation from λ = 1 will result in poor operation of the catalyst, and extremes can actually damage the O_2 sensor or the catalyst itself. This narrow range (1.01 > λ > 0.98) is the *only* range in which a standard three-way catalyst will work properly; too lean and NO_x is not well controlled, too rich and HC/CO is not well controlled. Other kinds of catalysts have been developed, but until emissions regulations demand the lower levels of pollutants found in cars, the extra weight and expense of having two different converters and two different kinds of oxygen sensors will not make sense for motorcycle manufacturers.

One of the few things not shown on the graph of pollutant gases is residual oxygen. Obviously, being lean of λ = 1 is going to leave you with increasing levels of excess oxygen. But some oxygen is going to be turned into NO_x, so as NO_x goes up, the oxygen level will go down. Also, beyond a certain point of richness, the excess fuel has more and more of a cooling effect, slowing combustion even more, which means that less and less of the available oxygen actually gets burned! So as you go to a lower and lower lambda, you slowly see residual oxygen increase. Three factors are in play: two working in one direction, and one in the other. This doesn't make for a very nice, smooth-looking residual oxygen curve, does it? Remember this. I'm going to bring it up again later on when we talk about oxygen sensors and what they really tell you.

Getting the Mixture Mixed

To burn effectively (which typically means less HC in the exhaust, as well as better fuel consumption and more peak power), the fuel needs to be as fully evaporated as possible. Atomization creates many times more surface area, which means much faster evaporation. So we want excellent atomization. Evaporation of the fuel (turning it from small droplets into a true vapor) requires heat, and it takes that heat from whatever it touches.

Air doesn't conduct heat very quickly, but it does conduct it, so some of the heat will come from the air around the fuel, causing the air to cool. This, in turn, makes it denser, which increases the ability to make power. Metal, however, conducts heat exceedingly well, so any warm or hot metal hit by the fuel will be cooled greatly and vaporize the fuel extremely well.

One remaining factor that can't be ignored is octane rating. There's a lot of conventional wisdom out there on octane ratings and what they mean to you and your engine. With pump gas, the main effect from changing octane is that the structure of some of the hydrocarbons is more resistant to being broken up. This makes the fuel more resistant to compression ignition. The advantage here is that you can then do whatever you like to speed up the burn rate without fear of runaway compression ignition at any point, and get better thermal efficiency. However, premium pump gas has *less* available heat energy than regular unleaded! The reason you can get more power from a higher-compression engine

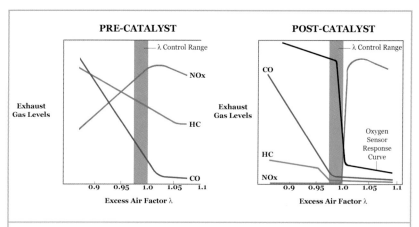

FIGURE 1-7: A graph of exhaust gases varying with mixture, both before and after a three-way catalytic converter. With use of a catalytic converter, note the huge drop in unburned hydrocarbons, especially when run lean, as well as the huge drop in nitrogen oxides when run rich. The optimal mixture for best emissions with a catalyst is always lambda = 1. Maya Culbertson

running premium is that there is less heat released, but you have turned more of it into useful work. The flip side of this is that engines that are running perfectly well on regular pump gas will actually make *less* power, all other things being equal, when being run with premium. Engines that run on the edge of detonation by means of additional spark advance may see slightly smoother running, better idle, and slightly more power with premium, all other things being equal.

Vaporization and Cylinder Filling

In the intake tract, while the intake valve is open (during aspiration), air moves into the combustion chamber based on pressure, density, temperature, and engine speed. Now, when fuel evaporates, it expands, since it is becoming a gas. This raises the pressure, but it lowers the density of the overall mixture. What's more, the pressure pushes in all directions as the fuel evaporates, so it works as much *against* airflow into the cylinder as it works *for* it. So this lowers density and does nothing to improve cylinder filling. Again, we need to find a compromise between excellent vaporization and cylinder filling, and that point of best compromise changes based on our goals (power, economy, emissions), and the conditions of the engine.

On the one hand, we want to keep the fuel in its dense, liquid form until near when the intake valve will close, at which time there is nowhere for the pressure to escape to when the fuel vaporizes. What's more, the vaporization can be used to help cool the very high temperatures of the metal parts in the combustion chamber to keep them from suffering thermal stress, and even to lower friction. If it takes too long, though, some of the fuel will remain liquid and won't burn. This increases HC emissions and lowers power and fuel economy. On the other hand, we want the best fuel vaporization, so we want to inject it as early as possible, both to allow more time to gather heat and vaporize and to take advantage of the sudden drop in manifold pressure when the intake valve first opens (the lower the pressure, the faster the vaporization).

So again, we have to find a compromise in design and timing to keep airflow as non-turbulent as possible in the intake system and keep fuel as finely misted as we can (but not quite vaporized) until the intake valve is about to close. Then we want a fair amount of turbulence and vaporization of fuel (which is aided by turbulence, hot combustion chamber components, and squish area) so we can get a good, homogeneous mixture that is as dense with oxygen as possible. Since the speed of the airflow is fastest in the center of the intake runner, and gets slower as it gets closer to the runner's walls, we also want to put this fuel as close to the center of the runner as possible.

One of the major things to note about mixture formation is the effect of lower manifold pressure (which decreases somewhat with engine rpm, but decreases at a much greater rate as the throttle comes closer to being closed). Low manifold pressure is our friend for a lot of reasons when it comes to mixture formation and cylinder filling. It somewhat increases manifold pressure through vaporization of the fuel, and thus makes for good cylinder filling and less energy wasted on the intake stroke, and it also greatly increases the rate of fuel vaporization. So lower emissions and higher thermal and mechanical efficiency are two of the great benefits of running at part throttle. But there's a fly in the ointment that I will come to shortly when I talk about thermal efficiency, compression ratio, and burn speeds.

Burn Speed—What Affects It?

This is a tricky subject, because a number of things can affect burn rate. And since burn rate determines best spark timing as well as power, economy, and emissions, we really ought to understand how it can be altered.

The main point here, as I mentioned earlier, is that we want a fast burn rate, but not too fast. So it needs to be within a controlled range. The fast side of the range borders on detonation, and this is the direction in which we are going as an industry. Faster burn means better economy *and* more power, although it tends to mean more NO_x in our emissions. Slower, cooler combustion reduces NO_x emissions and can help protect engine parts, but it also generally requires more spark advance to ensure that the fuel is largely done burning when the exhaust valve opens. Again, a compromise must be sought, because the hotter the combustion, the more power is available for our use, but the engine has thermal and structural limits, and there are emissions considerations as well. So keep these factors in mind when thinking about burn rate and how we might tune it to our best advantage.

Mixture and Combustion Speed

Obviously, how we put the combustion components together will have a sizable impact on combustion speed. Strictly keeping to mixture, it would appear that ? < 1 (slightly lean) would give us the fastest rate of burn. A mixture that has enough oxygen present and well-distributed to ensure that the maximum amount of heat energy is released from a given amount of fuel (which would be the mixture for best economy) should allow for the most rapid chemical reactions, and thus the quickest flame front travel. You'll notice that lean mixtures are more likely to cause detonation at a given spark advance—the increased burn rate is the reason why. However, the wasted oxygen means we are down on total power output, even though we're using more of the fuel's available heat energy.

Burn speed slows down on either side of the best economy mixture. As there are fewer HC molecules per intake charge with a leaner mixture, they are farther apart from each other, thus slowing combustion. Likewise, with a rich mixture, there is a lower density of oxygen molecules. Again, the burn rate slows due to the increased distance between $C–O_2$ and $H–O_2$ pairings (which release heat energy, increase pressure [which also increases heat], and produce work).

The Effect of Exhaust Gas on Combustion Speed

The nitrogen in our atmosphere slows down combustion speed over pure oxygen by spacing out the components of the intake charge (O_2 and HC) that combine to release heat energy. Nitrogen does this because it is a fairly inert gas and doesn't contribute energy to the chemical reaction taking place in the combustion chamber. The same effect can be attained by adding any inert gas. Automobiles can actually use EGR (exhaust gas recirculation) to intentionally slow combustion to prevent detonation, reduce NO_x (because a slower burn is a cooler burn), and reduce pumping losses (which is the energy used up by the engine when it has to pull against manifold vacuum during the intake stroke, moreso when the throttle is closed, thus costing us some power). Since exhaust gases contain a large amount of N_2 (nitrogen) and CO_2 (carbon dioxide), they work very well at this task. In addition, there is a second chance for unburned HC to be burned in the combustion chamber and produce useful work.

Another manner in which exhaust gases will be present in the combustion chamber of four-stroke engines, especially those with cam design and timing designed for high-rpm power, is incomplete scavenging. Modified cruisers with big cams and sportbikes tuned for top-end power tend to suffer more from this problem than bikes tuned for low-rpm and midrange running. This is because of increased cam overlap (like we talked about earlier in this chapter). Not only does increased overlap reduce the total amount of fresh mixture in the combustion chamber, thus lowering VE, but it leaves a large amount of fairly inert exhaust gas within the combustion chamber as well. This greatly slows the burn rate near idle, as well as increasing the variability of mixture distribution. This creates a very uneven idle condition, burn rate effects aside.

Charge Density and Combustion Speed

The same principle that creates changes in burn speed based on mixture or inert gases also holds when we are speaking of charge density. The closer together combustible elements are, the quicker the flame front will travel. This is why burn rate speeds up as combustion proceeds. The increase in pressure not only increases the heat of the remaining intake charge (thus bringing it closer to the temperature needed for combustion), but also presses the molecules into a smaller space, thus allowing faster flame front travel.

What else affects charge density? We've seen that diluting the mixture in the combustion chamber with inert gases reduces the charge density by keeping some intake charge from being pulled into the cylinder on the intake stroke. Tuning the intake and exhaust system can affect charge density differently at different engine speeds. Combustion chamber scavenging and valve timing both affect charge density. Are you beginning to see a pattern here? Yes, that's right—charge density is almost entirely based on VE (with the exception of EGR systems and one other factor). Motorcycles don't have EGR at this point in time, so for our purposes, we have VE, and. . . .

Finally We Come to Compression Ratio!

Compression ratio. Finally you know why increasing compression ratio means better power and better economy! By increasing the compression ratio, not only have we increased the starting point for combustion chamber presssure at the PPP, which will mean a higher pressure PPP, but is also increases the charge density. This means more power *and* more efficiency out of the same amount of fuel and air under the same engine conditions! A free lunch! Lucky us. So why don't all engines have a 200:1 compression ratio? Because there are mechanical limits to the strength of the materials from which the engine is made. A higher charge density means a quicker, hotter burn. That means a higher peak pressure, and higher temperatures as well. This can lead to detonation if we don't use less spark advance or a fuel more resistant to compression ignition (higher octane). And in any case, even if we avoid detonation, we could end up overheating the pistons or cylinder head, or damaging the head stud threads in the engine cases (these hold the engine top end together, so you know how important they are!). Within the limits of the materials and design of the rest of the engine, though, you get more for less with a higher compression ratio. Now you know why!

How to Alter VE?

Riders cannot change their compression ratio (unless we rebuild the engine). So what *can* we alter to change burn rate? Since motorcycles have increasingly changed their ignition timing maps to take MAP (manifold air pressure) or TPS (throttle position sensor) readings into account, we need to look at what control the rider has over MAP. And that control, of course, would be the throttle. Close the throttle and you reduce manifold pressure. Lower pressure means lower density, and that means lower VE. And that means lower charge density! Lower charge density slows burn rate.

What Do We Do About Changes in Burn Rate?

We've examined a number of things that affect burn rate in various different ways. Since burn rate changes, we need to find a way of keeping the PPP where it belongs. So let's see what we can do about changes in burn rate with the one element we can alter to change PPP: spark timing.

SPARK TIMING AND HOW IT WORKS FOR US

It's rather hard to visualize the two differing forces that are working together for the nice, smooth bell curve that represents combustion chamber pressure during combustion, because they are not always working together. At many points, they are working *against* each other. If the piston was not moving downward (thus increasing the volume and lowering the pressure in the combustion chamber) during most of the burn, we'd have detonation during every combustion event. The best way of thinking about it is to consider the charge density of the remaining unburned charge at any given point in time.

As we approach the point of spark ignition, the piston is still coming up on the compression stroke. Charge density is pretty good right now (given the mass we've ingested and trapped in the cylinder for this combustion event). We light off the mixture, and it creates a ball of burning mixture. The outside edge of that ball is the flame front, and as more mixture burns, the area of the flame front increases, thus speeding up combustion as the ball of burning mixture grows. Since it is still small and fairly slow-moving right now, it has not increased charge density by very much.

As the piston nears TDC, it pretty much stops moving in an up-and-down manner while the crank rotates past TDC and toward a point where the piston will come down quickly along with crank rotation. We definitely do *not* want the PPP to occur until *after* TDC. If it occurred at TDC, not only would the rapid increase in burn rate cause severe detonation, but it wouldn't even work to turn the crank. Instead, it would force the oil film out of the connecting rod bearing, causing damage to it (and possibly the connecting rod, crankshaft, and main bearings). This is a very bad thing. Thankfully, the ball of burning mixture is small at this point, and hasn't raised the combustion chamber pressure very much yet. As the crank continues to rotate, the piston begins to drop at an ever-faster rate. This reduces pressure in the combustion chamber, even as the ball of burning mixture is expanding and speeding up its burn rate. The increase in pressure from the burn outstrips the reduction in pressure from the increased combustion chamber volume (and note that as the pressure changes start to even out between piston falling and flame front expanding, the burn rate begins to fall off). Beyond a certain point, where most of the mixture has been burned and the piston is still moving downward pretty quickly, the pressure drops off, and the piston reaches BDC and begins the trip back up, increasing pressure to push the exhaust gases out of the combustion chamber and into the exhaust system.

You can see why timing of the PPP is so critical. Too early and the pressure will rise dangerously, causing too much heat and pressure and damaging the engine in a number of ways (not to mention wasting much more of the heat energy in other things besides useful work). Too late and the PPP will have a much lower peak (because the piston will be much farther along in the downward power stroke, with an accompanying pressure drop, and that lower pressure will slow the burn rate, exacerbating the problem). So we have a pretty narrow window for spark timing, and it depends on burn rate as well as engine rpm. Since the burn rate will be the same for a given charge density and composition regardless of any other variables, and the fact that there is less actual time used to cover a given amount of crank rotation at higher rpms, we need to advance the spark (start it sooner) at higher rpms so that the PPP will still occur at about the same crank angle, even though the engine gets there more quickly.

The shape of the combustion chamber often has a significant impact on burn rate, so we will want to adjust our timing based on how the combustion chamber is designed as well. And manufacturers need to take emissions into account, and can often make significant alterations in emissions without changing power output by very much, simply by altering ignition timing to suit (since it changes the rate, and thus temperature, of the burn). Now we have the knowledge and understanding to see the following: 1. Why very efficient engines (like diesels) generally run slowly (because a slower engine speed means more time for the fuel to be burned, and often a higher peak pressure unless the combustion speed is slowed somehow); 2. Why ignition advancers tend to make their biggest difference at part throttle (because the lower charge density slows combustion, and some power can be recovered from advancing the ignition timing somewhat); 3. Why engines are more likely to ping at full throttle and low rpm (fairly high charge density gives excellent burn rate, but slow crank speed means the PPP happens as early as it ever will, thus timing needs retard there); and 4. Why ignition advance at idle can smooth out idle speed (fairly low charge density means slow burn rate, thus and a more complete and efficient burn with more ignition advance).

SPECIAL CONDITIONS WE ENCOUNTER
Cold Starting: The Hardest Part

The most difficult special case of all is the cold engine. There is almost no heat to help vaporize the fuel as it enters the combustion chamber. Because of the cold temperatures of the metal surfaces in the combustion chamber, not only does fuel tend not to vaporize very well, but it also tends to stick to the combustion chamber walls, thus further reducing evaporation, and causing oil contamination and engine wear. There are quite a few large

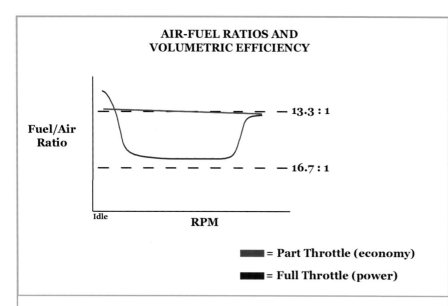

**AIR-FUEL RATIOS AND
VOLUMETRIC EFFICIENCY**

Fuel/Air
Ratio

— 13.3 : 1

— 16.7 : 1

Idle
RPM

▬▬ = Part Throttle (economy)

▬▬ = Full Throttle (power)

FIGURE 1-8: At part throttle, there is a great restriction on volumetric efficiency. Low VE means a slower burn rate, so leaner mixtures can be used without fear of detonation. When under load, however, the engine requires a richer mixture to make good power and avoid detonation. Acceleration requires extra fuel before there is a detectable change in airflow, so acceleration enrichening is a requirement with EFI, just like it was with automotive carburetors. Maya Culbertson

droplets of fuel that won't burn at all, and a lot of air without much fuel vapor in it. Since fuel is composed of many different compounds with different boiling points, only the lighter fractions (with lower boiling points) will tend to vaporize.

So we have a lot of extra liquid fuel and a lean mixture, both working against us. The throttle is closed, which helps us somewhat on the vaporization issue, but charge density drops significantly. Not only does this mean the engine is turning more slowly (allowing more fuel to fall out of suspension before getting to the combustion chamber), but it also slows the burn rate even more than it would be from the leanness alone.

The thick, cold oil resists the engine's turning over with the starter motor. This reduction in crank speed slows intake runner air velocity still further *and* drops system voltage because of the load being presented to the starter motor. Lower voltage will cause the injectors to behave sluggishly, thus *further* leaning the mixture. In addition, spark energy will drop unless we increase the dwell (essentially the "charging" time for the coil), since lower voltage means a longer period of time to build the same magnetic field!

As you can imagine, the factors involved in cold starts typically lead to the potential for high emissions, poor running, and fouled spark plugs, among other things. Looks like almost anything that could be bad for us to deliver and burn fuel to add some heat and engine speed to the equation *is* bad during cold cranking. EFI systems take some special steps to help cover cold starting, which will be discussed later. You can see, however, why small problems with the intake, exhaust, fueling, and spark systems sometimes manifest themselves for the first time during cold cranking.

Acceleration

The other significant special case is that of acceleration. Let's say we are cruising along on the freeway at a constant engine speed and we need to accelerate suddenly. The engine is in a nice, stable configuration, with it running at a set speed, getting air at a fairly constant density, and not much is changing. Suddenly, we open the throttle. What happens next? (1-19)

For starters, MAP will rise fairly rapidly as the "air pump" of the plenum filled with air at a given pressure starts increasing the density of the air in the intake runners. This will take a little bit of time, because it takes time for the molecules of air to move (as we discussed before). So MAP rises fairly quickly, which means fuel pressure has to rise a like amount; this also takes a little time. In between, we have a condition where the injectors are underpressurized, and the MAP sensor has not yet caught up with the increase in air density. Further, the increase in MAP decreases the vaporization of the fuel, making the mixture tend even further to leanness. So our engine goes lean and has a higher charge density, thus we end up with a stumble until the fuel delivery catches up with the air. This is not unlike the kind of issue people had back when cars came with carburetors. With carbs, an accelerator pump was added to squirt extra fuel in with the extra air until the vacuum-operated fuel metering caught up. We do much the same thing with fuel injection, but we can do it by either altering pulse width or adding extra pulses between normal injection events, to deliver more fuel until the ECU and fuel supply catch up. For this we use the TPS and watch for the delta alpha (rate of change of alpha, or throttle angle).

We may also wish to alter spark timing. We'll talk more about this in the section on ECU mapping philosophies.

WRAPPING IT ALL UP

We've made a long trip through the engine, we've talked about the chemistry of combustion and how fuel burns. In fact, if you understand everything you read here, you have about 80 percent of the knowledge it takes to understand the entirety of the four-stroke gasoline engine and its ancillaries. But it's necessary to know and understand all of it if you are to have any hope of being able to figure out why things are done as they are in an EFI system. If you ever want to troubleshoot, modify, or adjust your fuel injection or spark timing to meet *your* ends better, you need the tools I have given you here.

We will see how these factors shape EFI component design later on, when we talk about injectors and sensors and how they work to meet our goals and needs. But a key point we've already seen over and over again is that some of our demands work against each other, and, as always, we need the best *compromise* to achieve our goals. For instance, increasing the density of the air entering the engine (by, say, opening the throttle) means we can make more power. But decreasing the density of the air (by, say, closing the throttle) helps the fuel to vaporize more quickly, so we get a better quality of mixture, even though we get less mass. So even if looking at power alone, we have to look at how these many factors balance against each other to bring us as close as is practical to meeting our goals, regardless of whether we are a manufacturer, a consumer, or a racer.

FINALLY WE COME TO EFI ITSELF

Well, Chapter 1 was a lot of dry, difficult information. I hope I included enough photographs and diagrams to help make it more understandable. All the principles and information you read in the last few pages will form the foundation you'll need to understand why certain things will or won't work when applied to fuel injection, and why things are done the way they are done (as opposed to other possible ways). Now that a lot of the theory is out of the way, let's talk about what EFI really is.

Let me start by busting up another common misconception. Time and again, I hear people talking about EFI on motorcycles like it is a single entity—like all designs and systems are the same, they all work as well or as poorly as each other, and the differences in cost and effectiveness between them are based on some mysterious black art. Nothing could be further from the truth. EFI is nothing more than a general *category* of systems, and there are as many ways to measure and inject fuel electronically as there are molecules flying around inside an airbox!

Just like any other part of a motorcycle, you can design a fuel injection system to respond to any combination of factors you like, in ways that range from very simple and crude to incredibly detailed and complex. As I mentioned before, manufacturers start with a set of goals regarding drivability, emissions, economy, and power and then generally try to find the simplest, cheapest, most reliable way to meet those goals. These can include everything from manufacturing cost to reliability, from repair cost to ease of assembly, from flexibility in part interchangeability to promoting their technological prowess.

This tangle of often-conflicting goals usually means that some compromises are made along the way, even from the consumer standpoint. It also means that, to those who are prepared to spend the time and money, and possibly reduce reliability slightly, it is common to be able to improve on how well-met *your* goals are by the fuel delivery hardware on your bike. The drag racer, street rider, and road racer will each have a different set of goals and a different set of resources to work with. But to use another analogy, if you want a watch, you can buy anything from a cheap dime-store wristwatch all the way up to a TAG Heuer or a Breitling. Each has advantages and disadvantages, quirks and features, and different people find different watches to be the best *compromise* for their own needs.

Now let's take a look at the parts, how they work, and how they fit together into a system. Along the way, we'll discuss how the EFI system fits into the bigger picture of the drivetrain and the entire motorcycle.

FOLLOW THE FUEL

Well, we followed the gases and air backward through the system. Now let's look at fueling by instead following the fuel forward from the tank into the combustion chamber.

The Tank

The tank is pretty self-explanatory—not much to misunderstand. It's usually a metal shell (although increasingly, motorcycle tanks are being made out of special impact-resistant plastic like car fuel tanks, which cuts weight) that is sealed and holds fuel inside. A one-way valve allows air into the tank to replace fuel as it's depleted, and a charcoal canister typically condenses fuel vapors and prevents them from adding to HC pollution. The vapors are then drawn through the airbox and burned. Fuel-Injected bikes usually contain the fuel pump entirely within the tank, and there needs to be a fitting of some kind for fuel bled off by the pressure regulator to return to the tank as well.

The Pump

There has to be some kind of motive force to push the fuel into the intake runners (just like atmospheric pressure or ram pressure pushes air into the combustion chamber). This force is delivered by the fuel pump. Fuel pumps come in a variety of types and sizes, but as noted above, the pump can usually be found inside the fuel tank, and it will usually be of the roller cell type. Early systems had the fuel pump outside the tank, but having it inside the tank leaves more room for suspension and intake hardware, and has the added benefit of helping cool the pump itself, which helps extend its life. Typical pumps were originally of the vane type, but later the vanes were replaced with rollers to cut down on friction. Some Ducatis use a lobe-type pump mechanism, which is similar in design to most motorcycle oil pumps.

Pumps have to be capable of supplying enough fuel with enough speed to meet the demands of the engine without the supply pressure in the fuel rail dropping. Typical naturally aspirated port-injection fuel pumps are capable of delivering their

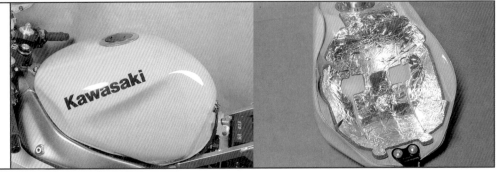

A fuel tank may not seem like much, but it is an important part of the fuel loop. This Kawasaki ZX-6RR tank contains the fuel pump. The foil insulation on the underside helps keep the fuel cool and prevents vapor lock in the fuel pump. Kawasaki Motor Corporation USA

A charcoal canister filters out fuel vapor from air leaving the fuel tank and introduces it to the intake, allowing it to be burned. This lowers evaporative hydrocarbon emissions. This one is from a Buell. Motorcycle courtesy of San Diego Harley-Davidson

rated fuel volume while maintaining a pressure in the 3–4 bar range (1 bar is atmospheric pressure at sea level, or 14.7 psi). Turbocharged applications require more pressure (sometimes in excess of 6-plus bar). To prevent the pump from being damaged in case of fuel-line blockage, it will usually have a high-pressure one-way valve, usually set at around 5 bar, to bleed off pump pressure if the output line is blocked. Since a fuel pump it draws a lot of current (more than we'd like to see going through the ECU itself), it is powered with +12–14v from the battery via a relay, which is switched by the ECU. Many systems will cycle the fuel pump for several seconds at key-on, then power down the pump until after the bike's engine is turned over. This ensures proper system pressure during starting.

Fuel pumps are sized according to the needs of the engine. The more power the engine makes, the more fuel will be required over a given time frame. The delivery characteristics of a pump are usually rated in pounds or gallons of fuel delivered per hour at their rated voltage. System designers will size a pump based on the needs of the engine. This is calculated from the total power output of the motorcycle, plus a set factor that takes into account the need to replenish fuel system pressure very quickly (to keep pressure at or near the desired level in the fuel rail). Typically, designers will use a pump that has a minimum of a 25–30 percent fuel delivery margin in excess of the engine's requirements. This not only provides for transient acceleration conditions, but also for aging of the electric motor in the pump, since over time, the

Roller-Cell Pump

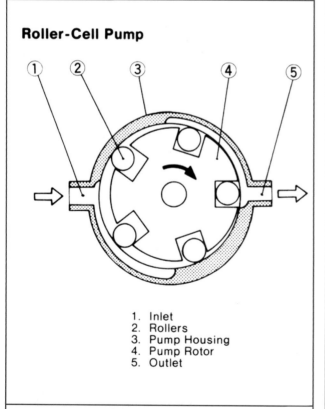

1. Inlet
2. Rollers
3. Pump Housing
4. Pump Rotor
5. Outlet

FIGURE 2-1: A roller-cell pump. You can see how each little compartment is compressed as the pump drive forces it toward the outlet. Kawasaki Motor Corporation USA

This external fuel pump is from a Cannondale ATV. Note the rubber shock mounting on the straps and the banjo-style fitting for the high-pressure fuel at the top of the pump. Vehicle courtesy of Alba Action Sports

Russ Collins of RC Engineering demonstrates a pump-testing rig, where flow volume and rate can be measured under varying voltages and loads. OEM fuel pups have capacity beyond minimum requirements, to allow for age-related reductions in pumping efficiency; however, an old OEM pump can cause a bike to run lean if it is too worn out. Testing rig courtesy of RC Engineering

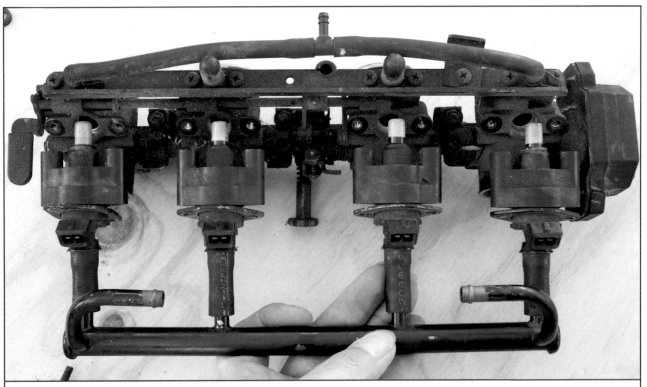

An early fuel injection rail, from a Kawasaki GPz1100. Injectors were held onto the throttle bodies with screws, and sections of rubber fuel line joined the rail to each injector. Note the inlet and return fittings on the rail itself. Sid Young

pump motor will become less efficient and incapable of delivering as much fuel as it could when new. Also, pump output drops substantially during cranking (starting) due to the drop in battery voltage, so there must be additional fuel delivery capacity to account for such a drop during cranking.

In the quest for additional power, some people raise the voltage used to drive the pump, which raises its capacity as well. This can be very important if one alters the stock pressure regulator. In some cases, two or more pumps may be used to either increase either the flow rate or the total delivery volume over a stock configuration.

The Filter

Since injectors are made to exacting tolerances, it is extremely important to prevent any solid contaminants from reaching and damaging them. Older bikes usually had their fuel filters between tank and fuel pump, while newer machines have the filter either inside the tank, or between the pump and the fuel rail. The

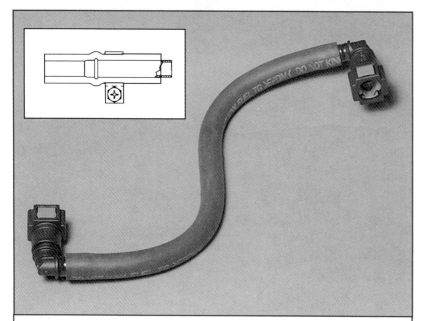

Maintaining a solid, leak-free connection is essential for high-pressure fuel lines. This photo shows one method for fuel line connection—a clip-type positive lock connector sealed by an O-ring. The inset illustration demonstrates correct technique for installing high-pressure fuel lines using a barb-type fitting. Note the generous overlap of fuel line and barb and the placement of the clamp just before the nipple. Kawasaki Motor Corporation USA

rider, the engine, the rear tire, etc. Rubber lines also deteriorate over time, requiring periodic replacement for the sake of safety, even if no cracking, bulging, or other damage to the lines has been observed.

The Pressure Regulator

At the far end of the fuel rail you will typically find the fuel pressure regulator. It is almost always a simple metal can with a spring and a pressure diaphragm inside it. On the spring side will be a vacuum line, which is almost exclusively attached to the intake runners. On the opposite side is a connection for incoming fuel from the fuel rail, and to one side of the diaphragm is an outlet.

The pressure regulator maintains pressure in the fuel rail at a given amount *above* the pressure in the intake manifold. Why is this? Well, given a certain motive force (differential pressure) and a certain-sized orifice, a liquid of a given viscosity will always flow at a given rate. In other words, if the difference between fuel rail pressure and manifold pressure is kept constant, then the injectors will deliver the exact same amount of fuel if they are opened for a particular period of time, no matter what the manifold pressure happens to be.

purpose of the fuel filter is used to screen out extremely small particles of sand, dirt, rust, or whatever else may have gotten past the mesh screen in front of the fuel pump (or in the petcock on older bikes). This filter must have a great deal of surface area to allow substantial fuel flow in spite of having very fine pores (to help trap smaller particles). Thus it is quite different in design from a filter for a carbureted motorcycle. This is an often-overlooked maintenance item on fuel-injected motorcycles, and despite the apparently high cost of replacement, it should be replaced on a regular basis to prevent fuel starvation and excessive wear to the fuel pump.

The Fuel Lines and Fuel Rail

Fuel travels from the tank to the pump (if it is externally mounted), then from the pump to the fuel rail or injectors, via a series of flexible hoses. Early on, fuel injectors were held into the intake runners or throttle bodies with clips or tabs and were connected via the fuel line. More recently, the connecting lines were replaced with a metal rail, which not only helped keep the injectors sealed into their runner/throttle body, but also reduced the number of joints in the fuel delivery system, as well as the total length of rubber hosing. Since rubber lines are more prone to failure with age and improper connection at junctions, reducing their length and number added to reliability.

The rubber fuel line used in EFI systems must be reinforced to deal with the comparatively higher pressures seen in such systems. Thus it is extremely important to ensure that hoses are properly connected to their junctions and that all hose clamps are installed as recommended in the factory shop manual. Equally important is not attempting to replace high-pressure fuel lines with those meant for carbureted systems, as this could result in the lines splitting and spraying high-pressure gasoline all over the

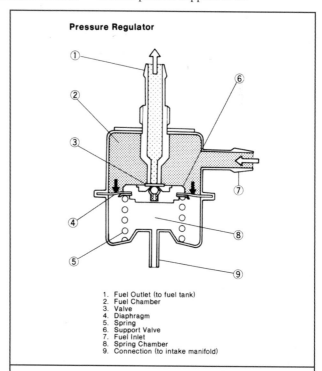

Pressure Regulator

1. Fuel Outlet (to fuel tank)
2. Fuel Chamber
3. Valve
4. Diaphragm
5. Spring
6. Support Valve
7. Fuel Inlet
8. Spring Chamber
9. Connection (to intake manifold)

FIGURE 2-2: A cutaway diagram of a typical fuel pressure regulator. Fuel coming in from the pump works against the pressure of the spring at the bottom. If fuel pressure exceeds spring pressure, the diaphragm opens, allowing excess pressure to bleed back to the fuel tank. Manifold pressure is applied to the spring side of the diaphragm to allow fuel rail pressure to reflect manifold pressure. Kawasaki Motor Corporation USA

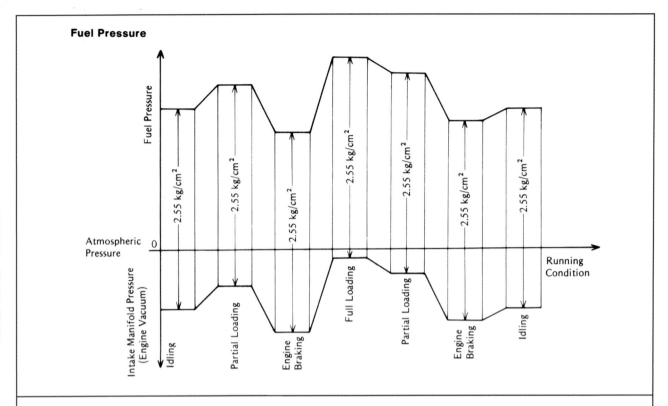

Fuel Pressure

FIGURE 2-3: *This chart demonstrates how injector pressure changes with varying intake manifold pressure. The difference between the two is always the same, so that the same volume of fuel is delivered for a given injector pulse width under all circumstances.* Kawasaki Motor Corporation USA

As you can imagine, this makes it very convenient for the ECU. No matter what the conditions are in the intake manifold, the injector will always deliver very close to identical amounts of fuel for a given injector pulse width from the ECU. Since pulse width is tied linearly to fuel delivery under the entire range of engine operating conditions, we do not need a translation table or multiplier factor to ensure consistent fuel delivery under various conditions. The pulse width directly reflects the fuel mass being delivered.

One problem with pressure regulators is that they may vary from machine to machine. With some makes, it is not uncommon to see variations of as much as 1/3 bar range of variations between regulators installed on the same model of machine. Since this directly affects the amount of fuel being delivered, it is important to maintain a precise and repeatable fuel pressure for many riders, most especially racers (who need to be able to take a tune from one bike to another without wasting time fiddling around with fuel pressure). The aftermarket offers adjustable pressure regulators, allowing not only precise control of fuel rail pressure, but the ability to raise it for increased fuel delivery on a highly tuned engine as well.

Automobiles are rapidly moving away from mechanical regulators and are instead using some ECU processing power to recalculate injector pulse width based on the fuel rail pressure and MAP. This eliminates a prime source of variability and mechanical failure, at the expense of putting more load on the ECU. As emissions regulations tighten, we will probably see this on motorcycles as well. It's a good place to get a little more precise control over fueling, but at added expense.

The Return Line

At the end of the chain is the return line, which takes excess fuel pressure and flows that fuel back into the fuel tank. On many motorcycles, you can not only hear the buzzing of the pump when you switch the key on after a recent ride, but also the trickling of fuel returning to the tank from the pressure regulator via the return line.

The Full Loop

So now we have seen the path that the fuel travels and how we maintain a fairly constant supply for the needs of the engine. It's a good base to build on. Now let's explore how we get that fuel from the fuel rail into the engine. It's time to talk about the injectors.

Now that we have established the flow path, from the ever-running pump through the filter, to the fuel lines, and into the fuel rail, with excess being bled back to the fuel tank, we have achieved a stable, responsive source of fuel to be metered. And thus we come to the electromechanical devices that actually do the metering and atomization of this fuel—the injectors.

Russ Collins, motorcycle drag racing legend, inductee into the Motorcycle Hall of Fame, and owner of RC Engineering in Torrance, California, has this to say about fuel injectors: "There are as many different injectors out there as there are different kinds of light bulbs." There is a wild assortment of sizes, flow capacities, methods of construction, attachment points to fuel rails, electrical connector types, and more. And like light bulbs, different sorts of injectors are best suited for different uses.

LITTLE TINY SOLENOIDS

All electronic fuel injectors in use today are of the electromagnetic valve type. They come in one of two basic configurations, but essentially they all consist of a body with a metering orifice in one end and an attachment to the fuel rail on the other. Inside, some type of stopper is held by spring pressure against the orifice to keep it closed. The body is wrapped with electrical wire that forms a coil. When current is sent through the coil, it generates a magnetic field that pulls the stopper off or out of the orifice, allowing pressurized fuel to pass through the orifice. When the current to the coil is cut off, the magnetic field collapses, and spring pressure forces the stopper to close the orifice, ending fuel flow.

So a fuel injector is basically just a solenoid. A solenoid is a mechanical switch that is activated by an electric current through a magnetic coil. The mechanical switch can be used to switch to a higher-current load (as is the case with a fuel pump relay or a starter solenoid), control flow (like a fuel injector or a pneumatic valve), or perform simple actions itself (like an idle air control solenoid).

The Injection Event

Because it is a coil of wire connected to a current source, it behaves electrically like any similar coil (called an inductor). As current is applied and begins to flow through the coil, the initial energy flow goes into establishing a magnetic field through and around the coil. As the field builds, it starts attracting the pintle or disc (which is the stopper mentioned above), and much of the energy flowing into the coil is used to physically move the stopper. As the stopper accelerates, it continues using energy until it reaches a limiting device that prevents further motion. If we continue to provide enough current, the magnetic field in the coil will eventually reach its maximum possible strength—at that point it is said to have reached *saturation*. (Note: We do not necessarily have to provide enough current for the coil to become saturated. We can apply less, and the stopper will still remain fully open.) From that point onward, current is only needed to offset losses from heat dissipation in the coil, wiring, and driver. Excess current (if we apply it) begins moving through the coil and out the other end of the wiring. When current is shut off, the magnetic field around the coil begins to collapse, feeding its energy back into the windings of the coil to produce current, which then leaves the coil through the wiring. With a spring pushing the stopper back to its closed position, the stopper then begins to accelerate back from where it came until the spring has forced it to its stop and it comes to rest.

What you have just witnessed was an injection event! We have now seen the mechanical part of our method for turning electrical signals into fuel delivery. That wasn't as complex as you thought it would be, was it? Provide appropriate fuel pressure, send an electrical signal to a little solenoid, and there goes our metered amount of fuel, off to be burned. But it's not quite that simple.

TAKING REALITY INTO ACCOUNT

As you see from the above description, it takes a certain amount of time for the magnetic field to build, and then time for the stopper to move out of the way of the fuel, allowing it to pass. Likewise, when the injector pulse ends, it takes time for the field to collapse and the stopper to close again. Since it takes longer to build the magnetic field than for it to collapse, and since it takes longer to open the stopper against spring pressure than to close it with the help of spring pressure, opening the injector takes longer than closing it does. The time between the beginning of the injector pulse and the opening of the pintle is referred to as the opening or dead time. For the purpose of adding fuel, almost nothing happens during the dead time. Some fuel continues to flow during the closing time, but very little. The timing of the injector pulse, and its width, have to be adjusted by a fixed amount based on these physical realities.

AND YOU THOUGHT YOU HAD IT ROUGH

So we have to do some extra math to accurately provide fueling. That doesn't seem like such a big deal, does

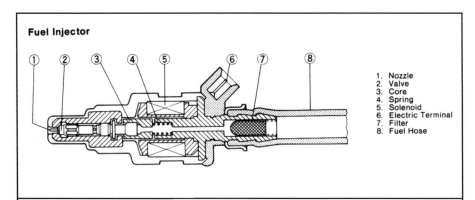

Fuel Injector

1. Nozzle
2. Valve
3. Core
4. Spring
5. Solenoid
6. Electric Terminal
7. Filter
8. Fuel Hose

FIGURE 3-1: A cutaway drawing of a top-feed saturated drive injector. Here you can see the various parts in relation to each other. Kawasaki Motor Corporation USA

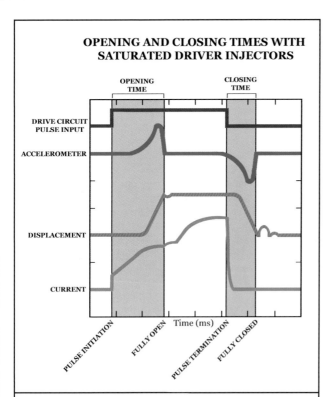

OPENING AND CLOSING TIMES WITH SATURATED DRIVER INJECTORS

OPENING TIME

CLOSING TIME

DRIVE CIRCUIT PULSE INPUT

ACCELEROMETER

DISPLACEMENT

CURRENT

Time (ms)

PULSE INITIATION

FULLY OPEN

PULSE TERMINATION

FULLY CLOSED

FIGURE 3-2: A comparison chart of injector events for a saturated driver injector. The red line represents the actual injector open signal being delivered by the ECU. The blue line represents the acceleration of the pintle or disc (opening acceleration is above the zero point, and closing acceleration is below it). The green line shows the actual physical movement of the pintle. The orange line shows the changes in current draw during the injection event. Maya Culbertson

it? How hard could that be? Consider that a four-stroke engine running at 14,000 rpm will have to have a *minimum* of 117 injector events *every second*. If it is a four-cylinder engine with sequential injection, that number *quadruples* to 467 injector events per second. The difference between open and closed for an injector is between 60 and 100 microns (about half the size of the period at the end of this sentence). This means that not only do the internal components of fuel injectors need to be *very* precisely made, but they have to be very light to accelerate and decelerate as quickly as possible. We'll discuss shortly the electronics necessary to calculate injector pulse width and many other functions at such lightning speed. Right now, let's talk some more about the physical and electrical properties of these amazing little devices known as injectors, which get put through such extremes of vibration, heat, and being banged off their internal stops a few hundred million times during the life of your bike. For kicks, I did the math—the stopper for each injector on your bike travels a total of about 43 miles during the lifetime of the bike, in increments of a tenth of a millimeter or less. Wow.

THE TWO TYPES OF INJECTORS

There are two main types of injectors available for EFI systems today. They are referred to as peak and hold driver injectors and saturated driver injectors. I will typically refer to them by abbreviation or acronym—either P&H or sat. type (or drive) injectors.

Their physical characteristics differ, as do the electronics in the ECUs that drive them. Since they differ so much in both electrical and physical characteristics, they tend to be used in different ways. Thus, they will each be dealt with independently.

One thing that all injectors used in OEM EFI systems have in common is that they are all connected to the battery's +12–14v (via often a relay) and the driver circuit actually serves as the ground path. ECU designers figured (and rightfully so) that it would make more sense to have a normal condition of no current passing through the ECU, rather than it being hooked to a high-current source all the time. This way, there is less chance of any damage to the ECU through heating or a short circuit. It does mean, however, that we are limited in the amount of power we can use to open the injectors quickly. At a higher voltage, we could use a lower amperage for the same amount of power available to open the injectors (or the same amperage to open them more quickly). This is one of the big limitations of the 12v electrical system we currently use. Cars are probably going to move to a 48v system at some point in the near future, but weight and space constraints may keep motorcycles at 12v for quite some time into the future.

Now that we know our limits (no more than a few amps of current at +12–24v to keep wire gauges and heating issues to a minimum), let's see what we can do within them.

Saturated Injectors

These are by far the most common injectors you are likely to see on a motorcycle. Nearly every stock injection system ever put on a motorcycle uses this design. There are a variety of pintle (or stopper) configurations, but they all use the same basic design. A metal needle that fits into a seat in the injector body is lifted off its seat when the coil is energized. A plastic collar is fitted to the pintle to limit its upward travel. The pintle returns to its closed position with the aid of a spring. Below the seat is an orifice and a diffuser screen that dictate atomization and spray pattern. A plastic pintle cap is then placed over the end to protect the pintle and screen and sometimes to aid in directing the spray pattern. A small fuel screen is placed at the fuel rail attachment to catch any debris that could clog or damage the injector.

The saturated injector's magnetic coil has a higher resistance (usually in the range of 13–18 ohms DC) than that of a P&H injector. It is operated by a constant current driving the coil to saturation (thus its name). This current is usually between 0.7–1.1 A. Saturated injector drivers are referred to by some as voltage sensing. Because sat. injectors have a lower current driving them, they take longer to build their magnetic field. What's more, they use a pintle with more mass than the disc-type stopper used in P&H injectors. This means sat. injectors require about 2–3 ms to

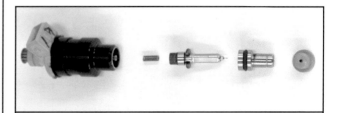

A disassembled saturated drive injector made by Weber. You can see the return spring and the pintle very clearly in this image. Note the plastic stopper clip on the pintle, and the gray plastic pintle cap at the bottom. Injector courtesy of RC Engineering

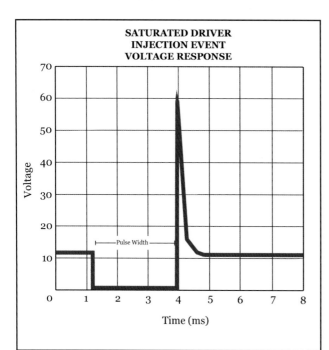

SATURATED DRIVER INJECTION EVENT VOLTAGE RESPONSE

Voltage vs *Time (ms)*

Pulse Width

FIGURE 3-3: Graph of a saturated drive injector event. Voltage starts at 12v (system voltage) and drops to zero as the injector is triggered (the energy goes to building the magnetic field). When the grounding is switched off by the ECU, the magnetic field collapses, sending the energy back down the line and generating the spike in the center of the graph. Maya Culbertson

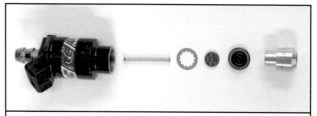

A disassembled peak and hold disc-type injector made by Delphi. Note the disc (the metal plate with six small holes) and the much longer spring. Injector courtesy of RC Engineering

open fully. In an engine that can see an injector event every 8.5 ms at 14,000 rpm, this is an eternity. It is this opening time that somewhat limits fuel delivery at high engine rpms. At idle, the pintle has to move far enough to provide sufficient fuel flow, and then close again as rapidly as possible. Since it is nearly impossible to control fuel delivery evenly based on electrical pulse width if the pintle does not open fully enough before starting to close, the minimum pulse width (and thus minimum fueling) we can guarantee for consistency is about 1.3 ms in length. Saturated injectors are only manufactured to a certain flow capacity. If you are already pushing the limits of what's available in a saturated injector and you still need more fuel at high rpm, your only option is to switch to P&H injectors (which are available with much greater flow rates than the largest of sat. injectors).

The good news is that the low current demands of this type of injector. The drive circuitry in the ECU (which must both switch enough current to energize the coil and dissipate the voltage spike produced when the magnetic field collapses) generates less heat than with a P&H injector, and the driver components can be less expensive and lower-powered. For mass production, this provides not only a cost savings and an improvement in reliability, but it also lowers weight requirements by eliminating heat sinks and larger components. For these reasons, the sat. injector is favored in OEM installations, despite its limits at either end of its fueling capacity.

Peak and Hold Injectors

Peak and hold injectors use a very different sort of construction from that of sat. injectors. Instead of a heavy pintle, the P&H injector uses a thin disc that looks similar to a small valve shim,

except that it has a number of holes cut through the flat section as if it were a movie reel. A much longer spring is used to help eliminate resonances that could prevent the disc from opening or closing at certain pulse frequencies. A very thin metal shim is used to adjust the maximum travel of the disc during operation. As with the sat. injector, the P&H injector has a body and a coil, a pintle cap and a diffuser screen, and, of course, a fuel screen at the fuel rail attachment.

The P&H injector has a much lower coil resistance (about 2.5–4 ohms DC) and is driven in a different way from the sat. injector—an initial current of around 4 A is used to rapidly build the magnetic field to yank the disc open very rapidly. Once the disc is opened, the current is dropped back to about 1 A to maintain a smaller magnetic field that will hold the disc up and out of the way to allow fueling. When the injection pulse ends, the field collapses, and the spring pushes the disc back to end fuel delivery. Some refer to P&H injector drivers as current-sensing or current-limiting drivers.

You can probably already see the advantages: less mass and more current mean faster opening times (about 1.5–2 ms), and less mass means faster closing times. With less dead time, this means more time for fuel delivery at high rpms. In addition, the rapid open and close times allow for more precise control of fueling at idle pulse widths, smaller than what's usable with sat. injectors (In this case, about 0.8 ms). This means better idle *and* more peak power from an injector with the same flow rate. Alternately, you could use an injector with a higher peak fuel flow to get the same idle quality, but more horsepower.

The disadvantages using P&H injectors lie in the driver circuit. With the high initial current demands of the injector, the drive circuit must be built with much larger and more expensive components to handle the added current flow. There must be additional circuitry to either use a timer to trigger the switch from peak to hold mode, or a current-sensing device that can switch the current level when it detects the full opening of the disc. And last, the transistors used in the drive circuit typically are not very efficient at handling current unless they are being driven at 100% of their capacity. This means they generate a lot of heat when in hold mode. This requires heat sinks, metal cases, and sometimes even forced-air ventilation to keep the electronics working reliably over time. All this adds weight, complexity, and tends to lower reliability, not to mention increasing production costs.

For high-performance applications, however, where warranty issues and manufacturing costs are less of a factor, P&H injectors rule the roost.

A Special Case: PWM Peak and Hold Injectors

Bosch uses the same design for their injectors as other P&H injector manufacturers, but they have a special driver circuit

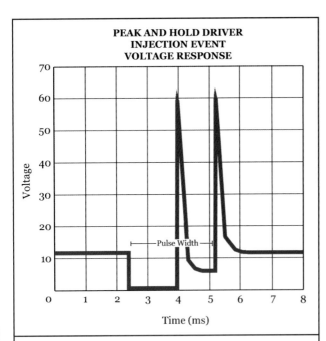

FIGURE 3-4: Graph of a peak and hold injector event. The beginning is the same as with a saturated driver injector, but after the pintle opens, the ECU switches to a lower-current drive. This switching point creates the first spike on the graph. After that, reduced current allows metered voltage to come above zero, but keeps it below 12v. When the ECU switches the injector off, the final spike occurs. Maya Culbertson

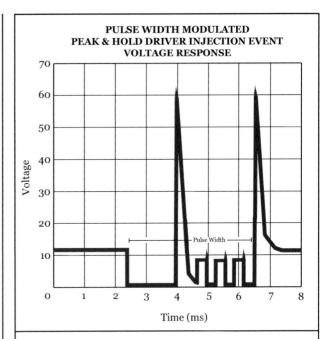

FIGURE 3-5: Graph of a PWM peak and hold injector event. This is the same as the graph for a regular peak and hold event, with one major difference. Instead of being held open with a constant, smaller current, the injector is being held open by on/off switching of the full current, as you can see from the square wave in the graph. Maya Culbertson

design for their systems. Instead of dropping the current to a steady lower level for the hold period, they instead switch the transistor on and off very rapidly. This switching on and off is called pulse width modulation (PWM), and it allows the transistor in the driver circuit to be operating at peak power the entire time it is switched on. This lowers heat generation, as well as lowering power consumption by a factor of four. The reduction in heat means more component reliability and less weight and expense necessary for cooling and heat sinking. The sole drawback is that the switching produces a great deal of RF (radio frequency) noise, which can interfere with radios, the ECU itself, or other electronics on board the vehicle. For this reason, the drive circuit and injectors need a certain amount of shielding to reduce the impact of this RF noise.

Swapping Injector Types

Since the high current draw of the P&H injector is related to its low impedance (which is the AC, or alternating current, equivalent of resistance), it is quite possible to build a P&H drive circuit and run it with sat. injectors. On most driver circuits, this would cause the driver to function in what amounts to a sat. drive mode. So it is safe (although of no real benefit) to run high-impedance injectors on a P&H drive circuit, but running low-impedance injectors on a sat. drive circuit will rapidly cause a great deal of smelly expensive smoke to pour out of your (former) ECU.

HOW BIG?

Well, now we have an idea of what kind of injectors we're looking at. But before talking about where to best put those injectors, we should

probably figure out what sort of a flow rate is going to be needed for our engine. Injectors have different limitations in their ability to flow fuel, so we need to determine the actual dynamic range of the injector type we'll be using, and then determine the flow capacity we'll need.

Dynamic Range

The differences in the two types of injector drivers are really only important on the injector side of the equation for one reason: the rise and fall times of the stoppers limit the low and high ends of the fuel delivery curve. At the low end, as we've discussed, the inability to get the stopper open and closed again in a short enough period of time is what limits minimum fuel flow. On the high end of the delivery curve, we have a different problem—past a certain pulse width, the stopper never gets a chance to close fully before it is being pulled back to the open position. This means that fueling suddenly jumps to a maximum rate at about 80–85% pulse width (in terms of available cycle time) and stays there. Both things are bad. On one end, fueling suddenly drops to nothing; while on the other, it suddenly jumps to maximum.

While a sat. injector might give accurate and reliable fuel delivery between 10 and 80% of its rated flow capacity, a P&H injector would be more likely to give linear fueling between 5 and 85% of its rated flow capacity. So you can see why a slightly larger P&H injector would be able to handle higher horsepower fueling demands without compromising idle quality and part-throttle drivability. You can think of these numbers as the dynamic range of the injectors. A P&H injector will have more dynamic range, making it a better choice for performance applications. What's more, they are available in larger flow capacities than sat. injectors.

If you build a motor making more horsepower, you will probably need to install higher flow rate injectors, like this peak and hold disc-type injector from RC Engineering. Injector courtesy of RC Engineering

Sizing Injectors

As I touched on above, injectors are calibrated to flow a certain amount of fuel in a given period of time and with a given differential fuel pressure. Since you have to burn fuel to make power, and fuel consumption is more or less related to power produced (here we will assume we have been tuning for best power), injectors are sized based on how much power you expect the engine to produce. A simple formula allows you to determine the size of injectors you will need, given your expected fuel consumption, power output, and number of cylinders. Injectors can be rated in cubic centimeters per minute or pounds per hour, depending on who is doing the measuring. They are always rated at a reference pressure (which is standardized at 3 bar) so one can figure out quickly and easily whether one injector flows more or less than another. Pump gas is fairly consistent in its density, so there's not as much variation between cc/min and lb/hr as you might think.

As you move to larger injectors, you increase the maximum horsepower for which you can provide fuel for, but at the same time, you increase the minimum amount of fuel you can deliver, too, since the minimum pulse width is a percentage of the flow rate. So it is usually best to size your injectors so they have as little extra fueling capacity as possible in the name of better idling and part-throttle fuel economy, drivability, and emissions. There are some clever ways around this double-edged sword that we will cover later in this section.

Since motorcycles have very stringent limitations on available physical space, making as compact a fuel rail and injector setup as possible is of some importance. The maximum available flow rate for sat. drive injectors is limited. In cars, this issue can be skirted by running two injectors in each intake runner, but the smaller runners and packaging constraints on most motorcycles make this a difficult option to implement. What's more, this strategy substantially raises the price of the EFI system, since it doubles the number of injector drive circuits as well as the number of injectors, and requires checking two main fueling maps per cylinder each engine cycle rather than one. It should also be noted that lower-flow-rate injectors tend to be physically smaller. Using the smallest injectors that can achieve our desired power output offers not only packaging advantages, but improved idle and cruise fueling as well. In cases where we can expect high final consumption, but also need for regular street drivability (and/or low emissions), we may have to look at clever ways of using various fuel delivery tricks to our advantage.

PHYSICAL INSTALLATION OF THE INJECTORS

So now we have our injectors correctly sized. But there is still a great deal of control we can have over throttle response, emissions, cold start, and top-end power that can be accomplished just through thinking long and hard about where to locate the injectors, how to aim them, and how the fuel actually comes out of them.

Connection to the Fuel Rail

The injectors illustrated so far are all of the top-feed type. That is, they have a connector with an O-ring at their very top that connects to the fuel rail (in some cases on older injected bikes, they have flanges attached that bolt to the fuel rail, or T-fittings to accept rubber fuel hoses). Top-feed injectors are the most common in the motorcycle world, largely because they allow the fuel rail to be set back almost two inches from the intake runner. This is important for packaging and servicing considerations on most of today's sportbikes.

Another type of injector feed is known as bottom-feed. While the internals of the injector are the same, the bottom-feed is open all around the lower half of the body and fits inside a banjo-style connection on the fuel rail. This setup is more compact and additionally helps cool the injector by always running fresh fuel from the tank through the injector bodies. Since it is difficult to mount these injectors and their fuel rail between the throttle body and the intake valve, they are more likely to be found in another location. It is extremely uncommon to see this style of injector feed on motorcycles, but it is increasingly used in automotive application.

Spray Pattern

Remember our old friend atomization, which leads to evaporation, which makes our fuel so very ready to burn? Spray pattern plays a large part in that equation. Keep in mind, though, that vaporizing the fuel too quickly can actually decrease power by displacing oxygen. Well, depending on the location of the injectors and the configuration of the intake runner, changing the spray pattern of the injector can have a profound effect on power, emissions, *and* fuel consumption.

As most motorcycles have a single injector per cylinder that is mounted near the intake valve(s), the most common spray patterns we encounter are the twin spray pattern and the pintle-type pattern. In the sat.-driven twin-spray injector, either the injector screen or the pintle cap will divert fuel into two narrow cones. Typically, they are aligned to spray directly onto the heads of the two intake valves (in a four-valve head). On bikes with a single intake valve, it's more common to see a pintle-type spray pattern, which tends to be a somewhat diffused single cone.

A Hilborn throttle body/fuel rail/injector/velocity stack assembly for EFI. You can see how the top-feed injectors are trapped between the throttle bodies and the fuel rail (which is bolted to the throttle bodies by a pair of black aluminum blocks). Assembly courtesy of Hilborn

In cases where there is a shower injector (which will be described later), mounted above the bellmouth of the velocity stack, we want a narrower spray pattern to help keep fuel from wetting the walls of the intake tract too much during the relatively long trip down to the valve. Since we have more travel time for the suspended fuel spray between the injector and the valve, we don't need to speed vaporization through a wider spray pattern. A typical sat.-driven shower injector will be either a modified pintle style or a needle and seat type with a single central orifice in the injector screen.

Disc-type injectors follow the pattern of non-pintle injectors, using the injector body, injector screen, or injector cap to control the direction, diffusion, and number of streams for the spray pattern.

The shape and spread of the spray pattern controls intake valve cooling, speed of fuel vaporization, and how much fuel ends up wetting the intake runner walls. People trying to eke the last bits of performance out of a system will sometimes try altered spray patterns to see if they can obtain a slight power advantage through subtle improvements in atomization and vaporization.

Injector Placement

The general rules about injector placement divide us into two camps that can be separate or combined: first, putting the injector between the throttle and the intake valve, and second, putting the injector in the center of the throttle bore, above the top of the bellmouth for the velocity stack. We've already talked a little bit about different spray patterns that are more or less suited to different mounting locations; now let's talk about the rationale for choosing one location over another (or even choosing both!).

The High-Mounted (Shower) Injector

When you look at a factory superbike in the pits and get lucky enough to see one with the tank and airbox cover removed, more often than not you can see a row of shower injectors strung along a fuel rail over the top of the velocity stacks. But until recently it has been quite rare to see them outside of this arena. What needs are being met there that don't exist on most street bikes?

When an engine is running at very high rpm, the air is moving through the intake runner(s) at very high velocity. While fuel pres-

Flow modeling of an injector spray pattern. Injector manufacturers are always trying to make their injectors work better for the people who use them. Here, Bosch engineers use computational fluid dynamics to model the flow capacity of a new spray pattern. Bosch GmbH

sure in the rail rises to match the increase in air pressure in the manifold, the speed of the air moving through tends to be fairly high, even very close to the runner wall. This means fuel injected fairly near the valve under those conditions might just get smeared down the intake runner wall, rather than making it out into the center of the airflow and vaporizing on the valve head(s). We need to find a place where air velocity is lower, so we can shoot our fuel straight down the center of the intake runner and not restrict

airflow in the process. Slightly above the bellmouth of the velocity stack, we find the perfect place to do this. There is very little restriction to incoming air, and we can introduce the fuel spray into the higher velocity air in the center of the throttle body bore, where it is unlikely to fall out of suspension before reaching the intake valve(s).

What's more, because the airflow into the combustion chamber is moving so rapidly, there would not be much time for

41

Shower injectors on a Yoshimura Suzuki GSX-R1000 AMA Superbike. You can see the brass-colored fuel rail above the V-stacks and the fuel pressure regulator on its right end. The four black connectors are for the injectors, and the black screw connector with the red stripe carries the injector signals from the ECU. The intake air temperature sensor is visible near the left end of the upper fuel rail; it is brass-colored and has a green connector.

the fuel mist to vaporize before being sucked into the engine; this could prevent full vaporization and lose us precious power (and increase emissions) were the injectors to be mounted on the runner or throttle body. Physically moving the injectors farther away from the valve head(s) (as is the case with shower injectors) allows more time for the fuel to atomize and begin vaporization before reaching the valve head(s), thus improving power, emissions, and fuel economy.

Large-displacement two-cylinder motorcycles can better benefit from shower injectors at lower rpm. Since they demand twice as much air per intake stroke as a four-cylinder of the same displacement, intake manifold pressure drops much farther during the intake stroke at low rpm, when compared with a similar four-cylinder. This additional pressure drop helps vaporize any fuel that has wetted the intake runner walls. In addition, the higher peak air demands when compared to a four-cylinder will tend to keep intake velocity higher than in a four-cylinder, which

helps keep fuel from falling out of suspension in the air and wetting the intake runner walls. Both of these effects work to provide better economy and emissions, as well as smoother part-throttle and idle, over what could be achieved with a same-displacement four-cylinder engine.

The big disadvantage of the shower-type injector is just what you would imagine: the large throttle plate right in the way of the fuel when the throttle is less than wide open. This can be a significant disadvantage to smooth power delivery and efficiency at or near closed throttle. It's probably the main reason why it is rare to see anything but racing motorcycles equipped *only* with shower injectors. The problem is greatly reduced with barrel-type throttle valves, but those are expensive and heavy and need to be designed specifically for the motorcycle on which they are used. Even in the racing world, they are rarely seen. Further, shower injectors create problems with intake runner wall wetting and pooling at low intake airspeeds, making for poorer idle and cruise, and

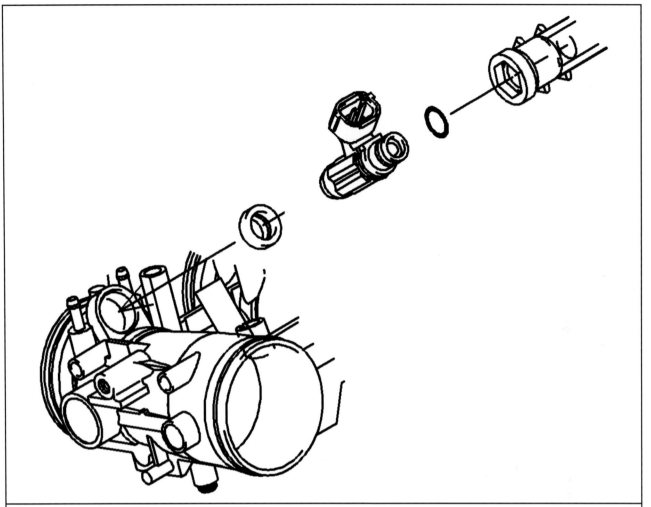

FIGURE 3-6: Installation of a low-mount injector. This exploded diagram shows how the low-mount top-feed injector is trapped between the throttle body and fuel rail, with O-rings to seal the injector and intake manifold on a Kawasaki Z1000. Kawasaki Motor Corporation USA

meaning that such a setup is unsuitable for motorcycles with smaller cylinders, as well as street use.

The end result of all these pros and cons is that a shower injector will tend to favor high air velocities (top-end on most motorcycles, and somewhat lower rpms on large twin-cylinder bikes) and give better atomization under those conditions; however, there is a significant handicap at or near closed throttle when using butterfly-style throttles. They are, however, growing popularity as one part of a two-stage injection system on larger-displacement sportbikes.

The Low-Mounted (Port) Injector

Those of you who have had a look at more than a few photos of intake runners on fuel-injected bikes with three- and four-cylinder inline engines have probably seen a great deal of consistency in how and where the injectors are mounted. On a typical single-injector-per-cylinder setup, the injectors will generally be top-mount with a fuel rail above them, and they will usually be held into their intake runners or throttle bodies (with sealing O-rings) at about a 45-degree angle to the runner. And if you look at a cutaway drawing of the intake tracts of most modern fuel-injected sportbike, you have surely noticed the slight upward bend of the intake runner, allowing

the fuel injector to be on the bottom of the runner, pointing straight at the head of the valve(s). This is as close to the ideal location for a single injector per cylinder as you can get with the throttled runner setup used on sportbikes, assuming you have to make good power, deliver adequate emissions, and provide for smooth operation at cruise and part throttle.

Two-cylinder engines where emissions and quick throttle response are a bigger issue than raw top-end power can also benefit from placing the injectors between the throttle plate and intake valve(s). At small throttle openings (idle and cruise), the low pressure behind the throttle plate works to increase vaporization greatly. When the airflow rate is fairly low, low-mounted injectors respond much more rapidly to changes in throttle opening, because the fuel has less distance to physically travel to reach the combustion chamber.

So low-mounted injectors tend to favor emissions and throttle response and are a good choice when your primary area of operation will be at fairly small rates of airflow. They lend themselves perfectly to most street bikes, which is why they are so often found in those applications. This configuration is also the best choice, by far, for use in smaller and less powerful engines.

GETTING THE BEST OF BOTH WORLDS

So is there a way to get great power out of an engine running wide-open at high rpms, and still get good transient throttle response and cruise emissions and smoothness? We can have all that *and* get more peak power in the bargain. Ducati figured this out some time ago, and has equipped a limited number of production motorcycles to capitalize on the best of both injector-mounting worlds and get extra dynamic range for fuel delivery in the bargain.

We've seen that injectors have a certain dynamic range formula: when you make them bigger to deliver more fuel, the smallest amount of fuel they can reliably deliver goes up as well. This tends to worsen part-throttle cruise and idle. What's more, different injector locations offer advantages and disadvantages that are very close to being opposite of each other.

So having both a high-flow and a low-flow injector will give the best of both worlds. The dynamic range of the two injectors overlaps, and having both a shower injector *and* a runner-mounted injector to capitalize on the benefits to engine operation can be had from each choice.

The most obvious possible solution would be to have a smaller, port-mounted injector that runs by itself when there are small throttle openings and/or a low fuel demand are required, and then switch over to operation of the shower injector at larger throttle openings and engine speeds, where the extra fuel delivery and physical advantages of the shower mounting can be utilized.

In actual use, the runner-mounted injector is typically run all the time, and when it gets close to its maximum usable duty cycle of around 80%, fuel is then added from the shower injector. At maximum fuel demand, you can have the full flow capacity available from *both* injectors combined. This allows a slightly smaller shower injector, which makes transitioning between its operation and single-injector operation a bit smoother, as well as cutting down on costs.

To prevent the engine speed from oscillating around the point where the shower injector gets switched on, the controller uses *hysteresis* to prevent the oscillation. In short, hysteresis causes the switch-on point for the shower injector is set slightly higher than the shutoff point for the second injector, in terms of fuel demands. That way, fuel demands have to climb a little bit following shutoff to reactivate the shower injector. This prevents the system from oscillating back and forth, with the accompanying drivability and power delivery issues you might expect.

A high/low injection setup allows for the excellent idle, fuel economy, drivability, and part-throttle response and performance of a small port-mounted injector, in addition to providing the extra power delivery available from a larger, shower-mounted injector. And the best part of all is that it allows a wider dynamic range of fuel delivery than any single injector could offer by itself.

The disadvantages, of course, are the added expense of an extra set of injectors, an extra fuel rail, and the extra injector drive and control electronics for twice as many injectors. In addition, to get best effect from such a setup, one should time the injection events so that the fuel from both injectors reaches the valve head at around the same time. This means even more additional work for the ECU. Such systems are found almost exclusively on racing motorcycles, or homologation specials like the Ducati SPS models. Honda has begun offering a street model in this configuration with its CBR600RR and CRB1000RR models, although it is clear that bike that both bikes are intended to serve as a racing platform in nearly stock configuration (much like the aforementioned Ducatis).

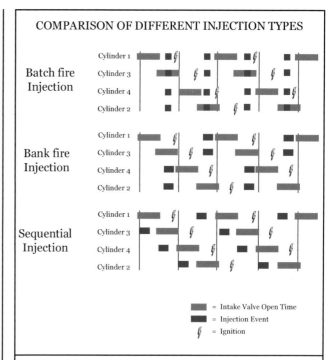

COMPARISON OF DIFFERENT INJECTION TYPES

Batch fire Injection — Cylinder 1, Cylinder 3, Cylinder 4, Cylinder 2

Bank fire Injection — Cylinder 1, Cylinder 3, Cylinder 4, Cylinder 2

Sequential Injection — Cylinder 1, Cylinder 3, Cylinder 4, Cylinder 2

= Intake Valve Open Time
= Injection Event
= Ignition

FIGURE 3-7: A diagram comparing the event sequences in the three types of injector event timing. Injection event timing has a large effect on idle quality and off-idle smoothness, but at higher engine speeds, the timing is much less critical, due to the intake air velocity and very brief time period available for a complete engine cycle. Maya Culbertson

DRIVING THE INJECTORS

So we've talked about where to put the injectors, how they work, how to size them, and how they respond to being "switched" on and off, let's look briefly at various strategies to control when they open. Especially at low rpm and low injector pulse width, *when* we deliver the fuel can be as important to idle quality and emissions as *how much* we deliver.

Since a full cycle on a four-stroke engine is 720° of crank rotation (two full revolutions), we need to be thinking in those terms when discussing injection events. One of the key points here is that a crank sensor can tell you where in its rotation the crank is (with a degree of precision based upon how many fingers the trigger wheel has), but cannot tell you the engine *phase*—that is, which cylinder(s) in an inline engine is/are at the top of the compression stroke, and which is/are at the top of the exhaust stroke (remember, the crank rotates fully every 360°; a full cycle is *two* rotations, or 720°). To give us information on what phase of its cycle a given cylinder is in, we need to measure something that only rotates 360° for every 720° of crank rotation.

Fortunately, we don't have to go very far to find something. Our camshafts rotate in just that pattern. You will find that most motorcycles have a cam position sensor (which some manufacturers call a cam phase or engine phase sensor). Engines with a V configuration often use two sensors set apart at the same angle as the cylinders, with a single finger on the cam's trigger wheel; this allows the ECU to know when each cylinder is at a certain rotational point in a given phase (and thus is used as a calibration point for fueling, and often for spark as well).

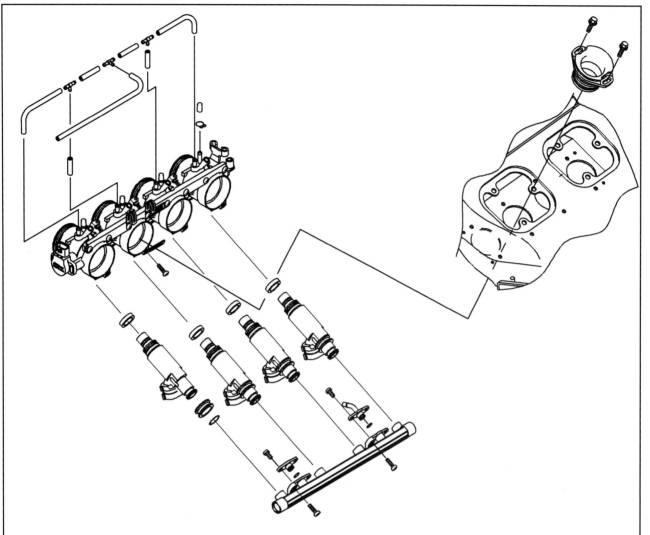

FIGURE 3-8: Port fuel injection lends itself wonderfully to sequential injection timing, since each cylinder has its own, separate injector. Here we see an exploded diagram for a Kawasaki ZX-12R, showing how the injectors, throttle bodies, and fuel rail install. Also note the clever use of a frame section as airbox and the mounting of the velocity stack. Kawasaki Motor Corporation USA

The speed at which things happen at higher rpm is very fast indeed. At 14,000 rpm, a complete engine cycle (two full crank rotations) occurs every 1/117th of a second, or every 8.6 milliseconds. In the time it takes you to blink your eyes, the crank has turned 68 *full* revolutions! At these kinds of speeds, it hardly matters when we inject the fuel in the cylinder's cycle—it will end up in an almost identical state when in the combustion chamber. But things happen much more slowly (relatively speaking) at lower engine speeds, so the timing of the injector pulses relative to cylinder phase here makes a much bigger difference.

There are three different ways we can group injectors for different cylinders together for the purpose of injection event triggering. They each have advantages and disadvantages, and to help you understand the differences, I've included a diagram to demonstrate the timing of injector events and intake valve open times for an inline four-cylinder engine. Again, different manufacturers and companies have various names for the different modes, but in this book, they will be referred to by their most common designations: batch-fire, bank-fire, and sequential injection.

Batch-Fire Injection Triggering

Batch fire is conceptually the easiest form of injection triggering to understand and implement. In a batch-fire system, all the injectors are triggered simultaneously. On an inline four-cylinder engine, this will require firing all the injectors once per crank revolution (twice per engine cycle). The clear advantage with this system is that there is no need of engine phase information—since the injectors are fired together on every crank revolution, that information would be redundant. Some bank-fire or sequential systems revert to batch-fire mode in the event of the cam position sensor failure. Another advantage is that you can use a much slower processor, since there is only one injection triggering event per crank rotation, and there's one less sensor to read and take into account. However, this advantage has been pretty well moot since the mid-1980s. You cannot even source a microcontroller any more that can't at least handle bank-fire operation or even better, even at high engine speeds. This, and the lack of need for a cam position sensor, was considered in economic terms when such a fuel delivery method was still a viable option for the OEMs.

The disadvantages are pretty obvious. Having two injector events per engine cycle doubles the fuel delivery at minimum pulse width (requiring smaller injectors for acceptable idle control), and it also means the peak injector output is cut another 15–20% (since there are two open/close events, the cap on pulse width is doubled). The dynamic range of the injectors is greatly reduced, relegating this form of injector triggering to engines that can accept poor idle quality or make little peak power. The other major disadvantage is that at least one injection event per cylinder will occur long before the intake valve is to open, thus wetting the intake valve and intake runner walls with fuel. Depending on engine and ambient temperatures, this fuel may not evaporate well, and in fact may puddle on the intake valve head. If the engine is warm, some of the fuel vapor could escape past the throttle butterfly and into the airbox. Cold starting, cold running, and idle control can all be severely affected by this method of injector triggering. Even under warm-engine operating conditions, at least some of that fuel will pass through the combustion chamber and out the exhaust valve during overlap. All of these negatives will also increase exhaust emissions.

Bank-Fire Injection Triggering

The next step above batch fire in the injection event food chain is bank-fire injection. Bank fire fires the injectors in two or more groups. On an inline four-cylinder, there would be two banks of two injectors each. It is most common to see the injectors paired for cylinders that have intake valve opening times that are as close as possible. In a typical inline four-cylinder engine, this would mean that the banks would consist of cylinder 1 and 2, and cylinders 3 and 4. This prevents the need to inject fuel into the intake runner and leave it hanging around to wait for a valve to open. At lower rpms, this strategy generally means less fuel lost out the exhaust due to valve overlap and less displacement of intake air by vaporized fuel. It offers improved idle and emissions over a batch-fire setup.

Bank-fire triggering clearly requires an engine phase sensor to operate in such a configuration as intended. However, there is still only one injector-triggering event every crank revolution, which means that processing capability is not taxed much more than with batch-fire injection.

Bank-fire triggering is suitable for microcontrollers of roughly the same speed and power as those suited for batch-fire operation, requiring only the addition of a cam position sensor and a little bit of extra code. It also offers the advantage of only having one injector event per cylinder for each complete engine cycle (two crank revolutions). The increased dynamic range means both better idle metering and increased maximum fuel delivery from the same flow rate injectors as compared with batch fire.

However, it still does not provide for optimum injection event timing for best idle quality and emissions at cruise and idle.

Sequential-Fire Injection Triggering

The most commonly used and best-performing method for triggering injector events is the sequential method. Using sequential triggering, each injection event takes place the same amount of time before that cylinder's intake valve opens (or after, should the

designers so dictate). This will give, by far, the best idle quality, as well as full control over fuel vaporization and loss through cam overlap. This has almost universally been the choice of OEM injection designers for most of the last 10 years, not least because a primary reason for moving to EFI has been to lower emissions.

Since this method has two discrete injection events per crank revolution (for a four-cylinder engine), it is most demanding of processing power, and of course requires an engine-phase sensor (which today means having a cam-position sensor). It offers the maximum dynamic range of the injector, just as with bank-fire triggering. It has the best ability to deal with high-performance cams (such as those found in many sportbikes), and it is the only injection event control method that allows a four-cylinder engine to run different maps for the inside and outside cylinders (which is necessitated by the use of different length inner and outer velocity stacks more than anything). Further, it's the only injection method that makes much sense for slow-revving twin-cylinder bikes. It also allows us a great deal of control over emissions, economy, and power output (since we can precisely time fuel delivery against engine events for all the cylinders on the engine individually). Advances in ECU design and increases in processor power and speed have made this the method of choice for current and future EFI development.

ALL FUELED UP

We've now taken the complete path from tank to pump to regulated fuel rail, through an injector (or two), and into the intake manifold. We talked a bit about injector pulse width, how injectors respond to triggering events, and how an ECU can deliver those events. We've got the actual *delivery* of the fuel down cold. That was the easy part, though. The hard part is finding a useful way to determine how wide that pulse should be, so that the bike runs, and runs within the parameters we (or the designers) intended. On the foundation of knowledge and awareness we have built in this chapter, we'll move on to tackling the heart of the matter, and by far the most challenging part: modeling the actual behavior of the engine and the gases and fluids that move through its intake and exhaust tract, as well as its combustion chambers.

Creating the Injection Pulse

Now we come to the most complicated part of the whole business: figuring out just how much fuel to deliver, when to deliver it, and in many cases, when to trigger a spark to burn it. The biggest issue we have to face is that an engine, and the behavior of the gases entering and leaving it, is a *dynamic* system. Its state changes depending not only on changing inputs and conditions, but often on the *rate* and *direction* of change as well. This means that any model we make of the behavior of this system will necessarily be pretty complex. Those of you who are familiar with tuning carburetors already know this in a roundabout way; if the system we were modeling (whether with carburetors or EFI) behaved in a simple, easily predictable manner, jetting carbs would be the very essence of simplicity. But the truth is that tuning carburetors, like tuning EFI, becomes a delicate web of balancing one sort of need against another and picking the best compromise (there's that word again!).

The big difference between carburetors and EFI is that carbs are "dumb". They only know about two things, throttle position and manifold pressure (which changes based mostly on the density of the air). They have no idea how fast your engine is

FUEL SYSTEM MAINTENANCE

Injectors are a marvel of technology. They operate under harsh conditions and function with very fine tolerances, despite being subjected to strong solvents, corrosive effects, and severe mechanical cycling. The passages through which the fuel flows are very small and are easily restricted by deposits. Further, deposits can obscure parts of the fuel screen or pintle cap, ruining atomization of the fuel as it leaves the injector. What's more, those same troublemakers can cause extra friction between the injector body and its stopper, which can cause increased wear or even injector failure.

The same factors that are a threat to the injectors cause other problems with power and emissions in the engine. Since they also cause uneven, heat-insulating buildup on the backs of the valve heads and inside the combustion chambers, this duo of deposits and corrosives is a significant enemy to proper fuel delivery and atomization, volumetric efficiency, and engine life. Deposits on the back of the valve heads can reduce VE by up to 15%! This means lost power and fuel economy.

Fuels today are significantly improved from those available in the early days of fuel injection. Thanks to the extensive use of EFI in automobiles, fuel formulations were changed to help reduce the formation of such corrosives and deposits. But fuels containing alcohol tend to bind water with the alcohol and contribute to corrosion of the injectors and fuel pump. Further, to meet emissions and volatility requirements, pump fuel cannot contain the ideal amounts of the additives that help to prevent damage and deposits.

Condensation from humidity in the air and water vapor from the combustion process make their way into the intake runners, airbox, throttle bodies, and even the fuel tank. That condensation mixes with nitrogen oxides, sulphur from fuel, and other compounds to create acids and gummy residue, plus the scaly, hard deposits that can be found on the back of a valve head after many miles. And fuel that leaks past the injector's stopper during the period immediately after driving creates the worst of these deposits. Thus, repeated short trips create more of a problem than a few longer ones.

An additional problem exists because the irregular surfaces of the intake valve deposits tend to hold a certain amount of fuel in their uneven surfaces, which creates a lean condition during startup. This causes one of the most common early symptoms of deposit problems, hard starting and poor running when cold. Combustion chamber deposits can cause pre-ignition and/or pinging from raised combustion chamber compression and localized hot spots of red-hot carbon that act like glow plugs in a diesel engine initiate combustion far from the spark plug.

A key to keeping the fuel injectors and intake valves in your system clean and free of deposits is regular treatment with a quality fuel additive that can combat the formation of acids, suspend water and carry it into the combustion chamber to be eliminated, and help thin and remove deposits that may already exist, especially within the injector bodies.

Ideally, you should be using a high-quality fuel system cleaner such as Motul's *Fuel System Clean* on a regular basis (a good yardstick here is a can in the tank with each recommended dealer service). Such a fuel additive will help to dissolve deposits that have already formed, thin the gummy precursors to injector and valve deposits (so they can be drawn into the cylinder and burned), and emulsify water in the fuel system (which allows it to pass harmlessly through the engine and out the tailpipe). If you tend to make more frequent but shorter trips, you should use such a treatment more frequently, since each time the vehicle is shut off while hot, the gummy precursors of fuel system deposits begin to form.

More than ever before, today's motorcycles require very clean components to function as they should. Removing sediment, varnish, gum, and water from the fuel and intake systems will help ensure low emissions, good cold starting and fuel economy, and maximum power from your motorcycle for years to come.

---

going (although intake air density at a given throttle position will change based on engine speed), and they don't know how hot or cold it is or whether your engine is warm or not. Given the fact that they are such simple mechanisms, it is a wonder of the natural world that they work as well as they do. We stumbled onto them by accident and refined them through trial and error until we got something that worked amazingly well.

With the continuing development of digital logic and the advent of affordable, compact microprocessors, we were offered a chance to do what could not be done easily (or reliably) by mechanical devices alone. We could watch for certain *sets* of conditions that appeared or changed in certain patterns and use those to trigger or alter our outputs. In other words, we could at least make cause-and-effect maps to describe the behaviors of our system in some way that worked at least as well as we needed them to. Being able to watch more inputs, watch them faster, integrate data between different inputs, and keep track of *trends* in these changes and patterns allows us to ultimately make more power while delivering better fuel economy and cleaner emissions from our engines.

But several challenges face us. Digital electronics are great, but a typical processor can only do one thing at a time. To stay a step ahead of the engine, keep track of all the data being gathered, and still provide accurate timing and duration of injection pulses, we need to run the microcontroller fast enough to do all the math before we run out of time to start the pulse, even when the engine is running at or beyond maximum speed or find another way to accomplish the same task. Beyond this, we need to have small, stable, reliable devices to gather useful data for us, and many times, to condition the signals from these devices so they are easily read by the microcontroller. We also need to make the sensors and the components in the ECU able to stand up to extremes in heat, cold, and vibration and last for years in the process.

None of this has been an easy task, and developments are happening every day to further these ends. Along the path of development, we've been able to obtain lighter, faster, and more reliable devices to do these jobs. And even better, at least from the standpoint of the manufacturers, they can be made *cheaper* now, too.

SENSORS

Having an ECU that can crunch numbers faster than a Pentium may be nice, but it means nothing without a reliable stream of useful data for it to work with. So before we worry about our ECU and how it will make use of the data, let's talk about gathering the data in the first place.

History, and How Far We've Come

The first EFI-specific sensors were developed in the mid-1950s by Robert Bosch GmbH in Germany for their D-Jetronic fuel injection system. D-Jetronic used analog processing circuits to cleverly combine a number of different waveforms from its sensors and output a pulse-width-based injector trigger signal. But the heart of the system was its clever method for measuring air pressure.

In analog circuits, a coil and a capacitor wired in parallel form what is called an LC network. When driven with a DC voltage, it becomes an oscillator at a given frequency. You can change the frequency by changing the value of the capacitor or the inductance of the coil. Cleverly, Bosch took advantage of the fact that moving an iron core in or out of a coil would change its inductance. They built a bellows that was connected to whatever you wanted to use as a source of air pressure (or lack thereof), and put an iron core on the back of the bellows. As pressure dropped, the bellows would contract, pulling the core out of the coil; as pressure rose, it would push the core back in. So the oscillator changed its frequency based on air pressure. Genius!

The downsides to this magical and clever device were threefold: First, they were about the size of a softball and weighed three pounds each; second, they were mechanical devices, and thus prone to malfunction due to dirt, corrosion, moisture, vibration, heat, and wear; and last, they were prone to being affected by stray magnetic fields.

The D-Jetronic system did not last very long before being largely replaced by the far lighter and more reliable sensors of the L-Jetronic system. But the principles of the D-Jetronic are still in use to this day on the vast majority of motorcycle EFI systems.

Today, there is a whole host of commercially available sensors, mainly designed around reliable, rugged solid-state technology. Almost anything you can imagine can be measured, from acceleration to pressure and flow, from stroke to torque, and so much more. The automotive field is again responsible for spurring development of stronger, smaller, and cheaper components from which we all benefit. The scale of mass production in the auto industry also allows us to ride their coattails to achieve cost benefits we in the motorcycle world could never realize on our own. Let's take a look at how far we've come, even across the 20-plus years that fuel injection has been available on production motorcycles.

The Two Types of Sensors

The D-Jetronic pressure sensor was a valiant early effort, but was impractical for many reasons. Over time, sensors have largely been confined to two categories, although there are a few that don't neatly fit into any category. I'll discuss each sensor individually in the next section and will note whether a particular sensor is a resistive or a signal generation sensor. But I'll talk about them as categories as well, since these categories will later relate to how those signals are

processed and conditioned, and, ultimately, how they are used.

For what it's worth, there's nothing in this chapter that is absolutely critical to understanding what fuel injection does or how it does so. This chapter deals with the varieties of sensor designs you will find on an EFI bike and some of the pros and cons of each one as you (or the manufacturer) might use it on a bike. Some may find it fascinating, and others boring. If you're not interested in physical science and what it takes to pick out particular sorts of sensors for particular uses, feel free to skip ahead to the next chapter, where I describe their actual uses on motorcycles.

Resistive Sensors

Resistive sensors tend to be pretty easy to categorize, because they all use some variation of the same sort of behavior. There are all manner of methods to turn the measured information into resistance values, which are turned into a voltage in basically the same way on all resistive sensors. How such devices are used to obtain a variety of data can be ingenious, as we shall see.

Potentiometers are one of the oldest sensor technologies still in use in EFI systems. Little has changed in the 20-plus years since this TPS was installed on a 1982 Honda CX500 Turbo. Note the frangible bolts designed to prevent tampering with the TPS calibration. Sensor courtesy of Greg Goss

Potentiometers

Potentiometers are variable resistance sensors that typically consist of a resistor with a lead on each end and a wiper that slides across the surface of the resistor. By applying a calibrated voltage to one side of the resistor and grounding the other side, we can measure the position of the wiper by measuring the voltage as measured at the wiper's point of contact. The farther the wiper goes toward the ground side of the resistor, the lower the output voltage will be. And as the wiper moves toward the powered side, the voltage will increase. Since these sensors need to be grounded on one end, they are connected to the ECU via three wires: calibrated input voltage, ground, and signal out. Isolating them from the rest of the electrical system helps reduce noise and other stray signals that might be conducted through the vehicle's electrical system or chassis. Variable resistors are great for measuring the motion of mechanical pieces (especially rotation). This makes them ideal for use to measure throttle position, or EXUP-style valve position. You can also find them in most float-type fuel level sender units, and in VAF (volumetric airflow) flapper-type airflow sensors as found on old Kawasakis and many Japanese import cars of the 1980s.

The advantages of the potentiometer are many. They have been around for decades and can be sourced cheaply and easily. Response characteristics can be tailored quite easily to suit the requirements put forth by the designer of the system. They can measure fairly small changes in position with good accuracy. And there are many manufacturers capable of making such devices, meaning there is basically no chance of running into a supply problem at any point. In addition, there are different grades and qualities of potentiometers for different prices. It is also possible to make them redundant (with two resistive tracks and two wipers) to help ensure a valid measurement.

The disadvantages primarily center on the potentiometer's mechanical nature. They are prone to wear over time, wiper contact area can degrade, and readings can be inconsistent due to dirt or worn bits of resistor track getting in the way. Potentiometers have a finite useful lifespan and should probably be replaced on high-mileage vehicles to ensure best power, emissions, and drivability, especially at or near closed throttle, where street vehicles spend most of their life.

There are other alternatives to potentiometers, but they are not currently being used on motorcycles. These alternate sensor types are typically solid-state, which makes them hardier for the long term; however, some alternatives require support electronics to process the signals into a form usable by the ECU. Between the increased cost of production and the cost of the support electronics, it is currently the position of the industry that potentiometers are a more cost-effective method of reaching sensing goals, while maintaining good long-term reliability. The automobile world is rapidly changing to special, variable-output Hall-effect devices (called non-contact rotary position sensors), which are more stable and precise than potentiometers. This is a likely future development for motorcycles, as well. Cars even use them for drive-by-wire technology, which is a technology likely to be adopted as well someday by motorcycles.

Thermistors

Thermistors form the next class of resistive sensors. The name comes from their method of operation: they are *thermally* sensitive *resistors.* This makes them ideally suited for measuring temperatures. Intake and coolant/oil temperature sensors are typically thermistors. The most frequently used form of thermistor is one whose resistance drops as temperature rises. This characteristic is known as *negative temper-*

NTC thermistors are well suited to a harsh life of dirt, oil, fuel, and other contaminants found inside the airbox. Here we see an IAT sensor being installed in a Kawasaki ZX-6RR's airbox. Kawasaki Motor Corporation USA

*ature coefficien*t, and you may find reference to this sensor type in literature about your motorcycle. It is commonly abbreviated as NTC. Since thermistors change their resistance internally, and not mechanically, they typically will have only two leads: one for calibrated input voltage, and one for output voltage. Internally, they are semiconductors, and they generally last a very long time.

Unlike mechanically variable resistors, they have no moving parts and are very resistant to dirt and other environmental contaminants. NTC thermistors are ideally suited for use on vehicles due to the fairly large changes in resistance that can be achieved by fairly small changes in temperature, as compared with other methods of turning temperature into an electrical signal. Like potentiometers, they have been around for decades and are available cheaply from a variety of sources.

Piezoresistive Sensors

This class of resistive sensor is excellent for recording very small mechanical movements. The most common use for piezoresistive sensors is in the small, reliable solid-state pressure sensors that are commonly used today.

Piezoresistive elements are part of the same family as piezoelectric elements. *Piezo* is from the Greek root meaning "to squeeze." Piezoelectric and piezoresistive ceramics are unique in their electrical behavior, which changes based on compression or flexing, and vice versa. With no moving parts to wear out, they last a long time and are very light. As you might infer from the name, piezoresistive elements change their resistance based on being physically compressed or flexed. Due to limits in the amount of physical deformation they can withstand before they shatter, they are very useful in measuring very small deflections, like those from small differences in gas pressure.

Development has brought us to the point where these piezoresistive elements are actually often built on a thick film substrate, making them incredibly small and light. They are constructed of a captive bubble at a reference pressure, with piezoresistive elements on top of the bubble (where they can flex) as well as nearby but off the bubble itself (where they can provide a reference resistance based on temperature change). These four resistors are combined in a circuit called a bridge (in this case, a Wheatstone bridge, for those who want to delve further into the actual electronics involved). The nature of a bridge circuit is such that applying a reference voltage to the bridge causes an output signal that is proportional to the difference in resistance between the four

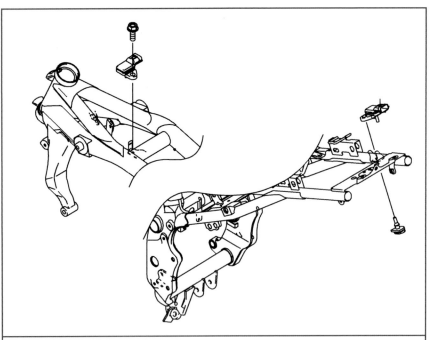

FIGURE 4-1: *Thin-film piezoresistive pressure sensors are light, stable, and hardy. They have brought us a long way from the early days of pressure sensing. Most motorcycles using speed density mapping have both an ambient and an intake air pressure sensor, as with this Kawasaki Z1000. The ambient sensor is mounted in the tail, while the intake sensor is mounted near the intake manifolds and is connected to the intake runners via vacuum hoses.* Kawasaki Motor Corporation USA

a ferrous (able to be magnetized) core wrapped in wire. When a triggering wheel passes a tooth close to the core, a voltage spike is generated (positive voltage at the leading edge of the tooth, and negative voltage at the trailing edge). These are as basic as you can get in terms of sensing position of a rotating device, like a crankshaft.

The advantages are the lack of moving parts and the simplicity of construction. Despite being a bit heavier than the alternative, they can be made for very low cost and are fairly reliable over the lifespan of a vehicle. They are also relatively insensitive to temperature extremes. Since they have been used as triggering devices in transistorized ignition systems for a very long time, a great deal of knowledge and hardware is already in place to handle the special parameters of these signals.

The disadvantages are more plentiful. Because the speed of the generation and collapse of the magnetic field determine the amplitude (height) of the voltage spikes, the voltage increases as the rotation increases in speed. On the other end of the scale, a very slow rotation could result in a very low signal amplitude, which could be a problem under certain conditions, especially during cold cranking. And regardless of the extremes, there will be a fair amount of conditioning required to make the signal usable to the ECU. Because of how the signals are processed, and the inverse square law (which you can look up in a physics textbook if you want the skinny), inductive sensors have a very low tolerance for variations in the gap between trigger wheel and sensor. Even a very small increase in the gap will alter the output such that there is no signal after processing. If you've ever had to troubleshoot an electronic ignition system on a motorcycle, you know just how sensitive to correct gap these sensors can be. In addition, since each pulse from the sensor is a slope, and the angle of the slope changes with the speed of the engine (which changes the *width* as well as the *height* of the pulse), the accuracy of something like a crank angle reading will typically be lower from this type sensor when compared with a Hall-effect sensor. It is possible to get a very precise measurement of the timing of the start of a pulse, but it requires more expensive electronics to do so.

resistors in the bridge circuit. Since resistors change value with temperature, having two of the resistors in the circuit be identical to the measuring resistors allows the sensor to essentially self-calibrate for temperature changes. A small amplifier then raises the signal level and passes it along to the ECU via the wiring harness.

A very similar sensor can be produced in slightly larger sizes for slightly less money. This sensor uses the identical principles, but replaces the thick film with a silicon base. These are used instead of thick film sensors when the pressure variations are higher (as in a turbocharged engine), or where it is desired to measure the difference between two pressures (by applying one to each side of the silicon base). The latter has occasionally been used to measure the difference between airbox and manifold pressures (which would give a strong indication of throttle position), among other things.

Generally, both types have about the same reliability, with the thick film style being lighter, more compact, and usually more expensive.

SIGNAL GENERATION SENSORS

We've looked at many kinds of sensors that indicate changes via resistance and need a calibrated voltage applied across them to extract the data they gather. But there is another class of sensors that actually generates a voltage based on its measurements. There are a wide variety of methods for generating such signals, but they all have the commonality of producing their own signal without reference voltages.

Inductive Sensors

These sensors have been used the longest for ignition and fuel injection, on both automobiles and motorcycles. They are quite simple—

Hall-Effect Sensors

Hall-effect sensors are used in many of the same sorts of ways that one might use inductive sensors. In an increasing number of cases, they replace inductive sensors altogether.

The Hall effect is a very unusual property of semiconductors (which are the basis for solid-state components). In most cases, semiconductor designers seek to minimize this tendency, since it can cause problems with microchips and other solid-state devices. But here, we seek it out, and use it to our benefit. The Hall effect is as follows: If you apply a current through a semiconductor (or any conductor, for that matter) in one direction, and then move a magnetic field through the wafer, a current can be measured across the wafer that corresponds to the strength of the magnetic field. This means we can make reliable solid-state sensors that can

Crank angle sensors are perhaps the oldest of sensor technologies used on motorcycles, but they still provide essential data on engine speed and crank angle to an ECU. The more teeth on the trigger wheel, the more precise the measurement of crank angle can actually be. This Kawasaki Z1000 trigger wheel sports 23 teeth, with one missing to confirm crank angle. The sensor is the black box to the right of the trigger wheel. Kawasaki Motor Corporation USA

detect a change in magnetic field, sort of the opposite of the way an inductive sensor works.

Since the sensors themselves are solid-state, it is simple to then build signal conditioning circuitry onto the same slab of silicon. But there is a trade-off here: Silicon is a great medium on which to make a small conditioning circuit, but it is not the best material with which to make a Hall-effect sensor. Making an "ideal" sensor on top of a silicon substrate with onboard conditioning circuitry dramatically increases the cost of manufacture.

There are a great number of different Hall-effect sensors that have various desirable characteristics. They can be designed to give a digital, fixed-voltage square-wave output (which is perfect for use in a sensor detecting rotation with a toothed wheel), or an analog output based on the speed or proximity of the triggering device. Multiple devices can be placed a fixed distance from each other in a single package (such a device is called a differential sensor) and used as the basis for such a square-wave output by comparing the differences in time of the triggering, which eliminates any issues with proximity of the trigger. This is a very common form of Hall-effect device in the automobile world to obtain rotational triggering signals. It has yet to be found on motorcycles, however.

Ultimately, Hall-effect sensors are very flexible and can be tailored for a variety of uses. They require less downstream signal conditioning due to their capacity for onboard conditioning without a substantial increase in manufacturing cost. This also gives them great flexibility in their internal configuration. Hall-effect devices tend to be fairly insensitive to the gap between the trigger wheel and the sensor, making them of great use where thermal expansion might change clearances.

Unfortunately, they do have their drawbacks. The most obvious is that even in their simplest forms, their cost is substantially higher than that of inductive sensors. Also, Hall-effect sensors (which are favored for cam position sensors) require a magnetic trigger wheel, and the fingers on the wheel must be relatively wide in comparison to those usable with inductive sensors. This means that a single Hall-effect sensor by itself is much better placed when a smaller number of triggering events is required per revolution, as is the case with most injection systems' cam-position sensors, which are only triggered once per cam revolution

(since they are only indicating engine phase, not crank angle). A gradient sensor, with two or more Hall-effect sensors in one package, can be used to measure rotational angles with a small-diameter wheel at a much higher resolution. As was discussed in the section on inductive sensors, Hall-effect devices have the edge for precision and stability.

PIEZOELECTRIC SENSORS

Like piezoresistive sensors, piezoelectric sensors respond to being physically stressed. In this case, they will either generate a current when flexed, or conversely, will flex when a current is applied. Piezoelectric elements are commonly used as small speakers and microphones in handheld electronics (because a voltage applied to them causes them to move, and vibration applied to them causes an electrical signal to be generated). As sensors, of course, they would be used in the same manner as with a microphone—they would convert small mechanical changes (or vibration) into an electrical signal.

One use for piezoelectric elements is in knock sensors. By layering a piezoelectric element with a thick layer of silicon, you can create a sensor that is sensitive to physical vibration. Since the silicon layer has more mass than the piezoelectric layer, vibration tends to stretch and squeeze the piezoelectric layer while the silicon layer is lagging in acceleration or deceleration due to its mass. This generates a voltage that is then filtered to remove expected vibration from the normal running of the engine, leaving behind a signal that corresponds to the amount of knock detected. These sensors have largely replaced the mechanical acoustic sensors that were once used for knock sensing. They are

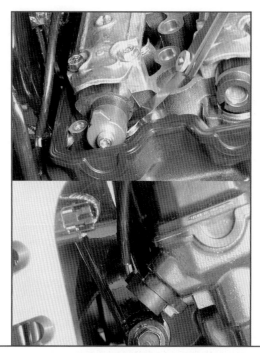

Hall-effect sensors are ideally suited for living in the hot environment of the cylinder head in the form of cam position sensors. Here we see the trigger wheel, with its one tooth, in the top photo and the sensor itself in the lower photo. The motorcycle is a Kawasaki Z1000. Kawasaki Motor Corporation USA

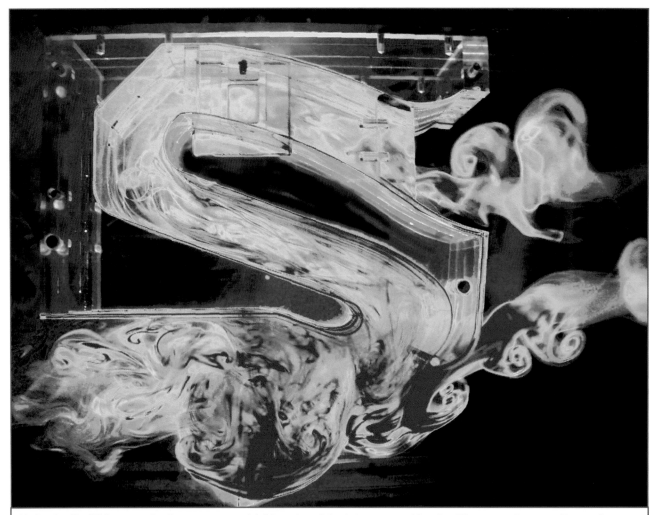

Modern hot-film MAF sensors often incorporate a special airflow channel that helps ensure unidirectional flow across the sensor. The translucent square at the top center shows the location of the actual sensor elements. Bosch GmbH

commonly bolted to the side of the engine, and look rather like a plastic coated GM side-post battery terminal.

Piezoelectric elements also make fine accelerometers, since they will flex from inertia when one end is accelerated. They are used quite frequently on today's cars due to their small size and reliability. For instance, they compose a key element in many automotive stability control systems, since they can be arranged to detect acceleration or rotation in any direction or on any axis if enough elements are used. In this way, they detect when a car is actually moving in a different direction from where it is being steered and can activate brakes or steering input to control it. We may someday see such systems (and their accompanying sensors) on our motorcycles.

HOT ELEMENT AIR MASS SENSORS

Like piezoelectric and piezoresistive sensors, the two main types of sensors in this class take advantage of special electrical properties of certain substances. All resistors are temperature-sensitive in their resistance, but certain metals can be heated by passing a current through them, and this change in temperature produces a corresponding change in resistance. This sensor class has only one purpose in four-stroke engines—to measure airflow. And

since the different types made have very different advantages and disadvantages, they will each be covered independently here, rather than in the next chapter on the actual use of sensors in various parts of the motorcycle.

The hot-wire mass airflow sensor was the first on the scene. It used a fine piece of platinum that was strung through many areas of airflow (to get as representative a measurement as possible) and connected to a heater control circuit. Early hot-wire sensors changed the current to try to maintain the same resistance at all times and sent out a signal based on the amount of current used by the heater. While this simplified things in terms of circuit design, its main drawback was the fact that the temperature of the wire changed rather slowly with changes in current. Therefore, it was a fairly unresponsive sensor speed-wise. It was also quite expensive to make and had a finite service life. Lastly, it also required the heater circuit to superheat the element after every shutoff of the vehicle to burn away deposits that would insulate the wire from the airflow and cause the vehicle to run lean.

A later version kept the current to the wire constant and used the changing resistance of the wire based on airflow to be the variable leg in a bridge circuit. Like with other resistive sensors, this allowed for another, non-heated platinum wire to be used to correct for differences in air temperature, making it self-correcting. The new design was a solid step up from the early sensors, but was still lacking in lifespan and speed of response (although not as much as the first version).

Then came the first hot-film sensors. They used the same principle as hot wire, but were made on a thick film like that used in piezoresistive pressure sensors. This allowed them to be much smaller and lighter. However, they were exposed to less of the airflow than a hot wire would be, so they had to be mounted in a location where the laminar (smooth) nature of the flow was relatively constant. They put a thick segment of calibration resistor in front of the actual hot film element, which gathered any deposits on its leading edge. This eliminated the need for the heating cycle at the end of each drive to keep the sensor clean. The new type of sensor was also much faster to respond to changes in airflow (on the order of 1 ms response time), and more robust as well (which increased reliability).

The last version of the hot-film sensor is the most recent, and is only now coming into substantial use. This version has compensation resistors upstream and downstream of the sensor

itself. This allows it to measure airflow in each direction independently, as opposed to the previous versions, which measured air mass passing by in whichever direction. The substantial advantage is clear—the sensor here can signal the air that is actually available for use by the engine, not just the passage of the air itself. Especially on vehicles with performance-oriented cams, this can be a very big issue, especially at lower rpms. Reversion can account for as much as 40% of the incoming airflow, which would mean a drastically over-rich condition with a bidirectional sensor. These new sensors are also smaller and lighter than the earlier hot-film sensors. On the one hand, this was better for the obvious reasons—but it has also made it more and more difficult to get a useful cross-section of flow, and thus runs more of a chance of delivering a measurement that's not representative of overall airflow.

The advantage of this class of sensor is very clear, and a major one: It can measure the *actual* air mass entering the engine. Since the cooling effect on the element is directly related to the total number of gas molecules moving past the sensor, it is a true measure of air mass, and it no longer needs to be calculated based on a number of different sensors. This makes mapping much

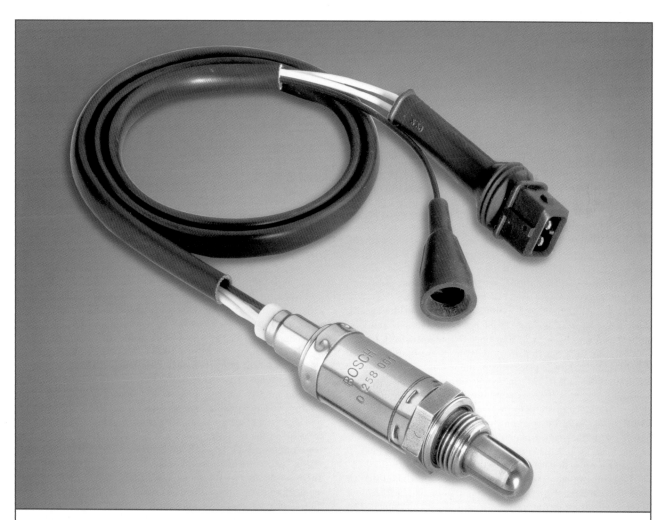

Heated oxygen sensors, like the Bosch unit shown here, allow closed-loop operation much more quickly after cold starting. As emissions standards tighten, more and more motorcycles will come from the factory equipped with O_2 sensors. Bosch GmbH

simpler and also frees up some processor overhead that was formerly devoted to checking several sensors and then doing math to calculate air mass. And as opposed to vane-type (VAF, or volumetric airflow) airflow sensors, they do not obstruct intake air.

Unfortunately, they are very expensive to manufacture and become more so as they get smaller and more responsive. Manufacturers have gotten quite good at making effective, responsive versions that are sturdy, but the cost, combined with the difficulty in finding a good location for an accurate, smooth signal, has limited their usage in motorcycles to date.

THE ODDBALL: OXYGEN SENSORS

This is the one sensor that truly fits in no other category. It operates under the *galvanic* principle, which is probably more than most of you wanted or cared to know. Suffice it to say that they are very clever little buggers indeed, especially in their wideband form. Let's take a look under the hood of these sensors and see what makes them tick.

Oxygen sensors come in several varieties, but they all operate by the same basic principle: oxygen molecules can be made to migrate from one side of a ceramic (typically zirconium dioxide) to the other at high temperatures. A typical oxygen sensor has electrodes on either side of a ceramic core, with air on one side and exhaust gas on the other. At operating temperature, oxygen molecules move from the open-air side through the sensor substrate to the exhaust gas, and the number of molecules that move is based on the difference in oxygen content between the exhaust gas and the outside air. By measuring the tiny current generated by the moving oxygen molecules, one can determine how much oxygen is in the exhaust gas (the more migration of molecules, the more current there will be).

Oxygen sensors have a fairly narrow operating range in terms of temperature. The first oxygen sensors were unheated. They relied on the heat from the exhaust gases to warm up the ceramic core to operating temperature, which is typically about 600° C (1112° F). At operating temperature, changes in exhaust gas composition are reflected in sensor output in as little as 50 ms; however, at 350° C (662° F) the same change takes several seconds, which is clearly useless for fine control of fueling in an engine that even at idle is firing nine or more times per cylinder in one second. And the sensor can be damaged from as little as several minutes at temperatures of about 850° C (1562° F).

These early sensors were mounted fairly close to the exhaust ports for good heating (they could not be used for closed-loop control until they were at or near operating temperature), but far enough away so as not to damage them from overheating at high engine load. This made placement of the sensor very critical. The warm-up time made for little or no pollution control on short trips.

Many of these problems were solved with the addition of an electric heating element into the sensor body. This brought the sensor up to near its operating temperature very quickly, and ensured that it stayed warm enough to work well even under low engine loads (which tend to keep exhaust temperatures low). It allowed for more flexible placement in the exhaust as well.

Later developments allowed for the removal of the outside air source requirement (by reversing the pump so that it would remove oxygen from the exhaust and pass it into a reservoir, which then releases it into the exhaust downstream from the sensor) and moved from a large ceramic structure to a much smaller planar sensor element, which is flat and has a number of layers. This advance made the sensors smaller, lighter, and, most especially, cheaper.

Standard oxygen sensors (now sometimes referred to as narrow band) have a response curve that is not very sensitive to changes in oxygen content, except in a certain narrow range surrounding the stoichiometric ratio for gasoline. Since we require a stoichiometric mixture to effectively operate our three-way catalytic converter, this works out very nicely. However, it does not give us an effective way of measuring oxygen in the exhaust outside of the narrow range of operation (about $1.01 > \lambda > 0.98$). Since the best economy in an "ideal" engine is leaner than the O_2 sensor can reliably read, and the best power would be richer than it could reliably read, this does not give us an effective tool to judge much of anything (never mind that we will have different "ideal" lambdas for any given goal, depending on the volumetric efficiency and spark timing in our engine!).

Scientists have cleverly found a method of using a narrow-band O_2 sensor as part of a larger sensor that can measure a very broad range of residual oxygen. They are called broadband or wideband sensors (WBO_2), and are known by a variety of designations, depending on manufacturer (Bosch has the LSU4, while NTK has the L1H1 and L2H2). Ingeniously, they use a small ion pump in a subchamber. Using the narrow-band sensor as a guide, a controller increases current in the pump to either add more oxygen to the subchamber (if the mixture is rich), or to remove it (if it is lean). The amount of current required to hold a stoichiometric mixture in the subchamber is measured, and is proportional to the actual lambda of the exhaust. Essentially it's a mini closed-loop system, but to maintain the mixture in the subchamber rather than at the tailpipe! WBO_2 sensors are capable of reliably and accurately reading mixtures from $\infty > \lambda > 0.7$.

The benefits of oxygen sensors again speak for themselves. WBO_2 sensors are a great tool for getting an initial map that's "in the ballpark" enough to tune an engine at the track or on the dyno; they are also sometimes used on lean-burn vehicles that often operate well lean of $\lambda = 1$. Narrow-band sensors are just the ticket for closed-loop idle and cruise operations, which reduce emissions without harming power or drivability (much). They can perform a number of invaluable emissions and timesaving functions, depending on the type of sensor and its use.

However, O_2 sensors are not terribly cheap, especially wideband units. They have a finite life; like a spark plug, they start wearing out as soon as they are installed. WBO_2 sensors are good for as little as 150 hours of use, depending on the exhaust environment.

AND WHERE DO WE PUT THEM?

So now we have covered all the kinds of sensors that have been used on modern EFI motorcycles and some potential uses. Now it's time for us to talk about where we would find these sensors and which types we might use. Don't worry, I know it seemed like we were on the track of how the fuel gets into the engine. But we have to give the ECU some input for the model it keeps locked inside—with that data, it can simulate the fuel demands of the engine and give it what it needs to run. To understand the models, we need to know where the data comes from, and then I'll tie it all together for you in a discussion about the models themselves and the strengths and weaknesses of EFI. So let's get through the next chapter on sensor locations and data-gathering and move a step closer to unlocking the mystery of how EFI works. It's not that hard to figure out!

CHAPTER 5

HOW IT WORKS:
WHERE THE SENSORS ARE

If you followed along in the last chapter, you know how the various sensors work and the benefits and drawbacks of the various types. This will help you unravel some of the mysteries of why certain sensors are chosen over others, or other types, on production bikes, and will get you started on thinking about how you might choose your own sensors, if you wanted to make your own system.

This chapter will discuss what sensors can be found on motorcycles, what they measure, and what types of sensor design they use. Some of these sensors (and the reasons for using them) might seem mysterious even after reading this chapter, but never fear—after one more chapter (on the ECU itself), we'll start to talk about the modeling strategies used by EFI. That is when it will all snap together into one big picture for you: the engine's opera-

tion, the data being gathered by the sensors, and the model that takes the sensor inputs and turns them into fuel delivery—delivery that *works* to achieve our goals for the engine (or those of the people who built it, at least!). For right now, just trust that we need to be taking measurements of some or all of the things we're measuring here. Soon you will learn why those measurements might be important.

MASS AIRFLOW SENSOR

The mass airflow, or MAF, sensor is not used very commonly on motorcycles. Despite giving a very accurate and direct indication of the air mass being used by the engine, it has a fatal flaw (even in the advanced designs now available)—it best responds to smooth, even airflow. Older designs cannot differentiate between air moving forward and air moving backward, so with high-lift cams where some intake air is being pushed back out the intake runner, there will be a reverse pulse that can result in an over-rich mixture. What's more, constant-temperature sensors need time for the temperature of the sensor to change when the current changes. Since the sensor is generally placed where it is less likely to get large, quick variations in airflow, it needs to have some kind of air tank between it and the intake runners on most high-

FIGURE 5-1: A fuel injection system is a complex web of multiple sensors, numerous other electrical components, the motorcycle's charging system and, of course, the ECU. All of these pieces must work in perfect harmony with the power production hardware on the motorcycle. Here we see a system diagram of a Kawasaki ZX-12R, showing air, fuel, and electrical flow, as well as component layout.
Kawasaki Motor Corporation USA

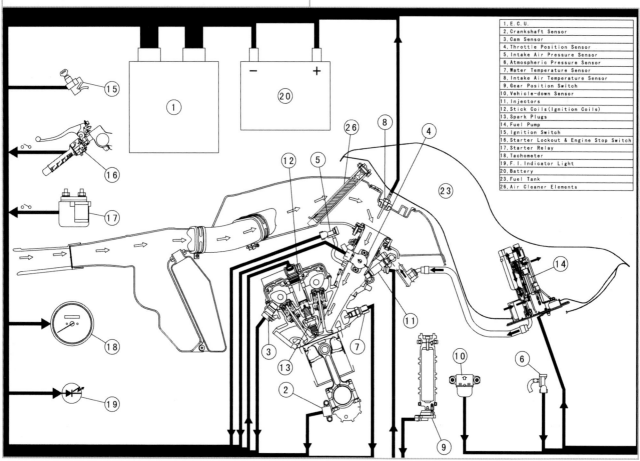

1. E.C.U.
2. Crankshaft Sensor
3. Cam Sensor
4. Throttle Position Sensor
5. Intake Air Pressure Sensor
6. Atmospheric Pressure Sensor
7. Water Temperature Sensor
8. Intake Air Temperature Sensor
9. Gear Position Switch
10. Vehicle-down Sensor
11. Injectors
12. Stick Coils(Ignition Coils)
13. Spark Plugs
14. Fuel Pump
15. Ignition Switch
16. Starter Lockout & Engine Stop Switch
17. Starter Relay
18. Tachometer
19. F.I. Indicator Light
20. Battery
23. Fuel Tank
26. Air Cleaner Elements

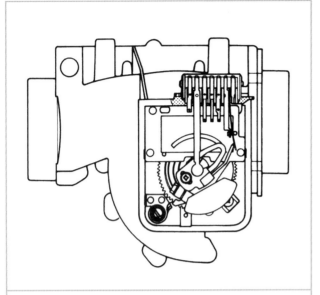

FIGURE 5-2: The flapper-type VAF was a carryover from automotive EFI and proved to be ill-suited to use on motorcycles. This early Kawasaki unit from a KZ1000G is nearly identical to the Bosch units seen on countless import cars of the 1980s. *Kawasaki Motor Corporation USA*

The round, black unit atop the throttle body on this Moto Guzzi houses the TPS. Almost all motorcycle EFI systems in history have incorporated this valuable sensor. Note the engine temperature sensor, with blue connector, on the upper right.

performance vehicles. This physically isolates it from the actual air that's entering the cylinders. Since air has mass and takes time to accelerate and decelerate, changes in engine demand take time before they will affect the amount of air coming into the plenum. These two delays combine to prevent the sensor from reflecting the engine's actual air demands at any given moment unless the engine cannot accelerate very quickly. Slow acceleration means a slow rate of change to the airflow, which lessens the effect of the delays from installation.

It is theoretically possible to install MAF sensors in each intake runner, either before or after the throttle. However, the closer the sensor is to the throttle, the less even the airflow will be through the cross-section of the intake runner. This would make it incredibly difficult to measure airflow accurately across the full range of throttle positions. Add to that the sensor's preference for more constant airflow, and the cost of these sensors, and it quickly becomes impractical to use individual MAF sensors on each runner.

Since having more cylinders will mean there will be more intake events in a given time period when an engine with more cylinders is running at the same engine speed, airflow to and in the plenum will tend to be more even as the number of cylinders increases. Combined with the fact that with a slow delta rpm (rate of change of engine speed), the sensor is more reflective of actual air mass entering the engine, this sensor is a good choice only on motorcycles that tend to have flat, even powerbands and many cylinders. You would be more likely to find them on four-cylinder touring motorcycles, for instance, over sportbikes or big V-twins. Only one manufacturer has used MAF sensors extensively.

VOLUMETRIC AIRFLOW SENSOR

The VAF (which has been commonly referred to as a "flapper" airflow sensor) consists of a spring-loaded flap that sits in the intake tract of a motorcycle. It can be found between the outside

air and the plenum, for similar reasons to those discussed in the MAF section. There is a second flap at a 90° angle to the main flap, which has a volume of trapped air behind it. Since the trapped air resists compression in direct relation to how fast it is compressed, it serves as a damper to prevent oscillation of the flap that measures airflow. The flap is connected to a potentiometer, which forms part of a bridge circuit. By including a temperature-sensitive resistor that is exposed to the intake air, this compensates for potentiometer drift from air temperature changes. It also provides the ECU with air temperature data.

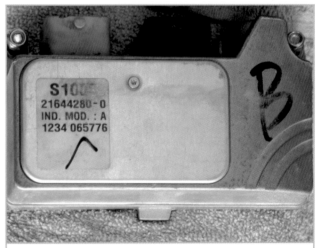

A number of ECUs past and present have incorporated an internal AAP sensor. This JCAE/SAGEM ECU from a Cannondale off-road motorcycle contains an internal AAP sensor housed within the case under the B marking. *ECU courtesy of Alba Action Sports*

Especially on turbocharged engines, it is of vital importance to have measurements of air pressure in various parts of the intake tract. This intake system from a Honda CX500 Turbo has no fewer than four pressure sensors, plumbed to the intake tract via the gray vacuum hoses in the center. System courtesy of Greg Goss

throttle plates to control intake air density and throttle the engine's power output, I'll just be describing how a TPS works in relation to butterfly-type throttle(s).

A TPS is a well-calibrated potentiometer that attaches to the end of the throttle shaft and measures alpha (throttle angle). Since there are no other mechanical parts inside the potentiometer housing (like the return spring used in the VAF), they can be sealed against dirt and corrosion. They are substantially hardier than the potentiometers used in VAF sensors, but they do eventually wear out. The automotive world has largely abandoned them in favor of Hall-effect rotation sensors, but even the remaining automotive potentiometers far exceed the quality and longevity of most current motorcycle potentiometers. Due to the shorter lifespan of motorcycles, this is a cost/benefit ratio that is found acceptable by the manufacturers at this time. We may see even better quality sensors on bikes in the future.

Now, the amount of airflow that the throttle plate allows is not linear with its angle. In other words, the difference between 1° and 2° open is much greater in terms of delta airflow (rate of airflow change) than the difference between 50° and 51° open. It has a non-linear response; small changes near closed throttle make a much bigger difference in airflow than small changes near wide-open throttle. This is one of the disadvantages of the TPS; it does not respond linearly to changes in actual airflow. However, this can be all but eliminated by using a potentiometer with a logarithmic response curve, which will more closely match actual delta airflow. This has advantages and disadvantages from a programming perspective, and many automotive applications use a linear potentiometer for its predictable behavior when faced with aging and temperature changes.

Since some systems require a very precise measurement of small changes in alpha, their potentiometers are available with multiple resistive tracks and better coupling to the wiper arm. These benefits combine to make for a more reliable and precise reading, in addition to delivering a longer life for the component. The downside, of course, is the increased price of such a sensor.

PRESSURE SENSORS

It may not be apparent just yet, but one of the most important classes of sensors on today's motorcycles is that of the pressure sensor. Solid-state technology has continued to advance over the years and has delivered smaller, cheaper, and more reliable sensors along the way. Today's sensors are about half the size of a candy bar, and weigh less. In most cases, they will far outlive the motorcycle itself.

All EFI motorcycles have a sensor that is used to measure barometric (or ambient) air pressure. Most have a sensor devoted to this function alone (as it is often cheaper to implement and/or requires less computing power), but some cleverly use another pressure sensor before startup, or during certain running conditions, to read and store a value for AAP (ambient air pressure). Air pressure is half of the density equation, making this a very important baseline measurement. In addition, we can also determine how hard the atmosphere is trying to push air into our engine. Ambient air pressure drops about $1/2$ psi (sea-level air pressure is about 14.7 psi) per 1,000 feet of increase in altitude. This equates to roughly half a main jet size change for every 1,000-foot

The drawbacks of this sensor are several. First, it's even slower to respond to changes in airflow than the early MAF sensors were. Second, the potentiometer is a wearable item, and will not only wear out over time, but is prone to getting dirty as well. And perhaps most importantly, it's a rather significant impediment to the airflow itself. This lowers the power a vehicle can produce and how quickly it can develop that power.

Flapper VAF sensors were cheap and easy to make, and cars used them quite a bit in the early years of automotive EFI (mainly in the Bosch L-Jetronic system). They were tried early on in motorcycle EFI, but the demands of the engines and intake systems being used meant they were rather quickly abandoned in favor of other sensors.

THROTTLE POSITION SENSOR

This has long been one of the most important sensors on an EFI system. Even systems that don't ever use throttle position (which is also known as alpha, describing the throttle angle) for primary mapping of fuel delivery will still have a TPS. And since nearly all motorcycle (and automotive) applications use butterfly-style

change in altitude. A bike jetted for a 15:1 AFR at sea level (which is lean of stoichiometric) will be running an AFR of 11:1 (which is very rich!) at 12,000 feet above sea level. Even if you changed fueling to compensate for the loss of air density with altitude, you'd still be down to 36% the peak power available at sea level! So you can see how important ambient air pressure measurement is for the determination of accurate fueling. Carburetors have a limited range of AAP compensation via the float bowl venting. As ambient air pressure drops, the amount of fuel being delivered drops as well, since it's not being pushed into the engine as hard as it would be with a higher AAP. EFI, however, needs to be told about such changes. Thus, the need for a measurement of AAP.

Pressure sensors can also be found in various spots along the intake tract, depending on the mapping model used by the ECU. On ram air bikes with sufficient airbox volume, there is typically a pressure sensor reading the airbox (plenum) pressure. Since ram air pressure can be in excess of AAP, it is important to know the density of the air in the airbox, as well as how hard it is trying to push its way into the cylinder. You will generally see this sensor referred to as the intake air pressure (IAP) sensor, although in some cases it is referred to as a throttle inlet pressure (TIP) sensor to avoid confusion about where air pressure is being measured on turbocharged applications.

Possibly the most important place to record pressure in mapping terms is between the throttle and the intake valve. A sensor located here will be called a manifold air pressure (MAP) sensor. This measurement is again half the density equation. We can use it to help determine how dense the air is as it is being ingested by the cylinder, and use that to determine the air mass inside the cylinder after the intake valve closes.

In some cases, a single two-sided sensor will be connected between the intake runner and the airbox/plenum. This sensor measures the difference between the two, and thus is a useful way to measure the throttling of the intake air without using any processor cycles. Since sensors are now smaller and lighter, and ECUs have plenty of channels for processing input data, this type of sensor is largely outmoded.

CRANK POSITION SENSOR

Crank position, or n (crank rotational speed, which is the engine's rpm), is another of the most important sensors on the motorcycle. It was used in electronic ignition systems some time before EFI appeared on motorcycles. Early on, it mainly counted engine speed and marked TDC (top dead center) so the ignition box would have a reference point against which to time ignition events. Early EFI systems actually used the primary coil triggering signal to count engine rpm (although because ignition advance changed based on rpm, the ECU would have been required to have a reverse map of ignition advance vs. engine rpm to be able to determine crank angle from such a signal; since it would have been more practical to simply install another sensor, we can infer that this methodology was never used).

Since electronic ignition came before the dawn of affordable solid-state sensors, they used one or more inductive pickup coils to produce their triggering signals. With the ignition box being an analog circuit in most cases, this fit in well with the analog signal produced by the inductive pickup(s). Not only did the voltage of the spikes increase with rpm, but the number and frequency of the spikes did as well.

When the switch was made to integrated ignition and EFI in a single box with shared sensors, the inductive pickup was retained. Its

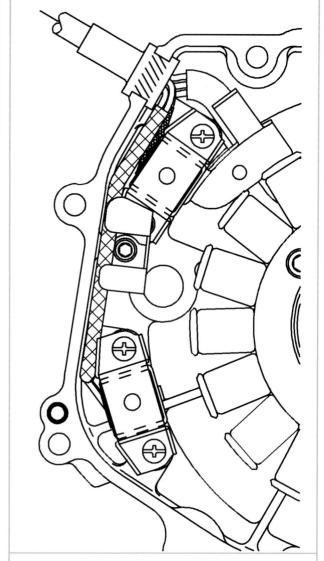

FIGURE 5-3: Some motorcycles incorporate crank position sensor triggering with the flywheel and charging system. Here we see the two crank sensors (the squares on the left of the illustration) used on a Kawasaki VN1500 Mean Streak. Having one sensor for each cylinder allows for a simpler ECU. You can see part of the stator coil (for the charging system) on the right. Kawasaki Motor Corporation USA

low cost and hardy nature were big advantages, and, at least at first, ignition was handled by a separate section of the ECU (it basically just had the old ignition module put next to the EFI section on one circuit board). When the switch was made later to microprocessor control of ignition timing, the sensor style was again retained.

As fuel injection becomes more complex and precise, it has become more and more important to know exactly where the crank is in its rotation. This has given rise to an increasing number of teeth on the trigger wheel, usually with a gap of two or more teeth to signal TDC (or another set crank position). This not only allows the ECU to register acceleration much more quickly, but also helps make it easier to trigger events based on crank angle (a trigger wheel with 58 teeth and a two-tooth gap gives a 3° crank-angle resolution). Auto-

WHERE THE SENSORS ARE

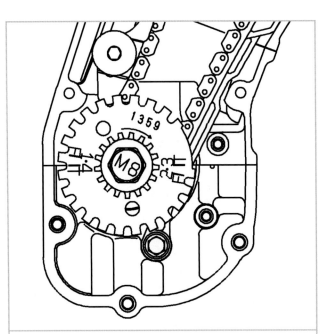

FIGURE 5-4: *More teeth on the trigger wheel means a more precise measurement of crank angle. More and more, motorcycles are increasing the number of teeth on the crank trigger. Here, a Z1000 crank trigger wheel sports 22 teeth, with two teeth missing to establish crank angle. Kawasaki Motor Corporation USA*

The cam position sensor gives us important information about engine phase on four-stroke engines. This Kawasaki Z1000 mounts its Hall-effect CPS on the front of the engine, to the left of the #1 cylinder. Kawasaki Motor Corporation USA

motive applications typically use a larger-diameter trigger wheel, which means more teeth can be physically fit on the wheel's circumference. Motorcycle trigger wheels are limited in their number of teeth by the maximum rpm the engine will reach and by the physical limitations of having a much smaller-diameter trigger wheel.

CAM POSITION SENSOR

This is a very handy secondary sensor (sometimes referred to as g) that runs from a trigger wheel that is usually found on the end of one of the camshafts (or the only camshaft, in the case of a single-cam bike). Since the crank position sensor already tells us where TDC is, where the crank is in its rotation, and how fast the crank is turning, we don't need to gather any of that data from the cam sensor. In fact, all we really need from the cam sensor is a single signal per rotation to tell us what phase the engine is currently in. Since the cams are typically chain-driven, and the torsional forces in the cam fluctuate a great deal due to the irregular nature of the cam lobes, cam position often cannot be used as a reliable measure of actual engine position. This further solidifies the use of the cam sensor to only deliver engine phase information to the ECU. This may change in the future, but for now it is uncommon for a motorcycle EFI system to rely on a cam sensor alone for engine position and engine phase. A cam position signal is, however, necessary for both sequential EFI and firing individual coils for each plug at the right times.

Since there is a lot of expansion and contraction of the top end parts from heading and cooling during engine operation, a Hall-effect sensor is perfect. Being relatively insensitive to changes in pickup gap, there are no real worries about thermal expansion. Since only a single signal is required per cam revolution (remembering the cams turn at half the speed of the crank), there are no worries about being able to fit enough teeth on a small trigger wheel.

The trigger wheel is magnetically active (which is required to trip the Hall-effect sensor) and has a single relatively fat protrusion (also required for high-speed operation with a Hall-effect sensor). The solid-state construction of the sensor means it should have a long life, even with the severe heat found in the cylinder head and being bathed in solvent-filled engine oil. Some V-twin motorcycles use dual sensors, set apart at the same angle as the cylinders, to help determine when a given cylinder is at or near TDC.

ROAD SPEED SENSORS

There are a variety of reasons to have a road speed sensor on a motorcycle. In lower gears, torque can be limited to help prevent accidents; in higher gears, speed limiting can be enforced through a gentle, progressive retard of ignition timing. But reasons even more important in terms of power and drivability bear discussing.

As already mentioned, torque limiting through ignition retard can prevent lowsides, unintentional wheelies, and damage to the transmission. This is pretty common on most EFI models. But another, bigger reason for having road speed sensing is to adjust spark and fueling based on the load that the engine will see. The higher the road speed, the more aerodynamic drag is experienced by the bike and rider. This takes more power to overcome, increasing geometrically as speed increases linearly. By tuning the engine to reduce emissions at lower road speeds, the bike can be made more fuel-efficient and more environmentally friendly without really changing 0–60 or dragstrip times by very much. As the OEMs are increasingly concerned about vehicular emissions from motorcycles, we've seen this appear on most motorcycles with EFI over the past five years or so.

There are a variety of ways to inform the ECU of road speed. Probably the simplest is the gear position switch, used most commonly by Suzuki. This consists of a rotary switch that switches a variety of resistors across a pair of leads from the ECU. By checking the resistance seen across those two leads, the ECU can determine which gear the bike is in. This is then used to switch between different ignition maps and, in some cases, different fuel maps as well.

Some ECUs simply factor in the wind resistance based on actual road speed. These machines use sensors that record the actual speed of the motorcycle, as opposed to simply indicating

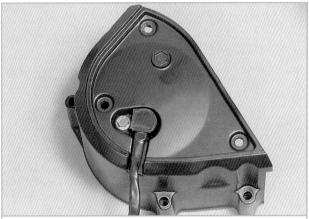

The front sprocket cover has become a popular place to measure road speed, due to its convenient, safe location. This Kawasaki Z1000 sprocket cover clearly shows its sensor location. Kawasaki Motor Corporation USA

Engine temperature is a critical measurement for proper fueling. This Moto Guzzi mounts its temperature sensor in a cylinder head, providing the best measurement of critical temperatures on an air-cooled motorcycle.

which gear is being used. There are two common locations for the sensors, which are both of the same design (typically a Hall-effect sensor): On the front wheel, or on the front sprocket cover.

The wheel speed sensor is most commonly found on motorcycles with ABS, where it is required to indicate wheel speed to the ABS controller. Thus it serves triple duty on such bikes, providing data to both the EFI ECU and the antilock braking ECU, and giving road speed data for the speedometer. The disadvantage of a front-wheel speed sensor is that the wire connecting the sensor to the ECU has to flex with the front suspension. This will eventually wear out the wire, necessitating replacement of the sensor. In addition, the sensor is susceptible to dirt, sand, and water from the outside environment.

The second location for a road speed sensor is on the front sprocket cover. This is an excellent location, as it is well protected from the elements and does not flex the attached leads during normal operation. It typically doubles as a sensor for the dashboard speedometer and is currently the most common form of road speed sensing used on production motorcycles. The primary disadvantage of this sensor is that if you change the gearing of the motorcycle, you are fooling both the speedometer and the ECU into thinking that the motorcycle is traveling at a different speed than it actually is. It is recommended that if you change the gearing on a motorcycle equipped with a road speed sensor in the front sprocket cover, you should obtain a "yellow box" or other similar device that can electronically alter the pulse speed to deliver corrected road speed information to both the ECU and the dashboard speedometer.

TEMPERATURE SENSORS

Depending on the motorcycle, there can be quite a number of temperature sensors for various purposes. As noted in the last chapter, these are nearly always cheap, easy-to-source NTC resistive sensors.

Typically, there will be some kind of engine temperature sensor to determine operating temperature. On an air-cooled bike, this can be mounted directly on or in the cylinder head (to measure CHT, or cylinder head temperature; also ET, or engine temperature), or it can measure oil temperature from an oil galley near the cylinder head. On a water-cooled bike, it will be found on the engine in most cases and it will intrude into a coolant-filled area to measure coolant temperature (CT).

The other common sensor of this type is used to measure the temperature of the intake air (IAT, or intake air temperature). It can be located in the airbox (which is fairly common) or in the intake tube for the plenum (which is less common, but still used quite a bit). The sensor is actually very similar (in some cases identical) to the engine/coolant temperature sensor above.

There are almost no downsides to this kind of sensor. They last a long time, are very reliable, and are cheap and easy to get.

KNOCK SENSORS

There are several different kinds of sensor we can use for detecting knock. Currently, the only real reason for detecting knock is to retard ignition to prevent engine damage; knock can be caused by overheating, lean conditions, or poor fuel quality. In the future, as motorcycles are required to run leaner and leaner mixtures for emissions purposes, knock sensors will become a critical part of the engine management system, allowing the engine to be run very close to detonation (which will allow for better power and economy), instead of the current method of erring on the side of caution with ignition timing settings.

The simplest form of knock detector is an acoustic sensor. Basically a small, very hardy microphone is placed against the cylinder block, where it picks up vibration from the engine's operation. A complex analog (or, in some expensive applications, digital) filtering circuit removes what amounts to normal engine noise, and any resulting signal will indicate knocking. The sensor then sends a signal to the ECU to warn of knock. Such a self-contained on/off signaling sensor is known as a "go/no-go" sensor.

Another current form of knock detector was discussed in the last chapter in the section on piezoelectric sensors. A small piezoelectric ring is attached to a (relatively) heavy silicon ring, and vibrations from the engine accelerate the silicon, stretching and compressing the piezoelectric ring to generate a signal similar to that from an acoustic sensor. Again the signal needs filtering, but since the sensor is solid-state, it is much easier to filter and process its signal with the use of digital electronics. By contrast, it is better for acoustic sensors to have their signals filtered by an analog circuit, ideally at the source. Piezoelectric sensors also have the edge in size, weight, and reliability, due to their solid-state construction. However, piezoelectric sensors are more expensive.

The last method of detecting knock has not yet come into much use, but may in the future. It is called ion sensing, and does not require a sensor as such. It actually uses the spark plug as a sensor.

After the spark event, the burning mixture works to turn as much fuel and air as possible into power and waste byproducts. Since each of those components in the combustion chamber conducts electricity differently, we can apply a small voltage across the spark plug electrodes while the power and exhaust phases of the cylinder are in progress. By looking at patterns in the change of the conduction, it is possible to determine many things about the quality, speed, and state of the combustion event. However, the more information you wish to obtain, the more filtering and complex math you have to do to extract patterns or signals that might be of use. There is only one ion sensing system currently found on production motorcycles, and it only checks for knock or misfire; what's more, it only does so at higher rpms and high engine loads. The cost for the support electronics to gather more data than that is prohibitive for OEM use at this point in time.

Acoustic and piezoelectric knock sensors can even be used to help determine which cylinder is knocking either by checking the

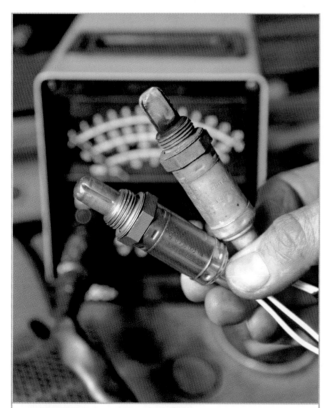

Oxygen sensors are a critical component for emissions control. On motorcycles so equipped, care must be taken to replace the sensor when it has reached the end of its life. Failure to do so will lead to increased emissions, and possibly poor running as well. Bosch GmbH

knock signal against crank angle and engine phase data (which will identify the cylinder that just had a combustion event), by the differential in apparent amplitude of the signals between two sensors located in different areas (triangulation), or by comparing the time delay between the signals being received (time differential).

OXYGEN SENSORS

As used on production vehicles, O_2 sensors are perhaps the least understood of all the sensors on the motorcycle. For some reason, people think that a motorcycle equipped with a narrow-band O_2 sensor is somehow better than one that is not. The fact is, most of the time, it isn't used at all. And during the time that it is used, it's not uncommon to get surging and sharp transitions to roll-on (on certain bikes). Follow with me now as I take you through what O_2 sensors can and cannot do for you.

Narrow-Band O2 Sensors

Obviously, the O_2 sensor will be found in the exhaust. The advent of heated O_2 sensors has allowed the sensor to be moved farther back from the engine, so overheating is now less of an issue. But just like the MAF sensor, the O_2 sensor is measuring data from some time ago; it takes time for the exhaust gases to travel down the pipe, and then longer again to stabilize a sensor reading, especially when the sensor is cold.

Riding in closed-loop mode is only possible when maximum power is not called for and conditions don't change very quickly, so the delay in sensor reading can be processed by the ECU before there has been much change in fuel demand. This limits O_2 sensors' operation to cruise and idle conditions on motorcycles.

Since they have a very narrow range of operation, narrow-band O_2 sensors are really useful for maintaining a proper mixture for a catalytic converter. And since that mixture is well lean of best power, the transition from closed-loop (using feedback from the O_2 sensor to control fueling) to open-loop running can be pretty abrupt. Big twins can end up with surging issues at small throttle openings in closed-loop mode; this is a common problem with BMWs, for instance. Narrow-band O_2 sensors are also used to help reduce emissions at idle on some bikes. This is being used more and more often, as emissions regulations are tightened.

So in short, narrow-band O_2 sensors are only useful where there is a requirement to reduce emissions through a catalytic converter, and then only when the engine running conditions (load and rpm) are close to constant. The vast majority of the time, O_2 sensor-equipped bikes are not paying any attention to the O_2 sensor. They are installed for the same reasons as catalytic converters—to cut down on emissions to meet government regulations. Narrow-band O_2 sensors have no other real use.

Wideband O2 Sensors

Now we come to an O_2 sensor that is much more useful. Since WBO_2 (wideband O_2) sensors cover a much wider (and more usable) range of λ with good resolution, they make an excellent rough tuning tool.

As I discussed in the chapter on how the engine breathes and burns its mixture, there are a number of factors that determine burn speed and completeness of combustion. All those factors combine to produce many different mixtures of exhaust gases. For instance, at part throttle, the burn slows down; at higher engine speeds, it can slow down enough that increasing spark advance will actually hurt power, as the peak pressure will occur too early in the power phase and work against the end of the compression stroke. In cases

Wideband O_2 sensors can deliver valuable tuning data, if used correctly. This standalone MoTeC unit offers integration with their line of ECUs and data loggers, giving data correlation that is extremely valuable to race tuners. MoTeC Systems USA

design, or after having made a major change in the VE curve of the engine (different cams or big changes in the exhaust system, for instance). They need a tool that can get them in the ballpark on fuel delivery, and fast. By using a WBO_2 sensor, they can find fueling where the engine will run well enough for either dyno or track testing, and find it quickly. For this, a WBO_2 sensor is a truly excellent tool. Get the fuel map so the engine runs at a certain speed and load point on the map, and watch the O_2 sensor as you make changes. When the O_2 sensor reads its lowest reading, move on to the next cell, until you have your map in place. And then you're ready for dyno tuning, or road testing, to further refine the map.

That's all. Really, it is. That's what WBO_2 sensors are used for by people who use them professionally. Sometimes they are used to get a rough picture of what is going on at specific load/speed sites in their maps, when running on a certain course with a certain driver; by combining logged data from a rider's practice laps, the trackside tuner can see which load/speed areas of engine operation are used most by this driver on this track. He can also see where on the track certain load/speed areas are in use. If the logged data or the rider's comments shows a problem at a certain spot (or spots) on the track on each lap, it's easy to put your finger on what needs changing, saving a lot of time and trouble in quick changes at the last minute. It can also be used to save expensive development time during a rented track day, or time rented on a dyno.

WBO_2 sensors are very expensive and have a fairly short lifespan (much, much shorter than narrow-band sensors). Tuners generally use them only when they deliver useful information (such as the two above-mentioned situations). They then put the sensors in a box and leave them there until they are in need of some quick general guidelines to keep them from wasting time trying to tune areas that are not being used.

Now, if they get the vehicle tuned to where a given rider is making his best lap times, then they can record that data using a WBO_2 sensor and use it as a target to tune to on, say, the "B" bike (which might need slightly different mapping to get the same response and power characteristics, because every engine is a little bit different). But until the tuner has a properly tuned bike from which to get baseline measurements, this is not possible. If you were to tune a bike to make best power everywhere, or deliver the fastest lap times, or the best fuel economy, you would see that levels of residual oxygen do not remain constant across the load/speed matrix. And each engine, intake, and exhaust combination will have a different map of residual oxygen when it has been tuned for the peak of whatever your goals are.

Mid-Band Oxygen Sensors

The mid-band sensor, as I refer to it, is really a special case of the WBO_2 sensor that has a broader range than a narrow-band sensor, but a much narrower range than a true WBO_2. These are not currently in use on motorcycles, but may start showing up in the future. Currently they are used on lean-burn automotive engines to help ensure that the two catalytic converters (which are required for low emissions on lean-burn engines) are functioning properly, and that fuel delivery is within the narrow range required to allow the catalytic converters to be efficient. While such engines are wonderful at providing very low emissions and excellent fuel economy, the cost of the required pairs of both O_2 sensors and catalytic converters on these cars is often second only to the cost of the engine. Between the cost and the weight, these systems will probably not appear on motorcycles until there is no alternative method to meet government emissions requirements.

like this, the mixture remaining in the exhaust will be increasingly unburned as there is less and less throttle opening. Even if you have the mixture for best power, the increase in unburned mixture will mean an increase in residual oxygen (as well as HC). So in addition to running lean, you can get an increase in residual oxygen in the exhaust from a slower burn. And as you approach either lean or rich misfire, you also increase residual oxygen levels.

The problem is there's no way to tell one cause from another just by looking at residual oxygen. In the case of a nearly closed throttle at higher rpm, you would need to run too rich a mixture to get a minimum residual oxygen reading. I cannot say this enough: *Using residual oxygen alone as an end-stage tuning tool does not work.* It cannot work, because you cannot separate the cause from the data you're getting. As mentioned earlier, CO (carbon monoxide) is a true measure of the amount of combustion that took place, and it serves as a much better gauge of proper tuning. Sadly, there is no cheap, portable, fast-reading sensor for CO. Since we have an O_2 sensor, we might as well see what we can do with it.

Many professionals use WBO_2 sensors in their tuning regimen. Accordingly, many consumers decided that if the pros could use them to their advantage, so could they. They proceeded to spend $500 or so on a WBO_2 sensor kit and found that they were not the fastest thing on the track after tuning with it. What gives? How come they can't get the same results pros do? The difference is, the pros understand what they are seeing from the sensor and only use the data where it is appropriate. If you're not armed with that basic understanding of what you're getting and what it's good for, you can't use a WBO_2 sensor as an effective tuning tool.

So, how do the pros use their WBO_2s? Why do they buy them? One simple answer: *to save time.* Professional racers and tuners are often putting an injection system on a completely new engine

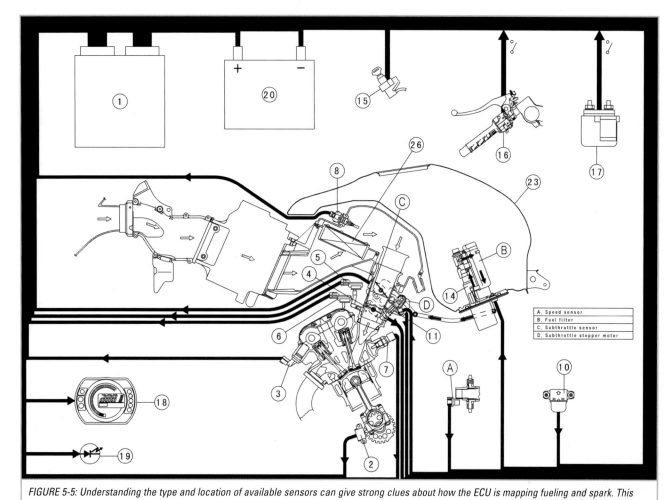

FIGURE 5-5: Understanding the type and location of available sensors can give strong clues about how the ECU is mapping fueling and spark. This system diagram from a ZX-6RR shows the complexity of modern EFI, but also gives us the information needed to unravel it. The numbering corresponds with the ZX-12R diagram at the start of this chapter, except where noted. Kawasaki Motor Corporation USA

A. Speed sensor	
B. Fuel filter	
C. Subthrottle sensor	
D. Subthrottle stepper motor	

Why Cover O2 Sensors in Such Detail?

The O_2 sensor is not terribly complicated, but it is probably the most misunderstood sensor. Since my job in writing this book is to teach people how fuel injection works, I am taking special care in areas where I have seen a lot of misunderstanding over the years. Now that you have a better understanding of what oxygen sensors are good for measuring, you can approach your choices (or those of a given OEM) with a much better idea of both the desired goals and the likelihood of being able to achieve them by using an O_2 sensor.

Remember, when professional mechanics are using gas sensors as diagnostic tools, their first choice is a four- or five-gas analyzer; if they can't use one of those, they will use a two-gas analyzer. Which two gases are chosen when the choice is critical for gaining information about mixture and combustion? CO (carbon monoxide) and HC (hydrocarbons). Any one gas by itself is not useful for tuning or diagnostics. If one had to list gases in order of importance for determining mixture, first would be CO, second would be either CO_2 or HC, then would come narrowband O_2, and finally NOx. Even wideband O_2 can only get you in the ballpark; from there, there is no substitute for the adjust/test/repeat methodology for meeting your goals.

SUMMARY

Now we know the players in the game. With little exception (system voltage and, in limited cases, ion sensing), all the information the ECU can get from the outside world comes through some combination of these sensors. Note that not all of them will be found on any given system. The actual sensors used will vary based on both the modeling method used by the ECU and the craftiness of the designers (who can sometimes get extra information out of existing sensors without adding dedicated sensors). I'll bet a lot of you are wondering why many of these sensors would be valuable to us. Some of you may have already made connections with ideas discussed in the chapter on how the engine breathes and burns mixture.

We're not quite ready to tie the sensors together with how they are used to meter fuel. Before we get there, we have to talk about the nerve center of the whole system, the part that takes all that raw data, and our maps, and turns it into pulse width and timing for the injectors, as well as ignition advance and dwell for the spark. It's time to take the plunge into the black box that we refer to as the ECU.

THE BRAINS OF THE OPERATION

I'll again start off by saying that this is another chapter you can skip. There is nothing in this chapter that is absolutely essential to understanding how EFI works when used in motorcycles. The chapter will explain some things that might be useful, like the difference between flash memory and an EPROM, and why some ECUs can do things others can't. I will warn you in advance, however, that there will be a lot of talk about how circuits are laid out inside ECUs, and some of you will get a syndrome that computer geeks call MEGO (for My Eyes Glaze Over). So those of you who don't care about the guts, but just want to know how the guts think, you can skip now to the next chapter.

This chapter of the book forced me to make the most difficult choices. For while I could write a whole book on digital logic, embedded processors, ASICs, and signal conditioning, that would not only be huge, it would lose the forest for the trees. But the less detail I include, the less complete the book will be, and the more people might be disappointed with the lack of detail. With that in mind, this chapter will explore the more common components of typical ECUs and how they work. I will also talk about signal conditioning, spark and injector driving, and the advent of ASICs (Application-Specific Integrated Circuits), without which we would not have the capabilities available to us today in factory and aftermarket ECUs. But before we get to the details about the individual components, let's take a look at how the building blocks of an ECU are arranged and how they do what we want them to do—turn sensor readings into actual fueling.

WHAT HAPPENS INSIDE AN ECU?

What happens inside an ECU? Sensor data comes in, calculations are made, and injectors are driven based on pulse width (the length of time a signal line has voltage applied to it). Almost all ECUs use a digital processor, but most of the input and output signals are analog. If several different things have to happen at different times during the engine's full combustion cycle, then you need enough computing power to get everything necessary completed at or before the allotted time has expired. And at redline on modern engines, this can be a very short period of time indeed. So what kind of internal architecture or processor speed will we need to make sure we can get things done when necessary?

These are the questions that shape the final form of an ECU's internal architecture. For OEMs, cost of components, emissions standards, and commonality of components among models also come into play as important factors. As I will demonstrate to you in this chapter, there are a lot of ways to skin a cat, and as long as everything gets done well enough to get the desired job done, there's no real need for anything more.

Even early ECUs had sophisticated electronics. This is the ECU from a 1983 Honda CX650 Turbo. Note the EEPROM on the left side of the left circuit board (it has a yellow sticker over the window carrying the number 13) and the five power transistors bolted to the far edge of the case to dissipate heat. ECU courtesy of Greg Goss

THE ECU

This Delphi ECU, made for Harley-Davidson, is the most advanced ECU on a production motorcycle to date. Powerful processing via integrated circuits make it light and durable as well. Motorcycle courtesy of San Diego Harley-Davidson

How Fast?

One of our primary considerations is the speed with which we can process incoming data. Along with speed goes a concern about how finely we can resolve time, meaning the faster we can check a given sensor, the more precisely we can determine the behavior of the engine. And the more we demand of an engine (in terms of redline, fuel economy, emissions, or power), the more important it becomes for us to have data with a fine resolution. As you may have guessed, resolution is a measure of the smallest change, or fastest change, in a system. Another factor in resolution is word size, but we'll come to that, as well as physical limitations of the EFI system, later on. For now, let's concentrate on time.

There are several ways we can increase the speed with which an ECU operates. The most basic is to simply use a processor with a faster clock speed. This means more computations in a given time frame, and it also means more *samples*, or checks on the data being delivered by the sensors, than with a slower processor. The downside to using a faster clock speed is twofold: First, a faster CPU (central processing unit, in most cases a microcontroller) generates more heat. And with few heat sinks and no fans to cool the ECU, heat can really limit the design envelope of the ECU. Some ECUs have metal cases that are used as giant heat sinks to help keep the circuitry inside from overheating. But metal cases are both expensive and heavy, and plastic cases are far more common. So we must balance our desire for speed against environmental parameters that limit our design.

How Flexible?

The next question is about flexibility. Most EFI systems are designed by companies like Mitsubishi and SAGEM, not motorcycle (or car) manufacturers. Flexibility in ECU design allows the designers to adapt the same design to many different possible uses. In fact, the microcontrollers themselves (which are made by other companies, like Texas Instruments and Motorola) are about as flexible as you can get. In most cases, they can be programmed to do a variety of very different things. The same microcontroller might be found running an automated assembly line, your home thermostat, or the fuel injection of your motorcycle.

However, the more flexible a piece of digital hardware is, the slower it does a given task, typically. Think of a home computer (which is an excellent example of a very flexible piece of digital hardware). You can run a variety of operating systems on it, and then you can run all kinds of different programs on it. These programs can do widely varied things, from computer games to spreadsheets to word processing. It's the flexibility of the architecture that allows this.

However, even an 850 MHz Pentium running Windows would be taxed running a fuel injection program on a running vehicle. That's not because the hardware itself doesn't have enough power; just that (most especially when using a multitasking operating system, like MacOS, OS X, or Windows) it's not well designed in its hardware and software to operate *efficiently* as a fuel injection controller. By having a great number of possible functions, it takes more time to sort through commands and execute them. Multitasking operating systems also make it very hard to maintain a rigid schedule of timing and events, which is of the utmost importance in a fuel injection system. Any of you who have kept pace with computers over the past 15 years or so know what I mean about the actual responsiveness of computers. As they have become more capable and more flexible, they often don't perform the same tasks any faster than in the past.

So again we are faced with a compromise: On the one hand, a flexible architecture for a microcontroller, or the ECU that contains it, allows the same design to be used in many applications (which helps spread out development costs); on the other hand, a design optimized for doing just one thing will generally do a much better job, and much more quickly; further, the actual manufacturing cost will tend to be cheaper. In the same vein, you can install a video card with a tuner in your computer and use your new Pentium to watch television, but a purpose-built television set does the same job for much less money.

Most ECUs strike a compromise: They use small, fast microcontrollers (which are fairly flexible, but are generally fast and pretty cheap) to handle tasks that require some flexibility (or that might need upgrading in the future), and add ASICs—Application-Specific Integrated Circuits—to do specialized jobs. By finding the parts of the injection program that require the most time and effort from the microcontroller and building special chips that do nothing else but handle those things, an excellent balance can be struck between cost and capability. In fact, it's often possible to use microcontrollers that are far slower, simply by taking the one or two really heavy load tasks away from the CPU itself, and handing them off to ASICs.

THE COMPONENTS, AND HOW THEY WORK

We've talked a bit about ASICs, and most of us already know there must be a microprocessor of some kind running a digital ECU. But what else is inside the "magic box"? What do we need to accomplish our goals?

The Nerve Center: Microcontroller

Before getting too far into things, it should be noted that pretty close to every EFI system ever made with a digital ECU contains

To remain affordable, manufacturers must limit the sophistication and processing power of their ECUs. This RC-51 unit is more than powerful enough to meet today's emissions requirements. ECU courtesy of Factory Pro Tuning

a microcontroller. A microcontroller differs from a microprocessor in that it has additional components right on the chip that assist in its controlling an electronic or electromechanical system.

A microprocessor has several buses (a bus is a connection or series of connections that allows data to pass back and forth between digital components) that allow it to store and retrieve information from memory (a data bus that carries information back and forth, and an address bus that tells the memory where to find or put that data), as well as one or more I/O (input/output) buses (which allow communication with the outside world of input or output devices). The microprocessor has a clock that not only controls how fast it can run, but also acts as a metronome to step it through its operations at a regular pace. And it will have interrupts (which, when activated, will cause the microprocessor to stop what it is doing, and do something else in a predetermined fashion) to help it respond to important events from outside. In fact, many microcontrollers contain watchdog circuits whose sole purpose is to watch for infinite loops that would cause the controller to cease functioning, and to reset it, meaning that it is essentially crash-proof. How's that for keeping an eye on what's going on?

So these are the connections the microprocessor has with the outside world. Inside the microprocessor, there is an ALU (arithmetic logic unit) that does all the math and an instruction decoder/register that executes commands from the program it is running (which is stored in memory). There is a stack where information is stacked up for later use, just like piles of paper on your desk—this makes it easy for the microprocessor to find what it wants, even if there are no more registers for it to use. Both the instruction decoder and the ALU have access to a series of registers, which are essentially scratch pads for data being manipulated by the ALU (or even directly by the instruction decoder). Having registers onboard the microprocessor greatly speeds up complex operations that are all done on a single datum.

In essence, the microprocessor is nothing more than a big calculator. It has a series of instructions that it reads and executes, and, according to those instructions, it performs math functions on data coming from memory or an I/O bus, and then sends that data somewhere else after the operations are complete.

Registers, buses, and the ALU can all have different sizes, which are measured in bits. Since microprocessors can't count, and only know V+ (usually +5 VDC) and 0V. They run in binary, where V+ is "1" and 0V is "0." On or off. To use those signals to represent numbers, the microprocessor counts in base two instead of base 10 like you and me. Each additional bit is another power of two, instead of another power of 10. So the number 1101 in base 10 would be one thousand, one hundred, no tens, and one one. In base two, that number would be one eight, one four, no twos, and one one, or 13 in base ten. So the width of a register, a bus, or the ALU can be counted in how many bits wide it is; this controls how large a number it can represent or handle. In the case of the 68HC11 family, which is commonly used in both ECUs and aftermarket "piggy back" boxes like the Power Commander, the data bus is 8 bits wide (so it can handle numbers up to 256 in base 10), and the address bus is 16-bit (so it can access up to 65536, or 64k, different memory locations). It has an 8-bit ALU, but can run some 16-bit instructions (by using 2 or more of its 8-bit registers), and can do some 16-bit math (although that takes two clock cycles at minimum). In addition, clock speed determines how many instructions can be carried out in a period of time. A 68HC11 microcontroller can be a 2, 3, or 4 MHz (megahertz, or millions of clock cycles per second) device, depending on model.

So we have some idea of how well this thing can crunch numbers—some big ones will take longer, but it has ways to handle a good bit. The more bits (width, or word length) in the ALU and the buses, the bigger the numbers it can handle (or sometimes it can work on two smaller pieces of data at once, saving time), and the more memory it can address.

That's pretty much all we really need to know about the microprocessor. So what else will be on a microcontroller besides the microprocessor itself? A microcontroller is essentially a stripped-down little computer, all on one chip. On any given member of the 68HC11 family, we would certainly find RAM (random access memory, which can be written over by the microprocessor, and which is erased when power is shut off), a timer (which counts digitally up to a predetermined point, adding to the counter for every cycle of the clock's oscillator), a serial communications interface (like an RS-232 or USB port, to allow it to be programmed or controlled from the outside world or feed data out), an EEPROM (electronically erasable programmable read-only memory) and/or ROM (read-only memory) (which does not get erased when power is removed), and perhaps most important, A/D (analog/digital) converters. An A/D converter takes an analog signal (like the varying DC voltage from a sensor) and changes the voltage into a binary number that has a numerical value that represents the relative voltage; as the voltage goes up, so does the numerical value output by the A/D converter (it should be noted that external A/D converters are commonly used as well as, or in place of, those onboard the microcontroller). And last, a PWM (pulse width modulation) generator turns our digital numbers into a pulse of a set width, the width rising with the size of the number. In actuality, these can simply be digital ports (channels for getting data into and out from a microcontroller or other processor).

Whew, that's a lot of stuff! What does it all do? Well, the A/D converters are probably the most important to us. They will take

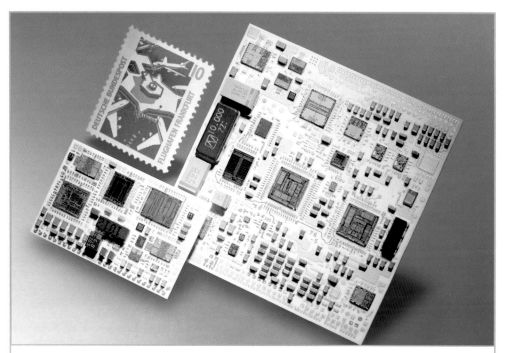

Amazing amounts of computing power can be fit on a single microcontroller. On the left is an MCU for an antilock braking system; on the right, an MCU for electronic fuel injection. The EFI MCU has nine separate integrated circuits onboard. Bosch GmbH

emergency condition has arisen that requires it to take other action. But as a rule, the code (program) that is run by the MCU (microcontroller unit) checks the values of some sensors, looks up a value in the map, does some math on that number based on the values of other sensors, and then sends a value to the PWM generator to cause an injector event. Along the way, it "listens" for a series of conditions (like a big change in throttle angle happening quickly) that might require it to behave a little differently, and the program can then branch (switch over) to another set of commands to handle the new condition.

Because microcontrollers can be programmed in a flexible programming language like ANSI-C, they are very flexible and can do all sorts of different jobs. It also means that they can be adapted to a variety of engine models and sensors as needed without too much trouble. This flexibility makes it simple to develop new ECUs for different motors. In some cases (as with many Suzukis), the internal components of the ECU are nearly identical between several motorcycles, with the only major difference being in the code and maps. Some newer microcontrollers were designed with automotive use in mind and have special capabilities that make it quicker and easier to do their jobs inside an ECU.

OTHER COMPONENTS

OK, so we have this spiffy MCU, with all its integration and capabilities. What else do we need? What is missing that a controller needs?

Signal Conditioners

For starters, not all of the signals that come into the ECU are nice and clean and consistent. Some of them need conditioning to be of use to us. A great example of this is the analog signal from the crank angle sensor. The spikes can range anywhere from a few volts during cranking up to over 80v at high rpm. We need to tame this signal through filtering and processing to get it into a form that will be of use to the ECU. So there will be some analog circuitry inside the ECU that takes the unruly raw signal from the sensor and conditions it into a form that can be easily handled by the ECU to calculate crank angle and TDC.

Many other sensors receive conditioning, although usually not to such a substantial degree as the crank angle sensor. The NTC temperature sensor, for instance, will usually have a logarithmic response; that is, the rate of resistance change is very steep at first and gets slower and slower for the same change in temperature as the temperature rises. It's usually pretty simple to create an analog circuit that fits the design of the sensor and give a linear

signals from most of our analog sensors (which we are feeding with +5v from the ECU) and turn them into digital numbers for the microprocessor to use. And the PWM ports will allow us to deliver a given pulse width to our injector and/or ignition drivers. No extra parts needed! So far, so good. We can use the timers (and there can be quite a number of them on some microcontrollers) to remind the microprocessor to do something at a certain time, or to sample a signal at a required point (although typically this is done with software or an ASIC). The EEPROM holds our program to be run and the data tables for our maps, and the RAM can hold anything from current tuning trims to logged data from our inputs.

Wow, that sounds like most of what we need on one chip. You can see why people designing ECUs would want to use something like a microcontroller. Since it's a tiny computer, it also has a programming language, in this case, assembly language. The actual instructions that can be understood by the ECU are coded as numbers when the program is compiled, and those numbers are loaded into the EEPROM and run in order by the microcontroller. However, since each microcontroller has its own assembly language, it is much simpler to write the programs in a higher-level programming language, like ANSI-C, and then compile it for a given microcontroller. This makes it easier to program a wide variety of microcontrollers, as well as making some or all of the code (the actual program) portable—that is, able to be used on several different microcontrollers by compiling it for each microcontroller.

All the microcontroller does all day is go in circles. That's right, as long as the key is turned on and the ECU is getting power, the thing is running in one of many possible endless circles. Some outside events can change what loop is being run or alter values that are acted upon by the microcontroller. Some tell the microcontroller what time it is in reference to engine rotation or when an

THE ECU

67

output (one that has a direct correspondence to temperature change) for use by the MCU.

A/D Converters

One thing I already noted is that most of the signals from the sensors are analog. Typically the actual measurement is represented by a change in voltage. MCUs are now digital, and they code numbers by timing pulses of voltage. Zero volts means a logical zero, and +5v means a logical one. Using a special form of arithmetic known as base two (where all numbers are represented by a string of zeros and ones), digital computers represent everything by watching for those ones and zeros. This is a little like translating from English into Morse code. We need devices that can take the analog voltage signal from a sensor and turn it into a base two number so that it means something to the ECU. Thus, there is a need for A/D (or analog to digital) converters. Typically, they will read an analog voltage (between 0 and 5 volts) and convert the voltage into a number in base two that is proportional to the voltage. This number is then read off by the ECU as needed.

Aftermarket ECUs often brag about the number of A/D channels they feature; more A/D converters mean more sensor inputs to use. Also, the more bits used by an A/D converter for a single "word," the finer a resolution the ECU has with a given input. For instance, a 4-bit word would give you 16 possible values; an 8-bit word would give you 256 possible values (each bit doubles the number of possible values). The more bits an A/D converter has, the more precisely it can represent the analog voltage it is seeing. Alternately, one can drop the least significant bits (the ones that represent the smallest numbers) to increase accuracy by reducing noise. It's typical to find a 10- or 12-bit ADC in EFI applications that is only used to deliver 8 bits of precision to the program running in the MCU.

ASICs

Application-specific integrated circuits (ASICs) can be almost anything; they can tackle almost any problem that would normally bog down the MCU. ASICs are chips that are developed to do only one thing, with no flexibility to speak of. Because they are optimized for this use, they are also very fast at their jobs. With recent increases in computing and manufacturing power, it has become much cheaper and easier to design a whole IC (integrated circuit) for a single purpose and to build a fairly small quantity. Less than 20 years ago, it would have cost astronomical amounts of money, and the chips would still have been fairly large and slow by today's standards. Thanks to the computer revolution, we can now design and build special ASICs for less than generic processor chips cost in the 1980s.

To show you what an ASIC can do, and why you might want to use one, let's take the example of a crank angle sensor again. At 14,000 rpm on our sample engine, our trigger wheel with 11 teeth and one tooth-wide gap (which allows us to know crank angle to within 30°, a very coarse measurement by current standards, and to see variations in crank speed at 1/2,800th of a second intervals, or every 0.3 ms) delivers an analog signal that goes through the conditioning circuitry and is now ready to be used for computing crank angle and engine speed.

Now imagine that if every time there was a pulse from the crank angle sensor we sent an interrupt to the MCU. Every 0.3 ms, the MCU has to stop what it was doing, check a timer to determine engine speed since the last crank angle event (signal), then check against the last cycle's time to see if it just registered the gap or not, toggle a flag to remind itself to run the TDC subroutine if it did just see the gap, reset the timer to start it over,

store the value of the calculated engine speed where the old one used to be, and then get back to doing whatever it was doing before it was interrupted.

Wow, that's a lot to do every 0.3 ms! With a 3 MHz clock speed, only 1,000 total instructions can be carried out in 0.3 ms. That may seem like a lot, but when you start to realize that there are requests for values from the map table, checking various sensor values, and a whole lot of math that has to happen for a lot of different reasons, the idea of dedicating up to 5 percent of your MCU time to nothing else but keeping track of the crank angle sensor is pretty hard to swallow.

This is where an ASIC comes in. A small, cool-running, high-speed set of solid-state (transistorized) switches arranged into what is called a gate array, ASICs take care of a single, dedicated task with absolute efficiency. In the above case, we could easily design a chip whose sole job was to run the little subroutine mentioned above, but coded in hardware instead of in programmed instructions. Check against a counter, determine crank location by counting the number of teeth since the last gap, store crank speed and crank angle values in memory locations where the MCU can check them when they are needed, and perhaps even toggle an interrupt line to the MCU when engine speed changes rapidly, or set a special flag when the ASIC believes there was a misfire that caused the crank to slow down very briefly.

With the ASIC, we have all our same data stored in memory locations where the MCU can look them up any time it wants to, and we freed up 5 percent of the total processor power available to us in the bargain.

Without ASICs, we would have to have very fast, powerful processors that were always being interrupted by something or other while trying to run their main loop. The high speed would be required to ensure that the main loop had enough processor cycles left over for it to use so that it would not drop behind the needs of the engine!

Think of it in terms of an office. If there is only one employee (the boss), and things start changing very rapidly in a lot of different areas (ordering, production, shipping, billing), the boss has to run around like crazy to keep up with all the demands and to get everything done himself; he will often have to drop one project in the middle so he can complete another that needs doing right now, and then get back to where he left off and finish what he put down, and so on. Eventually, our boss will either need to be upgraded to a faster boss, or face falling behind the needs of the business (which will then fail). The other alternative is to hire assistants. An ASIC is like a secretary, someone who is specialized in, say, typing and filing, and can handle all those tasks for the boss, and much faster than he or she could do them with all their other interruptions. Freed from doing all the typing and filing, the boss can now focus on getting more of his work done on time, and in a sensible order, knowing the secretary is handling the typing and filing and will only interrupt him if she has something very important for him to handle *right now*. The secretary can leave notes or messages with critical information for the boss, who can then look at them when he has the time or needs the information, all without having to hunt for or calculate data.

Drivers

In addition to getting the signals in to use them for computation, signals have to come out and activate electromechanical devices. Without such a system, the ECU could calculate fueling, but couldn't make those fueling events occur.

Connectors are often a weak link in an EFI system. These connectors, from a Honda CBR600F4i, have rubber gaskets on each pin to prevent vibration and water or other contaminants from causing excessive resistance. Motorcycle courtesy of Matt Keebler

This is a lot like the situation with the A/D converters in reverse. In this case, we need to turn a base two number (the calculated pulse width for the injector) into PWM (pulse width modulation). In other words, the length of the pulse needs to be proportional to the number represented in base two that is coming from the MCU. This part is relatively simple, but what is not simple is in driving the injector with enough current to move the pintle and allow the fuel out. Unfortunately, the circuitry in the ECU cannot handle the kind of current needed to move the pintle. What's more, since the injector uses an electromagnet to move the pintle, there is a lot of electronic noise sent back along the line. This noise is partly ringing/overshoot and partly flyback, which are terms used to describe the (mis)behavior of actual analog circuits. If you ever want to design your own EFI system, you'll need to learn about these terms, what they mean, and how to use them, but for our purposes, it is sufficient to say that noise will be generated by operating injectors and solenoids, and that this noise can adversely affect measurements made by sensors elsewhere in the vehicle. A circuit must be created that can amplify the PWM signal and deliver it to a solenoid (the injector, in this case) and also absorb any flyback or ringing without damage to the driver, the ECU, or the solenoid.

Drivers are increasingly available on a single chip, which can be configured for a variety of applications by adding external components. In most cases, these drivers are contained within the housing for the ECU, but some applications actually have a separate housing to contain them (usually to dissipate heat from the large power transistors used to drive high-current solenoids).

Drivers have other uses besides just ensuring injectors open and close when they should. They are also used to drive things like the solenoids (like an idle air bypass solenoid) and stepper motors (like the EXUP-style exhaust diverter, or the secondary intake butterflies found on some Kawasaki and Suzuki machines). Many times low-current drivers are used to latch relays, which are used to switch high-current devices on and off. An example would be the fuel pump; the high-current pump motor is powered through a relay, but the relay is triggered by a low-current driver in the ECU itself.

Voltage Regulator

Every signal going into the ECU that runs through an A/D converter needs to have a precisely controlled voltage feeding its sensor. If you were using a 16-bit A/D converter, then you would have 65,536 (which, to a computer programmer, is 64k, where 1k = 1,024) possible values available, all within the range of 0–5v. That means that a single-digit change in the 16-bit number coming out of the A/D converter represents a change in voltage of just 0.000076 volts, or a little less than 8 millivolts. Pretty darned small! With that kind of resolution, you can see how important it is to maintain a very precise voltage level with which to feed the sensors. There is a special voltage regulator contained within the ECU that delivers a very smooth, controlled 5v signal to all the sensors (and to power the chips within the ECU, as well). If you look at the wiring diagram for an EFI system, you will notice that nearly all of the analog sensors are fed with 5v directly from the ECU (two-wire sensors typically have a +5v lead and a signal lead; three-wire sensors typically add a grounding lead).

Something else to note carefully about this arrangement: As I am sure you are now aware, the voltage delivered to the sensors (and the quality of the ground connection on sensors so equipped) is critical to proper functioning of the fuel injection system. And of course, the +5v from the ECU is delivered to the sensors via the wiring harnesses that attach to each other, the sensors, and the ECU via connectors.

Connectors are pretty flaky when you think about it. They are prone to intermittent contact, dirt, and corrosion. Considering how unreliable they tend to be (even with corrosion-resistant pins and sealing gaskets), it's amazing they work at all. Given that, it should come as no surprise to anyone that issues with connectors can cause all kinds of strange problems and power loss in EFI systems. Several current-model high-performance Japanese race replica motorcycles were found to be down several horsepower from where they should have been—and were cured by replacing the wiring harness! Keeping connectors, sensors, and your

Powerful electronics generate a lot of heat. Most manufacturers choose plastic cases for their ECUs to save weight and guard against vibration, but MoTeC uses a machined aluminum case to act as a heat sink to prevent failure of the ECU under extreme conditions. ECU courtesy of MoTeC Systems USA

Mounting an ECU in the tail has been a favored choice historically. Even as early as 1980, manufacturers took advantage of wasted space in the tail, getting the extra benefit of improved vibration isolation and cooling. Seen here is the ECU from a 1984 Kawasaki GPz1100. David Vastag

charging system in perfect working order is essential to proper operation of a fuel injection system. Battery cables and such are one of the most commonly overlooked sources of trouble. Bad grounding and power supply issues should actually be checked *first* in most cases of trouble.

THE ECU CASE AND PHYSICAL LOCATION

As was noted earlier, the construction of the ECU case is an important part of the overall design. The location of the ECU is often just as important. There are more reasons for this than you might think.

First, cooling is one of the primary issues in both of these areas. The faster the processor, the more heat it will generate. In addition, the type of injector drive, and the location and number of other solenoid/relay drivers, play an important part in how much heat will be generated, and where. Companies like SAGEM turned to metal cases to solve the problem. Acting as heat sinks, you will usually find power transistors and other heat generators attached to or located very near the metal case. Metals conduct heat very well and make an excellent choice for heat sinks (essentially, radiators that draw heat away from components and dissipate it to ambient air). Plastic cases are much cheaper and lighter, but they tend to act as insulators rather than conductors, and their use can limit the capabilities of the ECU design.

As with analog ECUs, RFI (radio frequency interference) is an issue with digital ECUs. Again, metal cases have a big advantage in that they shield the ECU from RFI very well. Because of the fairly high clock frequencies of many digital ECUs, it is not uncommon to see them giving off a fair amount of RFI themselves. And of course, RFI generated by the ignition system, injectors, charging system, and environmental sources can all wreak havoc with sensor signals and internal current paths inside the ECU. Shielding and filtering can raise the cost of an ECU design, but failure to take such issues into account during the design phase can result in the ECU failing government certification, or worse, failing intermittently during actual service!

The same two issues need to be considered when choosing a mounting point for an ECU. Many modern motorcycles locate the ECU under the passenger seat. This separates the ECU as much as possible from ignition noise, and also moves it away from the hot engine and hot air passing over the radiator. However, such a location often does not provide very much airflow over the ECU, especially at low speeds. For this reason, as well as the above reasons, ECU processing power is often limited, simply to ensure that there are not reliability problems caused by too much heat.

THE ODDBALL SYSTEMS: ANALOG

Analog EFI systems are long outmoded, now that computing power is plentiful and cheap. But the first EFI bikes used analog computers, and I would be remiss if I did not cover them here.

The first EFI computers were masterworks, in my opinion. Taking inputs from sensors, they used oscillators and analog signal conditioners to generate injector pulses. This took significant ingenuity. Imagine trying to build a radio receiver that picks up signals from several places at once, and gives an output that corresponds to all the inputs, but not in a basic linear fashion! That's essentially what the crafty designers did.

Probably the biggest drawbacks to such systems were RFI and the limited ability to tune the system for fuel delivery. Since they were essentially pieces of radio circuitry put together in a novel fashion, they both generated and were susceptible to disturbance from RFI. And because it took so much creativity to get them to work in the first place, it was often outside the capabilities of the resulting ECU to adapt to changes in engine design. Ultimately, it was a no-brainer to switch over to cheap, efficient solid-state designs in the 1980s.

BLACK BOX NO LONGER

We've explored the parts inside an ECU, some of the things designers think about when developing them, and where the trade-offs are in the hardware. But we aren't any closer to understanding how the ECU determines fueling from sensor inputs. The answer is that an ECU uses a model of what's going on in the gas flow of the engine and delivers fuel based on what that model dictates. Several different kinds of models are used, and in the next chapter, we'll look much more closely at how sensors, ECU, and gas-flow dynamics come together to complete the picture.

ANIMATING THE HARDWARE

OK, so we have our engine, with its dynamics of gas flow and power generation. We have our sensors, to show us what the engine is up to. We have our ECU, our black box, to deliver proper fuel for the demands we exact on the engine. But how does that all work together? Where is the invisible hand that runs the marionette?

The unification of these components, the anima for the whole system, is the software—the program that converts sensor input into the needed output. And as always, we need to remember that what that output is, and how close to ideal it is, depends on the priorities and desires of those who designed the system. It doesn't need to be perfect, only good enough for the needs and desires of the designers. And that approach has given us a number of solutions for the problem of how to determine fueling, which work on a variety of levels. Some are better than others for a given outcome or goal, but they are all valid and all have their place. But you should be cautioned that there is no such thing as a "perfect" mapping strategy at this point in motorcycle EFI development. The car world is getting pretty close, and I'll discuss that at the end of this chapter; but there are pretty notable compromises made by the strategies in use today, and it's important to realize this at the outset.

How Smart Is Our Model?

One of the first things we need to think about is how precise and complex our model should be. The most successful mechanical fuel injection system for production cars was incredibly simple: It sprayed fuel continuously through injectors and had a mechanical arm connected to a metal plate. The metal plate was pushed down by an increase in air demand from the engine, and the arm allowed fuel pressure to increase, thus allowing the delivery of more fuel as airflow increased. It was simple and more than accurate enough to

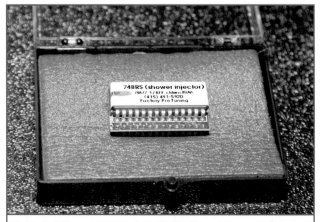

Both the computer program that runs the ECU and the maps that it uses to determine injector and spark event timing and duration are contained in one place, with very few exceptions. Older ECUs had a separate, socketed EPROM that could be replaced with a different one. This is a *Factory Pro Tuning* chip for a Ducati 748RS. EPROM courtesy of Factory Pro Tuning

meet fuel economy and emissions standards for many years. It isn't a perfect system by a long shot. The model is OK in terms of accuracy, but far from ideal at any point. Yet it was good enough to serve the purpose for a long time, and it was simple enough to be cheap to make and reliable over the long term.

Cheap, plentiful computing power has increased the precision and efficiency of modeling by leaps and bounds. With things like computational fluid dynamics, engineers can now predict with dazzling precision how a new chassis design will manage to slice through the air and where modifications need to be made in a car's body design to ensure that all four wheels are firmly planted at high speeds, that the radiator will receive sufficient airflow to cool the engine, that the doorframes won't make objectionable amounts of wind noise on the freeway, etc. These things were all decided long before a physical model of the car is ever built.

These same principles can be applied to any kind of modeling, including engine behavior and fuel injection. And they are, to varying levels of precision and complexity, as dictated by the needs of the designers. Computers used for computational fluid dynamics fill whole rooms and cost millions of dollars. Clearly, not everyone needs that level of precision, or speed of execution. The same holds true in the world of EFI.

But the thing we really have to remember is that we don't have any sensors that tell us exactly how much air is in the combustion chamber after the valves close, and how much exhaust gas is still in there (and what that is composed of). The models scientists use to work out actual combustion dynamics inside a cylinder (and these models don't even include gas flow outside the combustion chamber) are incredibly complex and cannot be packaged neatly into an ECU. So we're left with sensors that give us part of the picture and computing power that can come up with quick approximations, but not exact details. So the key element here is understanding how our sensor readings relate to what is actually happening in the combustion chamber, and how precisely we can approximate that given the limitations inherent in our computing power and sensor data. You may be surprised to find out that almost all ECUs, in both the car and the motorcycle world, don't really model engine behavior precisely. They cheat, and make a model that is quick and simple and close enough to get the job done. But if it works well enough to achieve the goals set out by the designers, then it can be considered a success.

The further a model deviates from actual physics, the more it will need a map of some sort to help bring it more in line with reality. What is a map, though? A map is an array of data, with reference points to help indicate correspondences between sensor data and desired fueling. What does this mean? Well, consider that none of the sensors we use to determine airflow can actually tell us how much oxygen ends up being trapped in the combustion chamber. With a given engine setup, with a given intake and exhaust, we can take measurements while running the engine on a dynamometer. We can look at the data from our sensors, and then experimentally determine what correct fueling will be for a given matrix of sensor readings. Many maps are 2D, meaning they have two axes; one of these axes is commonly engine rpm, since engine speed will determine the effects of pulse tuning and cam

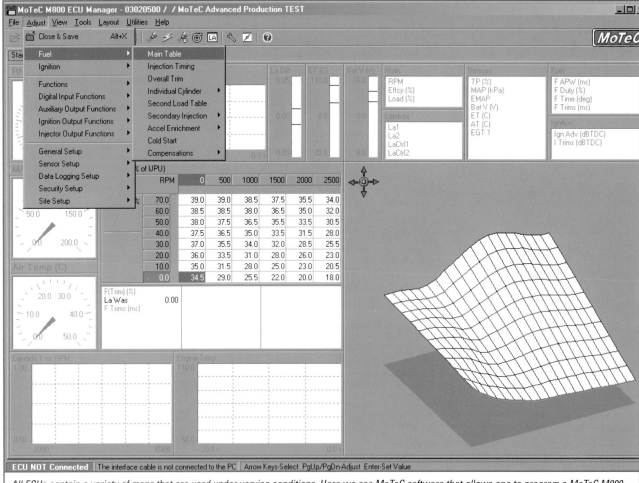

All ECUs contain a variety of maps that are used under varying conditions. Here we see MoTeC software that allows one to program a MoTeC M800 ECU with any combination of maps one desires. In this case, the main fuel table 2D map is being shown in three dimensions, with cell value being the Z-axis. MoTeC Systems USA

timing on volumetric and trapping efficiencies. By making a table with engine speed on one axis and, say, MAP on another axis, we can fill that table in with pulse width values that get us as close as we need for our goals. This table is called a map, and it can be stored in either permanent memory (some variety of ROM, or read-only memory) or temporarily in RAM (random-access memory); ROM maps are often shadowed or duplicated for use in RAM, since RAM can be accessed much more quickly than ROM. If a sensor reading falls in between the discrete points laid out on an axis for a particular cell (or intersection of axes on the map), then the ECU will typically *interpolate*; in essence it will draw a line between the value in the next cell above the sensor value and the one in the next cell below the sensor value; then it will pick a point on that line that corresponds to the sensor value, and use that. This allows the maps to be used smoothly instead of having huge jumps between adjacent cells. It also eliminates the need for very large maps, in most applications. Maps that only have a single component (like a coolant temperature map) are referred to as 1D (they have only one axis) such as those from the coolant temperature sensor. Likewise, they are interpolated for intermediate values. 1D maps are commonly correction factors—they modify the calculations in the same way at any point of the ECU's operation. For the simple models being used by most ECUs,

this is a necessary helper that keeps the operation of the vehicle relatively consistent over a wide variety of operating conditions.

Now that we have discussed the limitations of modeling and how we can get around them a bit with mapping, let's explore the most commonly used models and how they can be used to achieve the goal of making the engine run, and run reasonably well.

THE THREE MAIN MODELS

Now we have to refer back to Chapter 1 so we can figure out what we would want to use to guide us, and why. Since we are mainly concerned with what kind of mixture is available when the spark is ignited and how much oxygen is trapped in the combustion chamber at that point in time, our model must represent those concepts, and we must be able to measure (or estimate) those variables with fair accuracy. Fortunately for us, a gasoline engine can work over a reasonably wide range of air/fuel ratios, as long as the fuel is well-vaporized and the mixture is reasonably homogeneous.

MAF

The most common injection strategy found on cars is based on reading from a mass airflow sensor. In the sensor chapters, I covered many of the benefits and drawbacks of MAF sensors. The

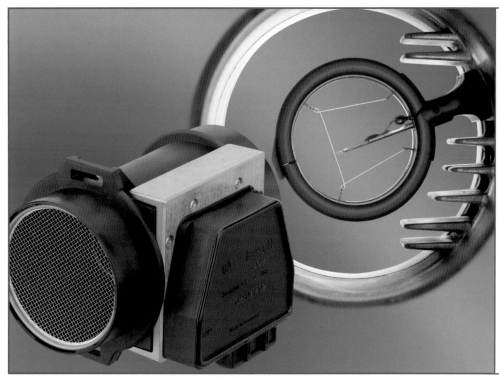

A Bosch hot-wire MAF sensor. Mass airflow sensors have some significant advantages when it comes to accurately measuring air mass entering the engine, but the limitations on installation location are the biggest drawback to their use in motorcycles. Bosch GmbH

primary reason they are seen infrequently on motorcycles is due to the different location of the intake components. The air mass ingested by the engine changes very rapidly with changes in throttle position, but the air mass entering the airbox is much slower to react, creating lag in the fuel delivery.

Benefits

To reiterate, using a MAF sensor to determine fueling is an excellent choice, since it actually determines the mass of air being ingested by the engine. This makes for fairly precise fueling, which can be tuned for emissions, power, or economy, or even a mixed bag of these priorities. Having the ability to distinguish between different engine dynamics (such as being able to see that a rider is engine braking, rather than running at cruise on the freeway) allows a seamless integration of priorities without it being obvious to the rider. They will simply notice better gas mileage with the same throttle response. Because MAF takes into account anything that changes the gas flow dynamics through the whole of the combustion system (by which I mean the engine, intake, exhaust, fueling and spark), it is the most adaptable of the fueling strategies. Changing your exhaust, or using an aftermarket air filter, would only make a very small change to the accuracy of fueling (the small changes would be due to the fact that measuring MAF does not measure trapping efficiency; some air will pass out the exhaust unburned, and this will cause the mixture to be slightly rich with an aftermarket low-restriction exhaust if run on MAF signal alone).

In addition, because a MAF sensor measures actual air mass moving through the combustion system, it is not necessary to establish ambient air density (which is typically determined through measuring ambient air temperature and ambient air pressure) in a well-designed MAF EFI system. This simplifies the wiring harness, reduces the number of potential failure points in the system (by reducing both the number of sensors and the number of connectors on the wiring harness), and simplifies the

program run by the ECU. In addition, it can deal quite easily with VE numbers in excess of 100%, as found in turbocharged engines, making it an attractive choice for highly pressurized intake tracts.

MAF sensors are typically self-cleaning and internally self-calibrating, thus making the system more robust and less likely to require maintenance or throw trouble/fault codes on the dash. This is especially inviting in the automotive world, where long service intervals are increasingly favored by consumers.

Drawbacks

As mentioned previously, MAF sensors are much more expensive than those used for other modeling strategies. Additionally, rapid changes in airflow to the cylinder cannot be measured in real time by a MAF sensor; so there is still need to approximate the transient changes in airflow during rapid changes in throttle opening (delta alpha), at least until the inertia of the air mass within the intake is overcome and the airflow is equalized throughout the intake system. As was noted in earlier chapters, the sensor is expensive, and intake design greatly limits the ability to install a MAF sensor on most bikes. Despite their advantages, MAF sensors are largely unused in motorcycle applications due to cost, design constraints, and their inability to respond rapidly to changing engine conditions.

MAF gives the best representation of gas flow into the cylinder, but it is still not completely sensitive to changes in trapping efficiency. This means that a simple map is still needed to factor in how trapping efficiency alters the measurement of air in the combustion chamber. MAF-equipped vehicles are best able to handle changes in intake, cam, and exhaust without changing the map stored inside the ECU, but they are not able to perfectly adapt without outside assistance in the form of altering their stored map.

Because MAF sensors are most accurate when airflow is fairly stable, they are best used in applications where there is a great deal of plenum between the sensor and the engine. This is often impractical on a motorcycle due to space considerations.

The four pressure sensors originally used by Honda in the 1982 CX500 Turbo. These are large and heavy by today's standards. Even Honda did away with several of them with the 1983 introduction of the CX650 Turbo. Sensors courtesy of Greg Goss

Speed Density

With the advent of stringent emissions regulations in the motorcycle world, the importance of leaning out idle and cruise mixtures has increased. This presented a problem for drivability, and a system was needed that would be able to follow changes in airflow near closed throttle with fair precision and great speed. Speed density sensing was the answer. (7-04)

Speed density is so named because it correlates engine speed to intake air density. By writing a map to correlate between measured MAP (manifold air pressure) and actual trapping efficiency at a given engine rpm, it is able to deliver proper fuel for a given engine state, despite the fact that it cannot actually measure the mass of trapped intake gases. It is an approximation, not an actual representation of trapping efficiency, so it requires some manner of map to account for intake and exhaust resonances, cam timing, and other factors that affect trapping efficiency. By measuring the air pressure in the intake runners, this metering method determines volumetric airflow (how large a volume of air is being ingested). Since a gas in motion will drop pressure in direct proportion to its speed of travel, it's a linear correlation based on sensor data. By combining data on ambient air density (via use of AAP and AAT sensors) with the data gathered on volumetric airflow, we can obtain a number for actual air mass entering the combustion chamber, and thus determine correct fueling. Most modern motorcycles utilize speed density mapping under at least some operating conditions.

Benefits

Because there is very little volume in the intake runner, changes in the engine's air demands result in nearly instantaneous changes in MAP. This is a good thing, because now we have a very responsive and accurate way of determining changes in the air demands of the engine. Very little guesswork is required to compensate for large delta alpha, and fueling is much more precise at very small throttle angles (where small changes make the biggest percentage difference in airflow). The two biggest winners from speed density mapping are cruise economy and steady-state emissions. Both of these factors are increasingly important in today's motorcycle market.

In addition, very accurate and stable pressure sensors are now available. They can be had for a very low price, especially when compared with MAF sensors. They are also small and light, and do not have limitations on their location on the bike (they need only be connected to the intake manifold(s) via a length of sealed vacuum hose). These factors combine to make speed density extremely inviting to motorcycle designers and engineers alike.

Keep in mind that the older, flapper VAF sensors give the same sort of data as a modern MAP sensor (and therefore must be included in a discussion of speed density mapping), but are much slower to react to changes in airflow, and have to be located before the airbox (which means they have a very slow response to changing alpha). They combine the disadvantages of speed-density with the drawbacks of MAF, along with adding mechanical reliability problems with aging of the potentiometer and the

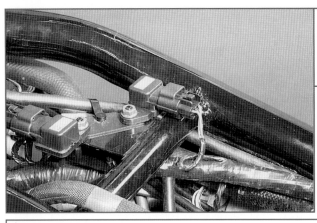

A pair of modern pressure sensors, seen on a Kawasaki VN1500 Mean Streak. Advances in plastics and semiconductors have made pressure sensors the preferred method of measuring part-throttle engine load. Kawasaki Motor Corporation USA

The flapper-type VAF, as shown here, gives basically the same data as a MAP sensor, but also has the drawbacks of both a potentiometer and a MAF sensor. They were not used for long on motorcycles. Kawasaki Motor Corporation USA

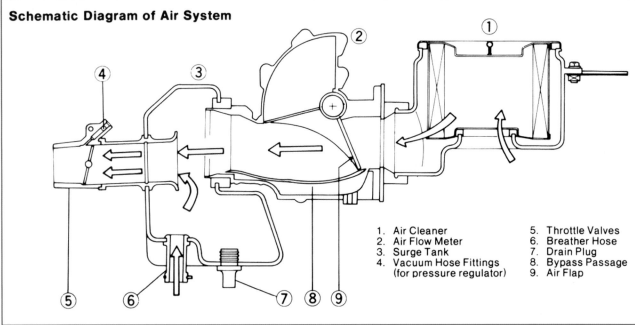

Schematic Diagram of Air System

1. Air Cleaner
2. Air Flow Meter
3. Surge Tank
4. Vacuum Hose Fittings (for pressure regulator)
5. Throttle Valves
6. Breather Hose
7. Drain Plug
8. Bypass Passage
9. Air Flap

spring resisting the airflow. They have been supplanted by modern MAP sensors for almost two decades, and are a special case that doesn't really play into our discussion (unless you're one of the few out there who still owns one of the old Kawasakis with an intact EFI system!).

Drawbacks

One of the big drawbacks of watching the manifold pressure and using that to guide our fueling is that the lower the engine rpm, and the fewer cylinders the engine has, the more fluctuation there will be in the manifold vacuum. Take the example of a single-cylinder motorcycle. In the course of a single engine cycle (two full crank rotations) at idle, the MAP will be highest right after the intake valve has closed. Air is rushing in past the throttle plate to refill the manifold, and its inertia continues after the intake valve has closed, but with the valve closed, it has nowhere to go, so it piles up in the manifold. And the MAP will be lowest not long after the intake valve has opened; the increase of volume in the cylinder lowers the pressure there, and the higher pressure in the intake runner pushes air into the cylinder, but the inertia of the air in the airbox resists it rushing past the throttle plate to refill the

manifold. So we end up with wild fluctuations in the MAP for each individual cylinder. How on earth can we get useful data from that?

There are two ways, but both of them require either an ASIC, or a decent slice of processor time. One is to use the crank position reading to determine the pressure just as the intake valve opens. This will give us a very good idea of what the density of the air is that is going into the cylinder. The other is to average the reading over an entire cycle, as the average will change as the air demands of the engine change. The first method requires keeping track of crank position and putting everything else on hold at a given crank angle so the measurement can be taken; the other requires constant sampling and then some math performed on the results. Depending on how you are designing your ECU, and how much processing power you can afford to include, each of these may or may not be a useful strategy. Of course, at higher engine rpms, the airflow becomes constant enough that you can usually take a reading almost anywhere in the combustion cycle without much variation in pressure. And if you have multiple cylinders, with each cylinder being at a different place in the cycle, it tends to even out the pressure reading between them; when one intake runner has a higher pressure, another will have a lower, and

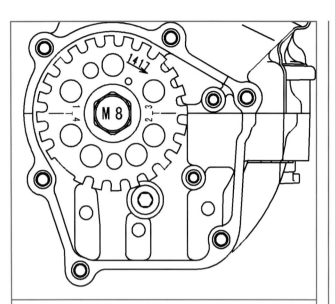

The more teeth a crank position sensor's trigger wheel has, the more accurately the ECU can determine crank angle. This Kawasaki ZX-6RR crank trigger wheel has 23 teeth with one missing, allowing the ECU to check its measure of crank angle every 15 degrees, and adjust its internal count as necessary. Such precision is very useful when one wants to sample certain sensors at certain places in the engine's cycle. Kawasaki Motor Corporation USA

so forth. Connecting vacuum hoses from all the cylinders to a single sensor basically amounts to averaging the signal without having to do any math. A V-twin engine will obviously not be able to use this method very well, while an inline-four using this method will give much closer to ideal sensor output.

Another disadvantage of this modeling method is that it cannot account very well for changes in intake, and especially exhaust, tuning. Since a MAP sensor can only tell us the density of the air entering the cylinder, and not how well it will be trapped there, anything that changes trapping efficiency will introduce some error. This is more of an issue than with MAF-equipped vehicles, simply because the data being relayed by a MAP sensor is less representative of actual airflow into the cylinder than a MAF sensor is.

The last big disadvantage of speed density is that it can only measure changes in intake pressure. At larger throttle openings, there is a fairly small change in MAP for a fairly large change in alpha. This lack of sensitivity to delta alpha when alpha is large tends to make it much more difficult to ensure accurate fueling under those conditions. Further, if volumetric efficiency ever exceeds 100% (i.e., due to intake and exhaust tuning, the combustion chamber takes in more than 100% of the air volume it could hold under static conditions), the MAP sensor stops reporting any information about intake air mass and cannot deliver any useful information at all. This essentially limits highly tuned motors to using speed density only when VE will be below 100% (in other words, at less than full throttle). It should also be noted that intake leaks between the throttle body and the engine will result in artificially high pressure readings, leading to a lean condition.

Alpha-n

This is the most primitive form of modeling trapped gases in the combustion chamber. But in some ways it is the most useful, espe-

cially for motorcycles with their short intake runners and individual throttle bodies. It is the simplest in terms of computing power and is probably the best-understood. Comparing engine speed (n) to throttle angle (alpha) is a much more direct correlation mentally—both are things that are easily measured and understood by the layperson. And for racing use, there is little reason to use anything else. Like speed density, it requires an AAP and AAT sensor to calculate ambient air density as a base to work from.

Benefits

The one clear benefit of alpha-n modeling is that it offers an instantaneous reaction to a change in alpha. Since I've covered the disadvantages of a slow reaction to delta alpha with the other two modeling methods, it should be apparent that there is a benefit here. In addition, the other two mapping methods will require a TPS anyway, so they can react to rapid changes in alpha that their own main sensors cannot provide.

The other huge benefit (which is slowly falling by the wayside) is that, due to the incredible simplicity of the measurements being taken, very little processing power is required to create a workable alpha-n system. The reduced complexity, number of sensors, and processing power required for putting such a system into operation is a vast benefit to the designers of such systems.

Because they don't actually measure airflow, but make assumptions about it in the map, they are often much easier to tune on large-displacement V-twin and single-cylinder engines where intake flow and pressure can have huge variations. What's more, since they can handle VE in excess of 100%, they are a good match with ram air systems at full throttle, or super- and/or turbocharged applications (although some kind of system for measuring or computing air mass is needed with a turbocharger, since it can deliver a wide range of air mass per unit of time, even at the same throttle position and engine speed).

For racers, who generally spend most of their time at or near wide-open throttle when wanting to make power, and who also want power over economy or emissions, the simplicity of alpha-n makes trackside tuning much simpler. What's more, the very

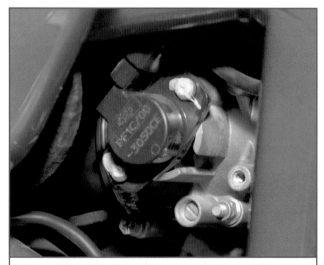

A Magneti Marelli throttle position sensor on a late-model Ducati. Alpha-n systems rely entirely on engine speed and throttle position measurements, while other systems use the TPS to determine changes in engine loading demanded by the rider.

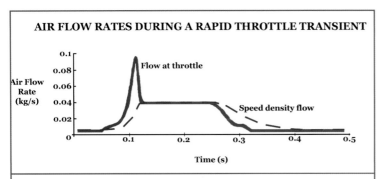

AIR FLOW RATES DURING A RAPID THROTTLE TRANSIENT

This graph demonstrates that there is a lag in intake pressure after changing the throttle position. This is why a TPS is really a requirement for all fuel-injected motorcycles. The ECU must be able to determine that the load demand has changed before it can react. Maya Culbertson

limited number of engine states that will be seen during a race means that the crudeness of the sensor data with an alpha-n system becomes a non-issue; racers don't care if they use a little more fuel during engine braking, as long as the spark plugs don't foul before full throttle is again applied.

Drawbacks

Since alpha only tells one small part of the story of engine conditions, it is by far the least precise modeling method. This means that gas mileage, fuel economy, and sometimes power, will suffer over other forms of injection modeling. It also means that it is the most sensitive of the models to changes in trapping efficiency. Even something as small as a slight change in exhaust backpressure will require remapping to retain smooth throttle transitions and good power. Since many assumptions about engine operating conditions and trapping efficiency are built into the map provided by the designer, alpha-n systems generally cannot take advantage of the fact that EFI can provide for different dynamic engine states (like cruise, idle, engine braking, and acceleration) that have the same alpha and engine speed. Alpha-n is very simple, but it is also fairly crude.

The other big drawback of alpha-n operation is based on the behavior of the butterfly throttle plate. The change in restriction of airflow past the throttle plate is an inverse logarithmic curve; in other words, at small alpha, a given change in alpha will have a much larger effect on intake mass than the same change would at large alpha. This is why there is relatively little difference in acceleration when one goes from 3/4 throttle to full throttle, comparatively. In fact, some manufacturers have even switched from round throttle bellcranks (which give a 1:1 response between alpha and actual throttle twistgrip angle) to bellcranks that are egg-shaped (which give more delta alpha at small alpha than at large alpha) to give their cars and motorcycles more throttle response when accelerating from a standing start, or from cruise (which are both conditions where one is generally using a fairly small alpha).

Because of this increased sensitivity at small alpha, it is *extremely* important that the TPS be adjusted to a very precise calibration. While not an issue on a race bike, which does not really need to idle or have smooth and efficient cruise operation, this is of paramount importance on a street bike, which spends most of its life at either cruise or idle. Maladjustment will also result in stumbles and surges during acceleration from at or near closed throttle, which again are of primary importance on a street bike. This alone tends to be most of the characterization of

drivability one assigns to a street bike. Since potentiometers change calibration due to age and dirt, and alpha-n doesn't actually measure anything about airflow, much maintenance attention must be paid to not only the TPS, but also to anything that would alter volumetric efficiency. Even something as small as a need for repacking the exhaust canister or a dirty air filter can cause drivability problems. And even more than with speed density, intake leaks between throttle and intake valve can cause significant miscalculations in fueling.

And last, due to its coarse measurements and assumptions about airflow efficiency, alpha-n generally provides both the worst fuel economy and the worst emissions of the bunch. As emissions regulations continue to march forward, straight alpha-n systems will drop entirely from street-driven motorcycles.

THE ODDBALL: CLOSED-LOOP OPERATION

I don't even consider closed-loop operation to be a mapping philosophy, since, in theory, there is generally no map to speak of (some applications, like those with SAGEM ECUs using O_2 sensors, build a table of correction factors based on O_2 sensor data, but that is using the O_2 sensor to gather data for open-loop running, and not true closed-loop operation). As I mentioned in the chapters on sensors, only a wideband O_2 sensor can give any useful data outside of an extremely narrow band of AFR right around lambda = 1. Even with a wideband O_2 sensor, one needs target data from a previous calibration for the O_2 sensor's data to

Oxygen sensors are a fact of life with emissions-controlled vehicles, but their only real purpose on production vehicles is to maintain a part- or no-load mixture that can properly feed a catalytic converter. Here, a new sensor is shown with one that needs replacement. Replacing your O_2 sensor when necessary will keep emissions low, and may improve rideability on some models. Bosch GmbH

be of use in working on fueling, which requires that one has tuned a similar engine to the user's goals previously using other measuring devices (such as a four-gas analyzer or a dynamometer).

Closed-loop, as it is utilized on motorcycles today, only operates at cruise, and in some cases idle, and only serves to produce correct mixture strategies (which are all referred to as open-loop, because they do not sense anything after the intake tract, and therefore are unable to provide feedback about trapping efficiency or the combustion process). Narrow-band closed-loop operation co-opts control of injector pulse width from the regular program in the ECU, and changes in pulse width are then based purely on feedback from the O_2 sensor. If the ECU detects a sudden change in alpha, it takes itself out of closed-loop mode, and resumes regular open-loop operation.

In some cases, data gathered from closed-loop operations are used to trim, or modify, mapping data for open-loop modes (as I mentioned above). The SAGEM ECUs that come equipped with narrow-band O_2 sensors are typically programmed to keep track of how far the mixture must be adjusted when shifting into closed-loop mode. If it differs consistently from a predetermined number, then the difference is written to a temporary memory location, where it is then applied to open-loop maps. Should this value exceed certain pre-programmed limits, the ECU will deliver a trouble code that signals either a problem with the O_2 sensor or some sort of problem with either fuel or air delivery elsewhere in the system (I should note that it can also signal extensive misfire, although it can be quite difficult to determine the actual source of the problem from such a reading alone). The temporary values are typically written in a table format that corresponds with the primary map used by the ECU; if the battery is disconnected (or the table is reset by a software command), the table is erased, and the ECU must begin again with its learning of the differences between the actual operation of that particular engine and the approximation that is coded in the permanent maps in the ECU.

INTEGRATION OF MODELS IN ACTUAL SYSTEMS

As has been noted, MAF operation favors engines that have a fairly small rate of delta-n, or acceleration/deceleration capability, speed density favors precision with small throttle openings, and alpha-n favors larger throttle openings. It is not uncommon for manufacturers to utilize different modeling methods under different operating conditions. Only one combination is prevalent in the motorcycle world, but a great number of OEM motorcycle systems use this particular combination.

You may have already guessed what it is, based on your own knowledge of the benefits and drawbacks, as well as taking an educated look at what sensors are typically found on modern FI bikes. Most manufacturers today use speed density for modeling at smaller throttle openings and switch to alpha-n at larger ones. This provides excellent precision throughout the operating range of the engine, which of course can be used to deliver superior smoothness and throttle response, along with excellent emissions and good gas mileage. It's a combination that is well understood by most OEMs and the Tier-One suppliers that design and build their injection systems, and it's quite capable of delivering excellent performance while still meeting today's emissions standards.

SPECIAL OPERATIONAL PARAMETERS

Setting up fueling for steady-state running (where alpha, rpms, engine temperature, and air temperature remain constant) is rela-

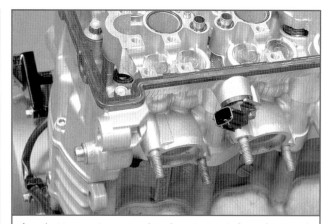

A coolant temperature sensor is an important part of ensuring smooth running and starting under a large variety of conditions. Here we see an installed coolant temperature sensor on a partially disassembled Kawasaki ZX-6RR motor. Kawasaki Motor Corporation USA

tively simple in the grand scheme of things. Changes in state happen very slowly, if at all, and trapping and volumetric efficiency remain constant. However, as I have noted above, an engine that is changing states (which could be a change in alpha, rpm, air temperature, or engine temperature, among others) often needs a little extra help. Especially with changes in alpha, there is usually a lag between a change in operating state and the change in airflow being relayed to the ECU. And a cold engine has a lot of differences that seriously affect its ability to atomize fuel and support good combustion. For these special cases, we need to alter our fueling to compensate.

Coolant/Engine Temperature

No single factor has more impact on engine operation than the engine's temperature. It plays into so many things in so many different ways, it can be hard to separate out individual causes and effects. But as I noted above with modeling methods that fold many different effects together to give a simpler way to get close to a "perfect" answer, we can do the same thing here. I'll try to offer you some insight as to what is going on, though, and how important it is to be able to change our fueling based on these things.

The Cold Engine

This is one of the most challenging cases for a fuel-injected engine. When the engine is cold, it will generally have more friction (mainly due to the oil being cold), which means we need to produce more power (especially for idle) under otherwise identical engine states. Further, we have special problems when it comes to ensuring vaporization, which forms the main difficulty in providing smooth throttle response.

Engine heat is the single biggest factor in fuel vaporization. As I have several times, it is essential for good, reliable combustion (not to mention power and emissions) that the mixture be as close to homogeneous as possible, that is, completely evenly mixed, with as much of the fuel in vapor form as possible. The further we get from this ideal, the worse everything about combustion will be. Failure to vaporize the fuel completely results in blobs of fuel being in suspension, which will not burn. If we chose a mixture designed for an engine that has been fully warmed up, this will also result in the remainder of the mixture being lean.

Let's follow the path of the fuel and see how a cold engine will impact its running, and what we can do about it.

Air enters through the airbox. On the one hand, a cold engine is an advantage here, as it will not heat the intake air as much, and will give us a denser intake charge. This means we have the ability to make more power. However, increasing the intake temperature will tend to provide for better vaporization of the fuel (since the fuel can "steal" heat from the intake, which will not only help vaporize the fuel more completely, but will also cool the air, thus making it denser). So we have a trade-off here.

As we progress along the intake tract, we come to the intake valve. Combustion heat that is conducted into the intake valve plays a very large role in helping vaporize the fuel, since that is where most of the fuel spray ends up after leaving the injector—on the head of the intake valve, prior to the valve opening and allowing the air/fuel vapor to enter the cylinder. Intake valve heads can reach temperatures of 350° F or more. A fully warmed engine can, however, achieve intake valve temperatures as low as 220° F from fuel vaporization alone. At peak, intake mixture passing the intake valve can be as hot as 150–200° F! This is a lot of heat transfer, and it moves an appreciable fraction of the injected fuel from liquid to vapor form. However, the intake valve heads do not reach a high enough temperature to affect vaporization until 20–50 seconds after starting the engine. Even then, it can take several minutes for the valve heads to reach their typical operating temperatures. During this time period, a much larger amount of injected fuel will remain in liquid form (which will increase hydrocarbon emissions, reduce burn speed, and can even cause plug fouling), necessitating a richer mixture to help compensate.

Even more important is combustion chamber wall temperature, including the piston crown. The effect is similar to that of the intake valve, but more pronounced, and what's more, the combustion chamber surface takes longer to heat up than the intake valve heads do, mainly due to having a much larger conductive heat path away from the surface in the form of the piston body, rings, cylinder liner, block/crankcase, and cylinder head(s).

To make matters even more difficult, gasoline is composed of a great number of different molecules, with a variety of shapes, sizes, weights, and volatility. Only the very lightest fractions will vaporize when the entire engine is at ambient temperature. These fractions have much more of a tendency to detonate, so mixtures must be richened even further, between the need to prevent detonation and the fact that only a narrow fraction of the injected fuel is being vaporized. As the engine warms, heavier fractions can evaporate due to increased cylinder wall temperatures, and things rapidly move toward a fully warmed state, where there is excellent vaporization.

So we need to richen the mixture greatly at very low temperatures and lean the mixture out as we get closer to normal operating temperature. Coolant temperature is a good gauge of the temperature change at or near the combustion chamber walls, since coolant is the primary path for moving heat out from the combustion chambers and dissipating it through the radiator. This is why a coolant temperature sensor is an important part of any fuel injection system. It is crucial to ensuring that the bike will be able to run well enough to be drivable until it is fully warmed up.

Typically, there will be a 1D map for coolant temperature that is additive—that is, there will be a numeric value for each of a range of coolant temperatures, and that numeric value will be added to the pulse width value already determined by the primary mapping strategy being used. At its coldest map cell, the numerical value will be highest, and it will drop as the temperature rises.

An overheated air-cooled engine is perhaps even more of a concern than a cold air-cooled engine. Here we see an engine temperature sensor installed on a Moto Guzzi.

At the map cell representing correct operating temperature, the value in the map cell will have dropped to zero. Some automotive ECUs use a formula for altering fueling based on coolant temperature, rather than a 1D look-up table, but this has yet to be implemented in the motorcycle world. It is inherently more accurate, but requires extra processing power and design sophistication over a LUT (look-up table, which is another name for a map).

The Overheating Engine

Overheating is one of the biggest enemies of modern motorcycle engines. It can easily warp cylinder heads, cause partial or full seizing of pistons and rings, and can even destroy spark plugs and pistons through detonation. Preventing overheating is extremely important in modern motorcycles. And as engines become smaller and make more and more power, we are seeing increasing demands on the cooling system. Small issues with the cooling system were once no cause for concern, but today even a small reduction in cooling efficiency can cause overheating and engine damage in short order. Some manufacturers choose to use ignition timing and/or the fuel injection system as a last resort to help lower engine temperatures. A side effect is often that the bike becomes so unpleasant to ride (without becoming unsafe) that the operator is prone to stop running the machine, thus allowing it to cool to safer levels before continuing.

Just as with the case of the cold engine, it's not terribly uncommon to find a coolant temperature map that becomes extremely rich once a certain high coolant temperature is reached. The additional fuel slows combustion, greatly lowering combustion chamber temperatures. The additional richness also cools the combustion chamber through evaporative cooling, as was mentioned in the section on cold running above. Honda in particular is fond of this strategy, which is prevalent on the RC-51. Ride it in traffic on a very hot day, where the small, lightweight fans cannot move enough heat out of the radiator, and you may well find yourself on a bike with extremely soft throttle response, very little power, and a rough idle. This is the manufacturer's way of helping to keep your motorcycle from being damaged by continued operation under such conditions.

Starting the Engine

As difficult as it is to get an engine to run when it is cold, it is perhaps even more difficult to get it to start in the first place. Even once the motorcycle is warmed up, trapping efficiency drops during cranking due to the very slow rotation of the motor (a typical starter motor with a freshly charged battery will only turn over an engine at a few hundred rpm). In addition, running the starter motor is a huge demand on the small batteries found in today's motorcycles. It's not uncommon to see system voltage drop to 10v or less during cranking, especially on high-compression engines. This can result in reduced spark, which will hinder starting. It can also cause glitches in the ECU. But most importantly, dropping voltage will cause the injectors to open much more slowly, and in some cases, to never open fully (when pulse width is already short, such as during a warm start). Also, the fuel pump will not be able to build and maintain as high a pressure, which in some cases can result in reduced fuel rail pressure. For these reasons, there is a 1D map for system voltage on every system I have encountered. As system voltage drops, pulse width is increased to compensate for the reduced amount of fuel being delivered by a given lower voltage pulse width to the injector(s).

One distinct advantage that we have during starting is that the throttle is closed. By lowering the MAP (by cranking the motor while the throttle is closed), we essentially lower the boiling point for the components of the fuel, thus aiding in vaporization. A good thing, too; without this effect, it might be impossible to start a cold high-compression motor using a small battery!

High-compression, large-displacement single- and twin-cylinder engines often need even more help during starting. Often such machines cannot get enough air into the combustion chamber to support combustion reliably. These engines need extra air during starting in addition to extra fuel. A common strategy is to use an idle air bypass setup. Honda experimented with a mechanical bypass controlled by a bimetal strip (as found in a home heating thermostat), which would allow extra air past the throttle plates in inverse proportion to coolant temperature. That design has been supplanted by an IAC solenoid (IAC for idle air control). This is usually not a solenoid at all, but a small stepper motor that can open a bypass channel in small steps depending on engine temperature. An IAC solenoid will typically self-calibrate, either using a sensor similar to a TPS sensor to tell the ECU where it is currently set or by running the solenoid through its entire range of operation and counting how many steps it takes to go from one extreme to the other. Some motorcycles will actually open the throttle butterfly or butterflies with a stepper motor to control idle speed, but an IAC solenoid tends to give more precise control and is mechanically separate from the throttle butterfly itself, simplifying design and installation.

Delta Alpha

As was noted in the sections about the three main modeling strategies, there is usually a lag between a change in alpha and a change in sensor readings (especially with speed density, and even more so with MAF). In addition, opening the throttle rapidly tends to increase MAP very quickly, which works against vaporization of the injected fuel. Clearly, when the throttle is opened rapidly, we need to deliver more fuel to overcome these deficiencies. Likewise, when the throttle is closed suddenly, we want to lean out our mixture to prevent excess unburned fuel in the exhaust (which produces the phenomenon we know as backfiring when it burns off in the exhaust system).

With an alpha-n system, this is less of a problem, as our primary mapping methodology relies on the TPS, so there will be no lag in responding to a change in airflow to the engine. However, some compensation is still needed for the change in fuel vaporization

Idle air control solenoids are typically found on motorcycles with slow idle speed and especially large cylinders—like V-twins. In fact, the Kawasaki VN1500 Mean Streak has two, one for each cylinder. They are labeled "A" and "B" in the accompanying photo. The arrow points toward the front of the motorcycle. Kawasaki Motor Corporation USA

from a change in MAP. Depending on how precisely we wish to control our fueling, and to what ends, we may even choose to ignore this most of the time, and only deliver additional fuel when there is a very large positive delta alpha (rapid opening of the throttle).

With a speed density system, it starts to become more important to alter fueling based on a measurement of delta alpha. Speed density reacts in a similar fashion to a carburetor in many ways, and if you have ever worked on a car carburetor (and even some bike carburetors), you'll be quite familiar with the accelerator pump. This is a small diaphragm that delivers extra fuel for a time as the throttle is opened; the faster it is opened, the more fuel it delivers. In a similar fashion, speed density and MAF mapping systems require an extra shot of fuel until the airflow measurement catches up with what is actually going on inside the combustion chamber. And in a manner similar to a carburetor, the more rapid the throttle angle changes, the more fuel is needed immediately, and the longer extra fuel will be needed before the airflow measurement catches up with the actual demands of the engine.

As a result, almost all ECUs are equipped with a function to measure changes in alpha, and to alter fuel according to the rapidity of its delta function. Generally, there will be a small subroutine in the runtime code (the actual program) in the ECU that will periodically check the value (position) of the TPS. When it sees a large change in TPS between samples, it calculates the rate of change based on the difference between the two samples, and then consults a small acceleration map that has a value for peak pulse width increase (which is the amount of enrichment delivered as soon as the throttle is opened), plus a decay function (which is the time period over which the enrichment is reduced until it returns to zero additional pulse width). These values are then used to trail off the enrichment by interpolating the value between peak and zero over the time span indicated in the decay function. This serves the same purpose, and actually works in the same manner, as an accelerator pump on a carburetor.

Gear Position/Road Speed

One sensor that factors into our mapping strategy, although not immediately obvious, is the road speed or gear position sensor.

A TPS is essential for proper throttle response on all fuel-injected motorcycles. Here, a 1981 Kawasaki GPz1100 proudly displays a cover over its TPS announcing D.F.I., or digital fuel injection. David Vastag

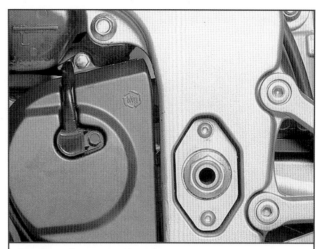

A road speed or gear position sensor can deliver a great deal of useful information to the ECU regarding the conditions it is facing. Here we see a road speed sensor on a Kawasaki ZX-6RR. It uses a count of revolutions of the front sprocket to determine road speed. Many motorcycles use this to drive a digital speedometer on the dash as well. Kawasaki Motor Corporation USA

Basically, these sensors are interchangeable; they deliver essentially the same information to the ECU (since road speed is easily determined by determining what gear the bike is in, and multiplying the gear ratio and tire rotating circumference by engine rpm). Why would this be important to us, or to the manufacturers? There are several reasons, which we will explore here.

Controlling Launch
One of the biggest challenges for racers is to leave the starting line without destroying the clutch, being slow, or losing control of the motorcycle. Since there is almost no air resistance at low speeds, the full power of most sportbikes would be enough to wheelie over backwards without any difficulty. Obviously, we don't want this on a race-track. Likewise, manufacturers don't want people suing them for crashing very powerful street bikes when launched hard. So the first important job of a road speed or gear position sensor is to allow the ECU to reduce the power output in first gear (and possibly second) to prevent the bike from behaving badly. This has grown to be basically mandatory on fuel-injected street and race bikes today.

Adapting to Ram Air
While an alpha-n or MAF injection system can handily adapt to a rise in intake air pressure, it's not a perfectly linear response. Often, VE will change in very slight but unexpected ways when the airbox is pressurized. This means that a slightly different set of fueling maps may be necessary to meet the goals of the designers. A road speed or gear position sensor will allow the ECU to switch between maps based on the amount of increase in intake air pressure as ram air comes into play.

Limiting Top Speed
For safety and liability reasons, as well as governmental legislation in some cases, manufacturers need to limit the top speed of their motorcycles. This can be done in a variety of ways, but typically is done via a soft limiter. This is not an actual device, but rather a way of describing its behavior. The ECU will either alter the fueling (usually by skipping an increasing number of fueling events entirely, leading to intermittent misfire) or retard the ignition timing incrementally as the bike approaches a given road speed. This way, power drops off slowly as the target speed is approached, rather than the behavior that would occur with a hard limiter (which would suddenly cap off the power right at the target speed, leading to a sudden change in the attitude and stability of the motorcycle). Most commonly, this job is done via alteration of ignition timing, so I will discuss it further later on in the ignition section.

Limp-Home Modes
As you may have noticed, there are a lot of components in an EFI system, which means that many things can potentially go wrong. Fueling is generally a pretty delicate balance, and it's not hard to determine when something has gone wrong (although knowing what exactly has gone wrong is another story entirely). With the attendant complexity of EFI systems, measures had to be taken to ensure that fail-safes were put into place and that failures or bad signals could be ignored, overridden, replaced, or otherwise corrected to enough of a degree to allow the engine to keep running reasonably well in as many possible failure modes as possible.

We're probably all quite familiar with the Check Engine light found on the dash (or in some cases, on the ECU itself) of nearly every EFI vehicle ever made. If it were not for limp-home modes, seeing this light would typically be your definitive signal as to why

Ram air bikes often make good use of a gear position or road speed sensor by allowing the ECU the ability to get a good idea of how much more air pressure it can expect in relation to the speed the bike is moving. Here a Kawasaki ZX-6RR shows off its central ram air duct, sans bodywork. Kawasaki Motor Corporation USA

the engine had just stopped running. But in practice, it is exceedingly rare for a fuel-injected vehicle to stop running entirely, based on a fault in the system. How has that been managed by the designers of such systems?

The simplest limp-home mode consists of a static value for a given sensor that replaces data from that sensor when it fails. Some of these substitutions work better than others, though. For instance, it's not uncommon for an ECU to plug in a value for a typical air temperature or coolant temperature if it receives no data from the sensor itself. This should, in theory, be good enough to allow you to at least drive the vehicle to a repair facility. And, in a fairly large number of cases, it actually is, although the operator of the vehicle may notice rough running, poor power, or drivability issues, among the most notable. Slightly more advanced ECUs can check to make sure the sensor data are within a certain set of parameters. This level of sophistication allows the ECU to determine partial sensor failures (where the sensor is delivering some data, but the data does not match the reality being measured). This is typically termed a plausibility check, since the ECU is trying to determine if the reading it is seeing is plausible. If, for instance, ambient air temperature was 100° F, and the coolant temperature sensor was consistently showing 55° F, it could safely be assumed that the coolant temperature sensor was unlikely to be showing a correct reading (since not only is it lower than ambient temperature, it is not rising as it should while the engine is running). This technique is still used with fairly great success.

More complex limp-home modes can sometimes offer fueling nearly as accurate as when there is no problem in the system at all. For instance, some ECUs are capable of synthesizing crank angle data from cam position data alone; while not as precisely timed as it would be with a functional crank position sensor, the vehicle can still be made to run at the expense of some of its maximum horsepower. Likewise, sequential injection systems can often be run in batch fire/wasted spark (having spark at the start of both the ignition and intake strokes, as on most carbureted motorcycles) mode should the cam position sensor fail. Here the victim of the failure becomes smoothness of idle and low-rpm fuel efficiency and power.

Occasionally fail-safe behavior cannot assist the engine in continuing to run, but can serve other purposes. Vehicles equipped with a catalytic converter are extremely sensitive to excessive unburned fuel entering the catalyst. Since catalysts run at a very high operating temperature, excessive unburned fuel has a tendency to light off inside the converter and burn, rapidly raising the temperature of the catalyst to damaging levels. Some ECUs are equipped to detect loss of spark and shut down fueling events immediately to prevent excessive unburned fuel from reaching the catalyst due to lack of combustion in the cylinder.

In a similar vein, some ECUs detect misfire (through a variety of means, including predictive crank angle timing and ion sensing), and will display a trouble code to alert the operator that there is a problem requiring attention, hopefully before damage is done to the catalytic converter.

It is also possible to use two oxygen sensors, one before and one after the catalyst. By observing the differences between the two signals, it can be determined whether either of the sensors or the catalytic converter is malfunctioning, and can then signal the operator of the need for diagnosis and repair.

THE FUTURE

Once again we turn to the automotive world for direction. While the above modeling methods are quite useful, they have clear limits. They only approximate what is actually going on in the combustion chamber in terms of VE, trapping efficiency, and combustion. For the emissions laws we currently have, they function plenty well enough for our purposes. However, emissions regulations have forced automakers to move to more complex models to maintain high levels of performance, drivability, and efficiency, while achieving increasingly low emissions levels.

To do this, the ECU no longer works on oversimplified modeling strategies that are good enough. To meet the needs of today's manufacturer, some automotive ECUs actually run on models of the physics of gas flow and combustion dynamics. In fact, these are much more precise mathematical models of what is really happening to the intake and exhaust gases, as well as in the dynamics of the combustion process itself. This strategy allows improvements in every area that an automaker would want.

The drawback is pretty obvious from the description of the challenge—software that models the actual physics going on in various areas of the combustion system, and how they all interact with each other, ahead of the actual need for the data, requires a very complex program for the ECU. This, in turn, requires a very powerful and fast MCU, typically with a number of ASICs to handle sensor processing and ancillary tasks. This makes such ECUs very expensive by current motorcycle ECU standards. As emissions regulations become stricter in the future, we should expect to see ECUs that work under these principles. That, however, is likely to be at least 5–10 years down the road.

SO THERE YOU HAVE IT

Short of talking in extreme detail about map encoding and software loops (for which there are already a number of excellent books and articles available), I've given you the gist of what goes on inside an ECU to determine proper fuel delivery, which dovetails with the chapters on sensors and injectors to fill in the big picture of what the system is really doing and how it does it. Next up: ignition timing. There's a lot more to it than you might think. Ignition timing is one of the least-heralded but most important factors in emissions in particular, and it plays into nearly every facet of engine operation, from power to fuel economy to (in some cases) engine longevity.

WE HAVE FUEL, NOW WE NEED SPARK

There is no question that the larger part of the evolution of fuel injection has revolved around delivering fuel. That sort of makes sense, doesn't it? Otherwise, they probably wouldn't have called it electronic *fuel injection*. But over time, control of the ignition system was integrated into the same box, and eventually into the same circuitry. To see why this would be a natural evolution (and yet did not occur right from the start), we have to look not only at the factors and devices used to control ignition, but what can be achieved through ignition control, and how it fits into the bigger picture of the combustion process. It probably won't surprise most of you very much to learn that many of the control factors and obtainable goals are similar to or identical with those connected with injecting fuel.

WHY IS IGNITION SO IMPORTANT?

Those of you who have dealt with motorcycles for a long time may be questioning why we would bother making the already-complex ECU even more complex just so we could handle ignition timing. After all, even the most advanced of carbureted motorcycles have a fairly simple method of determining ignition timing, typically relying on engine speed alone to calculate the ignition parameters. Who needs more?

To answer this question, we have to take a look at both the production of the spark itself and how spark timing affects events within the combustion chamber. As we will see, the issue of spark is more complex than it might seem on the surface. For spark timing is important in power, emissions, and even in ensuring the longevity of the motor itself.

What Is Spark, and How Do We Make It?

Sometimes the best way to get a solid understanding of something is to go back to the most basic parts of it and ask the questions that seem incredibly obvious (but often aren't). In the case of ignition, we have to start by asking ourselves, "What is a spark?" The answer may seem self-evident, but really, what is that blue fizzle in the spark plug made from?

Before we can talk about how we generate and control the electrical energy that ends up making the spark, we need to understand just what happens when that electrical charge reaches the spark plug. For right now, let's concentrate on what happens to that electrical energy once it makes it to the spark plug gap. We need to have an understanding of that critical event to really get to the heart of spark control.

Changing the State of Matter

The spark that we can see in a plug gap, the very one that ignited the fuel, is actually the visible result of changing the state of a small thread of air, atomized fuel, and exhaust gases remaining in the combustion chamber after the exhaust stroke. These molecules are changed from a gaseous state into *plasma*, a superheated, ionized matter stream. So how does this happen? The answer comes in the form of a large electrical charge applied rather suddenly. The initiation of a spark takes place as follows:

A potential difference (voltage) is created between the spark plug electrodes.

The gas (mostly air and fuel) molecules near the electrodes are ionized, forming charge regions (groups of molecules with their charged areas physically aligned).

The charge regions intersect, creating one or more conductive regions that bridge the spark gap.

Current begins to flow through the conductive region of least resistance.

If there is sufficient electrical energy, the current flow will increase until a critical point is reached; the gas molecules in the current flow path become super-heated and create a highly conductive plasma stream.

The plasma stream persists until there is insufficient energy to sustain it.

So we are actually generating plasma, the fourth state of matter (the other three being gas, solid, and liquid), between the spark plug's electrodes. The heat in the plasma keeps it strongly ionized, which keeps the current flow going as long as there is electrical energy available, which keeps the plasma heated. In other words, as long as there is electrical energy available at the plug gap, the plasma will be maintained. This will become an important point later on, when we start looking at the effects of spark duration. For now, we can say that there are two components in the spark equation, and they are the creation and maintenance of the plasma stream. The total electrical energy available at the plug gap is split between ionizing the mixture between the plug's electrodes and maintaining the plasma stream once it has been created. It is not electricity or ionization that actually ignites the mixture here; it is the incredibly high temperature of the plasma itself that initiates combustion.

Applying the Spark

So now we have our super-hot plasma, created and maintained by a high-voltage potential across the gap in the spark plug. That's

The spark plug itself is a very important part of making reliable power with low emissions. This NGK plug uses a narrow iridium center electrode that helps create a clean, hot spark over the life of the plug. Iridium stands up to higher heat with less erosion, thus allowing the plugs to last longer and maintain a like-new performance over time

step one; but what about our reason for having a spark in the first place? It's time to discuss exactly what happens in the combustion chamber, and along with it knock, pinging, detonation, and how the state of the combustion chamber can actually change our spark. It's time to talk about combustion itself.

Let's Look at the Hardware

Spark-ignition engines have been around for well over a hundred years. And in that time, very little has changed in the manner in which we generate the spark. In fact, one of the two circuits used in spark generation (the secondary circuit) is basically identical in just about every non-magneto spark-ignition engine out there. It uses a coil and a spark plug to do the job.

At its most basic, spark is created by building a magnetic field in a coil (which in this case is essentially a transformer, changing low voltage/high current to high voltage/low current). This is done by applying electrical potential (voltage) across the primary side of the coil. When the current flow is shut off and the magnetic field is allowed to collapse, the energy contained in the field is turned into electrical potential in the coil windings. And electrical potential is always looking for the fastest, easiest way to get itself to a ground. With the coil and plug wires being heavily insulated, the path of least resistance to ground is through the gap in the spark plug. So that is where the electrical potential goes. Since the mixture between the plug electrodes does not tend to conduct current very well, a lot of the electrical energy is used up in pushing through the resistive gases, which generates heat. The electrical energy tends to ionize the gas, as well as the rising heat in the region of the electrodes. A cascade begins, where the gas between the electrodes gets hotter and hotter, and if everything goes as planned, the plasma stream is created, remaining until all the available electrical energy has been discharged to ground via the ground electrode. If there is sufficient energy available to generate a hot enough spark, which lasts long enough, and occurs at the right time, combustion of the fuel is initiated.

What we have just described is the behavior of the secondary circuit; this is the secondary winding of the coil, any plug wires and boots, and the spark plug itself. But how do we end up with a magnetic field collapsing around the windings of the coil secondary? That's the job of the primary circuit, which controls dwell (the amount of time we use to build the magnetic field in the coil) and spark timing.

The coil itself has two windings, a primary and a secondary. The primary winding has many times more individual windings around the iron core than the secondary; the primary winding takes low-voltage, high-current input and the secondary offers high-voltage, low-current output. This is important because lots of voltage (which would be the equivalent of pressure in a flowing stream) is needed to push through the resistance of the gases in the combustion chamber. Think of it as the difference between a slow-moving but wide river (electrical energy at the primary coil) versus a very narrow, high-pressure water source (like the wand at a self-serve car wash). Both pass the same total number of water molecules in a given time (the equivalent would be having the energy to move the same number of electrons down a circuit), but the car-wash wand will be a lot better at blasting through the mud on the fender of your 4x4 after a day in the mud pits.

But it gets even better—all that electrical energy going into the coil doesn't just get converted between the windings, end of story. Some of it is lost in heat, of course, but here's where the iron core comes in—electrical energy coming into the primary winding generates a magnetic field, and some of the energy is used to create

and maintain this magnetic field. It takes time to build up the field, and once it is as strong as it will get from the available electrical energy, the coil is said to have reached saturation; continuing to flow the same amount of electrical energy through the primary winding will not make the magnetic field any stronger. When the current flow through the primary winding is stopped, there is nothing left to support the magnetic field, so it collapses, which turns the energy stored in the magnetic field back into electrical potential in the coil. This change of energy from magnetic field to current in the wire of the coil happens very quickly, which creates a sudden surge of electrical energy that is available on both windings of the coil. This sudden change of energy into electrical potential is what generates the spark at the plug gap.

So how much potential energy is available in the coil's magnetic field at the time of field collapse is entirely a factor of coil design, assuming we have enough system voltage and enough time to build the magnetic field to saturation. Dwell (the amount of time electrical energy is applied to the primary winding of the coil) is controlled by our ignition box; too long a dwell will overheat the coil primary, possibly damaging or destroying the coil, but not enough dwell will mean the coil never saturates, reducing the amount of potential energy we have to create a spark. The latter can cause misfire (and is almost always related to high-speed misfires, due to the much shorter time available to build the magnetic field).

What we are primarily concerned with in controlling this spark are two things: First, the amount of energy available to the coil primary winding to build and maintain the magnetic field; and second, the timing of the collapse of the magnetic field, to deliver the actual spark. It only takes about 2 milliseconds for combustion to occur once a spark is delivered. That may seem like a painfully short amount of time, but remember that at 10,000 rpm, a complete revolution of the engine takes place every 6 milliseconds! That's 6 milliseconds for us to determine the timing and duration of both spark and fuel, and deliver them. Not much time for everything that happens!

Dwell Angle

The amount of time that electricity is passing through the primary side of the ignition coil is called the dwell time, and it is usually measured in degrees of crank angle. As the engine turns faster, it will still require the same amount of time to build a strong magnetic field in the coil, given a certain amount of electrical energy passing through it. Thus, all other things being equal, dwell must *increase* as engine speed increases, just as spark advance must increase (since the burn rate will remain about the same, but the crankshaft will rotate more at higher engine speeds). This means that using a given coil and system voltage, there is an eventual limit on engine speed; beyond a certain engine speed, the coils won't be able to build enough magnetic field, leading to a weak spark and low reliability of combustion past that limit.

But there is another factor involved in calculating dwell angle. And that factor is charge density (which is one of the most important factors in working with spark timing and power). With a greater charge density, we need a hotter (or more powerful) spark to reliably ignite the mixture. Since charge density will change over a range of crank angles (based on mechanical compression; the closer we are to TDC, the greater the charge density) and throttle position (a closed throttle will allow less mixture into the combustion chamber, lowering charge density), as well as engine speed (based on changes in VE over the rpm range), we have a lot of factors to keep track of when ensuring that we have sufficient power in our spark to reliably ignite the mixture.

The Mechanics of It All

Well, now that we've established how important spark timing can be beyond simply approaching best timing of the PPP, let's take a look at how it is determined, and why.

The Old Way of Doing It

For years, motorcycles have relied upon the fixed mechanical advance style of ignition mapping; a simple 1D map of advance of spark angle versus engine rpm. This system is fine when all you are concerned about is best power at wide-open throttle, but it falls short at any part-throttle condition (since cylinder filling, and thus charge density, is lowered as the throttle is closed, thus slowing combustion). With slower flame front travel at part throttle, the spark occurs too late to make best power, and hydrocarbon and CO emissions are greatly increased (due to incomplete combustion).

The first major advance (which was made mainly for emissions reasons, but helped roll-on and part-throttle power as well) was to fit a throttle position sensor to carbureted motorcycles. By providing data about throttle position, it was possible to make a 2D map with alpha (throttle angle) on one axis, and rpm on the other.

Coincidentally, this 2D map is generally proportional to a VE map. And we have learned where we might find the same thing (a 2D map roughly approximating VE) with an EFI system. Yes, that's right. This is essentially the same "shape" of map you would find in an alpha-n EFI system on the same engine. Now you begin to see why ignition control dovetails so nicely with EFI!

How It's Done Today

Making ignition timing dependent on a 2D alpha-n map was only the beginning. Fuel economy and part-throttle emissions are most affected by small changes in alpha near closed throttle and under load (during cruise, in essence). As we so astutely noted in the fueling sections, a much more precise way of measuring small changes in engine load at small throttle openings is with a MAP sensor. Since what's good for the goose seems to be what's good for the gander here, we can safely assume that for economy and emissions at cruise, a 2D map featuring MAP versus rpm on the axes would be a good way to go. And indeed it is. Some manufacturers use this strategy for ignition timing as well. And just like the fueling setup found in most modern Japanese motorcycles, some machines even switch between alpha-n and MAP-n ignition mapping, using each in its area of greater precision (alpha-n during more open throttle conditions, speed density during more closed throttle conditions).

Several available systems even use a 3D mapping table, with one axis each for engine speed, alpha, and coolant temperature. Why coolant temperature? That will become clear later, in the Special Cases section. But as you can see, control over spark timing is becoming increasingly complex. For good reason!

Further, we have a whole host of other sensors that can come in handy for us. Since we are interested in volumetric efficiency and charge density (which, not coincidentally, are some of the big names in mapping fueling), we have opportunities to utilize a lot of data we have already gathered for fueling purposes.

Integration and Its Benefits

Modern EFI with ignition control has become the standard, and for reasons far surpassing the desire for more power. We have a bevy of sensors feeding useful information to the fuel injection system, so it only makes sense that we take advantage of this fact when timing spark. In the section below, where I will discuss mapping methods and strategies, it will become clear which sensors are being used and why. For now, it's enough to say that for ignition control, we have the ability to easily integrate sensor data that has already been gathered for use in calculating fueling. Further, we have the option of having a separate bit of hardware controlling spark, or of using the existing microcontroller to handle this.

A common way of handling spark control is to develop an ASIC for that function alone, and then to feed it with either pre-processed data from other ASICs, or sensor information (or even multiple-sensor calculations) from the microcontroller. As we have seen with the rest of the ECU, there are a variety of possible answers that have various costs and benefits associated with each. Designers look at a number of interrelated criteria when choosing a particular method; for instance, the cost of developing an ASIC for ignition control may be offset by the need for a faster processor if the ASIC is not used. Furthermore, there are the considerations of durability, mass-production, and all the other factors we previously discussed about the ECU.

The Component Pieces

Many of the components in a modern ECU-controlled ignition system are no different from those found on carbureted machines. Still, many of the innovations being seen on motorcycle ignition systems are running in tandem with integration of ignition into an EFI controller. What's more, most of these advances in components came about because the automotive world required them to meet its own emissions, power, and drivability needs. And as the components were mass-produced and costs came down, they were handed down to motorcycles as well. Again, we have governmental regulations and the auto industry to thank for modern motorcycle ignition systems. For now, let's take a look at how the hardware has changed over time, and what advantages today's components offers us.

The Origins—Points and Condenser

The very first modern spark ignition systems found in motorcycles (beginning in the late 1960s and early 1970s, by and large) were of the points-and-condenser type. A small single-lobe cam on the end of the crankshaft (or in some cases, the camshaft) drove either a single or dual set of points. Points are basically a mechanical switch; when closed, they allow battery power to build a magnetic field via the coil's primary winding. When the cam opens them, the field collapses and delivers a spark to the spark plug via the coil secondary. Just like with a fuel injector, the sudden collapse of the magnetic field causes voltage spikes to travel back through the points, causing arcing and damaging the points. Therefore a condenser (also called a capacitor) was introduced to absorb the flyback from the primary side of the coil (this is the voltage induced in the primary side by the collapse of the magnetic field), which prevents arcing across the points. This significantly extends the life of the points. Dwell was determined by the number of degrees of crank angle that the points remained closed; timing and dwell were both altered by changing the clearance between the point's rubbing block and the cam (as well as the shape of the cam itself), and timing could be adjusted by rotating the mounting plate for the points relative to the engine cases (or cylinder head, depending on where the points were mounted).

While automobiles utilized a distributor, motorcycles typically did not. There have been some exceptions (old V-twins, for instance, and magneto-fired ignitions), but the mechanical complexity, extra weight, and reduced dwell timing available at high engine speeds has generally precluded their use. Instead, most motorcycles relied on a waste-fire system. For inline engines, this was eminently practical. Since inline engines and parallel twins always have a set of pistons that are on opposite halves of the combustion cycle, it is possible to connect spark plugs from both cylinders to a single coil and trigger that coil once for every crank revolution. Since it takes two revolutions of the crank to complete a single combustion cycle, each of the involved cylinders would see one spark at the correct moment for combustion and one near the end of the exhaust stroke. Since there is so little resistance in exhaust gases as compared to a highly compressed intake charge, only a small amount of the electrical potential stored in the coil gets used up by jumping the gap in the waste fire cylinder, leaving the remainder of the electrical energy available to create the spark for the other cylinder's power stroke. On parallel and flat-twins, this allowed for a single set of points and a single coil; on inline four-cylinder engines, two opposed sets of points were commonly used, with two coils (one feeding each pair of opposing pistons). V-twin engines commonly used separate coils and two sets of points set apart identically to the angle between the cylinders; some used a single waste-fire coil driven by both sets of points, and some used dual coils.

Spark advance was handled the same way as it was in mechanical-advance distributors in cars: A set of weights attached to arms, and retained by springs, was attached to the crankshaft. As engine speed increased, centripetal force moved the weights farther and farther from the crankshaft. The movement of these weights rotated the points plate relative to the crankshaft, thus advancing or retarding the timing. This is known as mechanical advance. The advance curve could be altered by changing the weights or the strength of the retaining springs.

Avoiding the use of a distributor removed potential oil leaks, a number of mechanical parts that required regular replacement, and reduced the number of areas where there could be a current drop due to resistance (thus reducing available spark energy for a given dwell angle). In addition, each coil in a waste-fire system for an inline four-cylinder engine had twice as long to achieve coil saturation (since the task of spark creation was being shared by two coils, each of which fired half as often as the single coil in a distributor-style system). This allowed both smaller, lighter coils and an increase in maximum engine speeds.

The downside of the points-and-condenser system lies mainly in its mechanical nature. The rubbing block riding on the cam lobe would wear down from lack of lubrication and friction, increasing dwell while altering ignition timing. If the block wore far enough, or the set screw for setting point gap loosened, the points would collapse, thus staying closed all the time and never delivering a spark. Points are susceptible to wetness, since water conducts electricity. Beyond a certain engine speed, the spring for the points could not close them quickly enough to follow the cam lobe, making the points "float," which reduced dwell where it was needed the most. And in systems where there was more than one set of points, it was a trial to be constantly adjusting dwell and spark timing so that all four cylinders had the same output.

Next Steps: Electronic Ignition

The points-and-condenser system was used for a long time, due to its simplicity and general reliability. But being mechanical, it has some inherent failings. In addition, motorcycles were needing hotter, longer-duration sparks as compression ratios rose and mixtures became increasingly lean; additionally, dwell times were dropping as redlines increased. Something more was needed. That something was electronic ignition.

Although it comes in many flavors, the most popular has been the CDI, or capacitor discharge ignition system. This system uses a big switching transistor to charge up a big capacitor, which is then discharged into the coil. This builds a very strong, very sudden magnetic field that collapses very quickly after capacitor discharge. The resulting spark is hotter and quicker than anything that can be produced by battery voltage alone. It cuts down dwell times a great deal, which together with the hotter spark provides more reliable ignition at higher rpms.

Early CDI units were still triggered by points, most with a mechanical advance mechanism. These systems still had many of the flaws inherent in the points-and-condenser system. But very quickly, two changes were made to the CDI systems in use on motorcycles, which have remained with us right up to the present day.

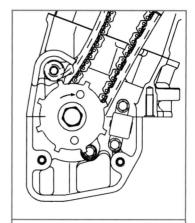

The switch from mechanical points to a trigger wheel and pickup allowed the crank signal to be used for fuel injection as well as ignition. The more fingers there are on the trigger wheel, the more precisely the crank angle can be determined from actual measurement. This illustration shows the pickup and trigger wheel of a Kawasaki ZX-12R. The trigger wheel has fewer teeth than many other fuel-injected motorcycles available today. Kawasaki Motor Corporation USA

The first was moving from mechanical to electronic advance. It was relatively simple and inexpensive to design and build a circuit that would advance the spark based on a measurement of engine rpm. This circuit eliminated mechanical advance, and the reliability and longevity issues associated with mechanical advance mechanisms. Weight was saved, spark timing became more precise, and there was much greater flexibility available in creating spark advance curves.

The second was the switch to an electrical pickup to replace points. While using the points as a mere sensing device (as with points-outfitted CDI systems) significantly prolonged the life of the contact surfaces on the points, there were still the problems with the points floating at high engine speeds, as well as changes in ignition timing from wear on the rubbing block. And of course, moisture was still an issue for reliable spark triggering. All that changed with the advent of a simple magnetic pickup to replace points. By using a trigger wheel to create a voltage in response to engine rotation, a number of benefits were apparent. Magnetic triggers did not require regular adjustment and were impervious to moisture. They did not wear out, and they had a long service life. And with electronic advance, it was possible to remove multiple triggers and use a simple timer to control spark timing for multiple coils. With the use of trigger wheels that had multiple teeth, it was even possible to increase the accuracy and repeatability of spark timing from cycle to cycle.

This simple system, with a magnetic pickup, removed almost all the negatives of a points-based system. Small, light, and reliable, it provided well for the spark needs of almost any motorcycle engine, and continues to do so through to today. Many of the other recent advances in ignition systems have been applied to independent CDI units as well as those integrated into an ECU.

Changing Coils

As noted above, using two coils in a waste-fire system provided a number of advantages over using a single coil and distributor. The biggest advantages were being able to use smaller, lighter coils and having the ability to generate a hotter, more powerful spark at higher rpms. And these advantages generally increase along with the number of coils.

Increasingly, motorcycle engines with three or more cylinders are being seen with individual compact coils for each cylinder. Commonly referred to as stick coils, they appear as large plug caps; the entire coil assembly is housed in a tiny package, one sitting atop each spark plug. While there are the obvious benefits of weight savings and increased dwell time at a given rpm, there are additional benefits as well. The smaller coils, fitting so well within the volume of the cylinder head on four- and five-valve-per-cylinder models, offer a great space savings over traditional coils. By eliminating the high-voltage lead from the coil to the spark plug, the amount of electrical energy that actually reaches the plug is higher. In addition, RF (radio frequency) interference is reduced. This not only helps meet governmental standards, but also helps prevent glitches in the ECU's operation. And last, there is no chance of any spark energy being lost to a cylinder that is not at its ignition point, as is possible with a waste fire system.

The major disadvantage of a coil-on-plug setup is that, if fired individually, there is a requirement for some manner of cam timing sensors to determine which cylinder of a given pair is at the end of its compression stroke, and which is at the ends of its exhaust stroke. This datum can be obtained through a traditional EFI cam position sensor (which is typically the case when stick coils are used with an integrated EFI/ignition ECU), or through simple forms of ion sensing. Stick coils can of course be triggered in a waste-fire fashion as well, but they lose some of their high-rpm capacity due to dwell times being cut in half for each coil.

Integration

So there you have the major developments in ignition technology over the past 35 years or so. We've come a long way, even leaving the ignition system as an independent unit from the EFI's ECU. But as some of you probably noticed, we already have at least one sensor providing data to both the CDI and the ECU—the crank position sensor. With the necessity for increased control of spark timing (first required for the long-term health of the early factory turbocharged motorcycles), attention turned to integrating the ignition control with the EFI ECU. And from there, the sky quickly became the limit, as manufacturers switched from having two separate systems in a single box to using the existing ECU to control spark events as well as fueling.

But why would we want to move to this level of complexity? What is important in system design, and why? To answer these questions, we need to look at what a spark really is, and what happens when we create one—and even examine the life of a spark and the energy used to make it. It sounds a lot more complicated than it is, but it is something we need to examine in detail to discover just why systems have evolved into what we have today—integrated fueling and ignition control, coil-on-plug setups, and the use of our control over fueling and ignition to create reliable power with low emissions.

The Burning Question

Sorry about that, I just couldn't resist the pun. But in all seriousness, what transpires in the combustion chamber is the point of

Modern coil development has given us the stick coil, also known as coil-on-plug. It is ideally suited for use on engines with four valves per cylinder, as it fits neatly in the center of the four valves. The move away from waste fire and toward sequential ignition has allowed these coils to do the same job, in a much smaller package than with traditional motorcycle coils. Shown are two views of a Denso coil taken from the front cylinder of a Ducati Monster S4. Components courtesy of GP Motorcycles

this whole exercise. The correct spark temperature, duration, and timing are essential to avoid engine damage, make power, and even manage emissions. You can see why this is of critical importance to manufacturers, and as you read more of this chapter, it will make more and more sense to have ignition control integrated with fuel injection control.

A Sample Ignition Event

Let's start off with a brief overview of an ignition event, so you have a solid understanding of the principles and timeline. Once that is done, I will explain how making changes in spark timing and quality will affect the combustion event. This is a critical part of the combustion process, largely because it has such a wide range of adjustability.

How Does Fuel Burn?

Once again, we are faced with a question that may seem obvious on its surface, but in reality is anything but. How is combustion initiated? How does it progress? What is the difference between knocking and detonation? How does the mixture change things for combustion?

Initiating Combustion

Well, let's start with the most basic question: How is combustion initiated? The answer is simple. Our vaporized fuel has a temperature at which it will begin burning. We need to keep the mixture from reaching that temperature until we are ready to begin the combustion process, then add enough heat to begin combustion, and it will progress from there.

So how does this heating occur? The first step is compression, in point of fact. Compressing a gas by a given percentage will raise its temperature in proportion. This is the (General) Perfect Gas Law. If you take a certain quantity of a gas and heat it, the pressure will go up, assuming the volume remains constant. If the temperature is kept the same, dropping the pressure requires an increase in volume. And so forth. In our case, we are reducing the volume *and* increasing the pressure. The temperature of the mixture climbs accordingly. What's more, the temperature will climb higher as the compression ratio increases. The idea here is to get the mixture pretty close to the point of combustion, but to keep it a little bit short of that point. We can then light off the mixture by adding a little localized heat in the form of our spark.

The Gradual Burn

Voilà! We have combustion. But there's more to it than that. Assuming that we timed our spark well and have a good mixture, a whole chain reaction occurs until almost all of the mixture is consumed by combustion, delivering its released heat energy to the crankshaft by way of the piston crown. Let's start with the moment of spark and follow from there.

Once the mixture in the immediate area of the plug gap begins to combust, a few things happen. The piston is pretty close to top dead center right now, so we have a few degrees of crank rotation before the volume of the combustion chamber will change substantially. For now we are only dealing with heat and pressure. The combustion of the mixture right near the plug gap creates a great deal of heat. This heat begins to radiate out from the point of ignition, lighting off the remaining mixture as it travels. The expansion of the combustion gases also raises the pressure in the combustion chamber, which raises the temperature of the remaining mixture as well. The boundary between unburned mixture and mixture being combusted is called the *flame front*, and how quickly it moves is of great interest to us, as you will soon see.

Since initially we are adding a fair amount of heat and pressure from the start of the combustion event, and the piston is basically stopped at TDC, the flame front accelerates as it moves away from the plug tip. We don't want it to accelerate too much, because increasing the pressure too much at once can damage the engine in very short order. The great heat from a sudden and complete burn of the mixture will literally melt the piston crown until there is a hole right through it, and the incredible sudden increase in pressure will squeeze the oil film out of the crank and rod bearings, causing rapid bearing failure. So we need to control the rate of flame front travel. How can we do this?

The first thing to remember is that the combustion chamber walls are pretty cool compared with the actual heat of combustion. Some of the heat will transfer to the cooler cylinder walls and be removed by the cooling system. Reducing heat is the same as reducing pressure (if the volume stays the same, which it is for now), so that helps us slow down flame front travel a bit, as well as helping to protect the engine components from damage.

But the real thing that helps keep the flame front from accelerating out of control and causing detonation is the fact that very soon after combustion, the volume of the combustion chamber begins to increase. We are at the start of the power stroke, and the piston is beginning to accelerate downward. This increase in volume both cools the remaining mixture somewhat and lowers the pressure as well. In fact, the pressure is being fed through the piston crown and connecting rod and is used to turn the crankshaft and propel the vehicle. The more mixture is consumed, the more heat is released, and this happens at the cube of the distance the flame front has traveled from the ignition source. In other words, the temperature rises more quickly as the flame front moves farther and farther from the point of origin. If this were to continue for very long, all the remaining mixture would ignite simultaneously, causing severe detonation. But by increasing the volume of the combustion chamber from the downward motion of the piston, pressure is lowered, and temperature along with it. So the flame front is, in reality, slowed to a reasonable rate, and detonation (and severe engine damage) avoided. The trick here is to keep the temperature in the as-yet-unburned mixture *just below* its ignition point, so it will burn readily once the flame front reaches it, but won't spontaneously light off (which would radically raise both pressure and temperature, creating a detonation event). This is a very delicate balance to maintain, and of course changes as mixture, engine speed, and charge density vary; this is one of the primary reasons we require ignition timing control.

It should be pretty clear now why ignition timing is so very important. Too early and you will have too much mixture burned before the piston begins its downward stroke, causing detonation; too late and you lose most of the ability to make power, and in severe cases, you leave notable amounts of unburned mixture leaving the combustion chamber (since combustion chamber volume is now increasing at a rate greater than the increase in temperature/pressure from flame front propagation; in essence, the flame goes out because the mixture on the other side of the flame front is not hot enough to be lit off).

Factors Affecting Mixture Temperature

Since one of the critical factors in achieving reliable combustion is the temperature of the mixture at the point of spark, we have to be aware of how environmental factors can affect this.

Heat and cold are enemies here. A cold engine will take heat from the compressed intake charge more quickly than a hot one. Combined with thick, cold oil and reduced battery capacity at low temperatures, plus a greater drop in battery voltage due to more cranking resistance (which will reduce the amount of electrical energy available to create a spark), this can be enough to keep an engine in marginal condition (which could be anything from a tired battery or starter motor to low compression) from starting at all. Likewise, cold air will be at a lower temperature after compression than warm air will. Combined with cold oil and a cold battery, this can spell real trouble (and it's the main reason that so many cars refuse to start in really cold weather). Note that a hot engine will help warm the intake air somewhat, offsetting much of the negative effect of cold air on reliable combustion; this is the reason almost all cars are equipped with ducting that allows the engine to aspirate air warmed on the outside of a hot exhaust header.

Heat provides the opposite problem: the risk of pre-ignition or detonation, especially under load. Heat the intake air enough, and it will reach the point of combustion from compression alone, without the aid of a spark. Heat it somewhat less and there won't be pre-ignition, but there will be knocking as the remainder of the mixture combusts simultaneously midway through the normal combustion process. The same effect can occur from an overheating engine, except this time the engine provides the heat rather than the air itself. The effects, however, will be the same. This is the reason why some vehicles will knock under load in the desert, but not otherwise.

One Last Factor

There's one more thing that can be important in the ignition process, and I present it here for the sake of completeness when discussing combustion and the conditions in the combustion chamber. That last factor is the possible presence of an ignition source besides generation of a spark.

One way is by having a carbon hot spot in the combustion chamber. Carbon deposits are bad for the engine for a number of reasons, but this is probably the big one. Carbon deposits take up some of the room in the combustion chamber, which increases the engine's compression ratio. Over time, this can really add up and make a pretty noticeable difference in intake mixture temperature when fully compressed. What's more, carbon buildup that occurs on sharp edges in the combustion chamber can end up glowing red-hot like charcoal and serving as a second source of ignition. In cases where there is a secondary ignition source, the pressure in the combustion chamber will increase at twice the normal rate and increase from there, which typically will produce noticeable detonation.

A similar secondary ignition effect can be achieved by using a spark plug of the wrong heat range. I will discuss spark plugs in greater depth later in this chapter; however, I do wish to note here that a spark plug that is in too hot a heat range for the engine load and mixture can reach a temperature where it can become an ignition source without needing a spark to be delivered. This will destroy the plug fairly quickly and will often take some internal engine components along with it to the scrap yard. Always ensure that you are running spark plugs of the correct heat range.

What Else Is There?

So, we have now seen how combustion actually occurs and that it is a cascading process, not an event that happens instantaneously. But how do the compression ratio, the cylinder filling, or the richness of the mixture affect the initiation of the burn? These are all important factors that will be covered here, and they will arise again when we discuss the spark-generating hardware and what we will ask of it.

The Name of the Game Is Resistance

Ultimately, the big deal in delivering spark is resistance. Whether it is resistance in the primary or secondary circuits (which is called internal resistance, composed of everything outside the combustion chamber), or in what is between the spark plug's electrodes (including the shape and composition of the electrodes, and the conditions inside the combustion chamber; this is called external resistance), raising the resistance has basically the same effect— less electrical energy is delivered on initiation of the spark, but more is left for spark maintenance. Some electrical energy will be lost in the form of heat, and if that heat is created outside of the combustion chamber, it is wasted energy.

Resistance Factors, and How They Come Into Play

Let's take a further look at how resistance can affect each part of the electrical and physical circuit first, and then go on to how that works together with burn rate to give us an overall picture of spark control and what the compromises are when making system design choices. There's that word *compromise* again.

Primary Circuit Resistance

Primary circuit resistance is a measure of the resistance between the voltage source and the ground on the primary circuit. This will include the ignition switch and/or ignition relay, the primary winding of the coil, and whatever the triggering device is (points in

older motorcycles; CDI or transistor switching in newer systems, including EFI bikes). On the one hand, keeping the resistance as low as possible will allow for much quicker saturation of the coil; this will raise the maximum rpm for reliable spark, which is a good thing. However, the enemy here is coil overheating; lower primary resistance means more electrical flow (current) moving through the coil's primary winding, which will cause it to heat faster.

Many motorcycle coils over the last 25 years are filled with oil to dissipate heat and thus allow lower primary resistance. In addition, having four individual coils on a four-cylinder motorcycle (like those found on late-model EFI sportbikes) means that each coil only fires half as often as the old-style waste-fire dual coils found on most carbureted inline four-cylinder bikes. By allowing more cooling time between power application events to the primary winding, these coils provide an advantage in this area.

Secondary Circuit Resistance

Of even greater importance is resistance in the secondary circuit. The secondary circuit will consist of the coil secondary winding, plug wire, plug cap, and spark plug (which includes the plug gap, electrode design, and electrode composition). Typically, manufacturers are trying to balance low secondary resistance with low radio-frequency interference (the sudden discharge of high voltage for spark generation tends to make nasty radio waves that can interfere with radio communications, as well as digital electronics —like the ECU itself).

Another key point in considering secondary resistance is the composition and density of the combustion chamber contents. Since this electrical energy is being used to build a bridge of charged particles to allow plasma generation, the resistance of that charge becomes important and can be considered (for our purposes) to be measurable like any resistance in an electrical circuit. We'll come back to the resistance of the combustible mixture a little later, when I will discuss the factors that alter that resistance. For right now, I just want you to keep the idea in the back of your head.

Ultimately, there is a trade-off in working with secondary resistance. Lower secondary resistance makes for a lot of the available energy in the coil to be used up with initial spark generation; in other words, a quick, hot spark. Now this may seem like a great thing for us to have in most cases, but the one thing we *don't* get under these conditions is a lot of spark duration; the more of the energy used in the generation of the spark, the less remains for spark maintenance (which is keeping the spark going once it has been created). In rather the same way that we can keep an injector open with less current than it takes to open it suddenly, it takes a lot less energy to maintain the plasma in the spark gap once it is created.

So a greater secondary resistance will result in more energy being devoted to creating the spark, but the resistance will limit the speed at which the energy is dissipated to ground, thus allowing the spark to stick around longer (assuming there was enough electrical energy to start it at all). And naturally, as resistance increases, there comes a point where so much electrical energy is expended in creating the spark that there's very little left to maintain the spark (this is generally perilously close to misfire). Why would all this be important to us, you may wonder? And the answer is simple: Different mixtures, under different conditions, will require different amounts and durations of heating (via the generation of plasma by our spark plug) to reliably ignite and burn well. This is perhaps *the* key point to understanding secondary resistance (and answering questions like, "Do I want to use a resistor or a non-resistor spark plug?") and how ignition characteristics might need to be changed in response to the changing parameters of combustion chamber environmental factors (such as, "What do I need to do if I raise the compression in my engine by changing deck height or even valve timing?" or "What changes do I need to make if I lean out my mixture to meet emissions regulations?").

Critical Point Voltage

Perhaps the most important question when figuring such things will be, "How much electrical energy do I need to have on tap to create a spark in the first place?" Obviously, if you can't make the spark bridge the spark gap, the rest of your plans are meaningless.

This is why so much effort is focused on building the magnetic field of the coil to saturation as rapidly as possible (to allow for higher engine speeds), and in designing the coil to produce a strong magnetic field at saturation (so that there is the right amount of energy available to create and maintain the spark).

As we have discussed, the voltage applied to the plug gap to create a spark at all will vary based on the composition and density of the contents of the combustion chamber. At the very least, our available voltage must meet that minimum requirement throughout the operating range of the engine (and this does change, based on changes in mixture [including the percentage of exhaust gas in the mixture, and the percentage of fuel vapor] and changes in cylinder filling caused by intake, exhaust, and cam timing adjustments) or it fails in its initial requirement, to generate a spark at any engine operating condition. And the general rule here is that critical point voltage will increase as pressure increases (from higher-compression engines, for instance) and/or as the mixture becomes leaner. And this is probably the key point for modern, fuel-injected engines: they run leaner (sometimes much leaner in certain areas), and so the minimum requirements for voltage generation by the ignition system have gone up compared with days past.

How Much Is Enough, How Much Is Too Much?

But here is where the balance between spark generation and spark maintenance comes into play; if there is a great deal of voltage available initially, and a lot of it is used up in spark creation, then not much is left for spark maintenance. Now, why would this be a problem for us?

The answer is simple: Leaner mixtures require higher temperatures to create and maintain ignition. What does this mean in practical terms? It means that flame front propagation will be slower during the initiation of the burn, all other factors being equal. And it is during that critical initial ignition point that we need to keep the pilot light burning until there is sufficient pressure (and accordingly, temperature) generated in the combustion chamber to make the combustion event self-sustaining, without accelerating out of control.

Higher engine loads have a similar effect. More load means more power output, and the richer mixture is balanced in terms of flame front speed by the higher density of the mixture. A richer (power) mixture tends to burn more rapidly, but a denser mixture tends to burn more slowly and requires a higher critical voltage in the balance. So at higher engine loads, spark duration *shortens,* due to the increased energy needed to create the spark. This leads to an increased chance of misfire and requires more precision in spark control to walk the fine line between misfire and detonation.

The special conditions of lean running or high load mean two things for engine management: First, we need to have enough electrical energy remaining to keep the spark alive for a longer time (to ensure that the chain reaction has been firmly established and is self-supporting). And second, we have a much finer margin between ensuring the chain reaction ending in a successful combustion event and causing a runaway chain reaction that will result in detonation.

So as we run leaner (or under heavier load, or even both), we have to balance a lot of factors. First and foremost, we need to balance our desire for maximum available electrical energy at spark initiation with our need to maintain the spark for a longer period of time. Therefore, the energy available in the saturated magnetic field, as well as the factors creating secondary circuit resistance (including the internal resistance factors of the gases in the combustion chamber), must be carefully controlled by designers to achieve the best compromise between spark duration and available voltage. Too much available voltage and the spark will peter out before a chain reaction is established, causing misfire; not enough available voltage and the initial spark event won't occur at all in the high-resistance environment of a lean mixture.

Because of these restrictions, it is vital to maintain as closely as possible the designed-in resistance in the secondary circuit during actual engine operation. Design improvements (such as coil-on-plug designs, which eliminate the plug wire and up to two variable resistance connections for the wire) help maintain the desired, engineered-in resistance, but perhaps more important is the frequent maintenance of these components (ensuring a clean connection and ground for the spark plug, as well as maintaining the correct gap), and not substituting parts (such as different coils, or non-resistor spark plugs in the place of resistor plugs). Failure to maintain the designed-in secondary circuit resistance will not only alter exhaust emissions (typically for the worse), but can also result in potential misfire, detonation, and even long-term engine damage.

Emissions

Earlier in the book, we saw how changes in combustion temperature altered the composition of the exhaust gases. Reading the previous sections on ignition control, you may have surmised that changing ignition timing will directly affect combustion temperatures. While to some extent we are limited by misfire and detonation in choosing the average temperature of combustion (based on changes in combustion chamber pressure due to flame front travel), we still have a fairly narrow window of timing during which we can make power without damaging the engine. And interestingly enough, making slight changes within that window can make for fairly major changes in the composition of the exhaust gases, even given an identical, homogeneous mixture!

So precise control of spark timing gives us much more control over final emissions in the exhaust than we would have from controlling fueling alone. What's more, we need to be able to alter ignition timing along with fueling to fully control exhaust emissions, within the range of available control. So as emissions standards have tightened, the need for more and more precise control of spark, as well as the linking of spark to engine load (which is the primary determinant for fueling), have taken a front seat in our system design.

Misfire, Our Enemy

We've already talked a bit in previous chapters about how misfire increases emissions of hydrocarbons and can damage catalytic converters. And we've talked a bit in this chapter about how mixture and ignition timing affect the potential of misfire and what designers need to do about it. But there's one more component we haven't covered yet—closed-throttle conditions, especially at low engine speed.

At higher engine speeds, we generally have better cylinder filling, and we have less time for compression heat to leak out through the walls of the combustion chamber. These things help

Misfire hurts fuel economy, creates backfiring, and increases emissions. But perhaps the worst result from ongoing misfire is damage to the catalytic converter. Shown here is a cutaway of a ZX-6R catalytic converter. Misfire can cause unburned fuel and air to cook off in the catalyst, radically raising its temperature. This can melt the converter in areas, leading to exhaust restriction and a vast reduction in normal catalyst activity. Nolan TA—Sydney, Australia

prevent misfire by helping ensure the burn reaches the point of chain reaction more reliably. But at idle, the throttle is closed, leaving us with a very hard-to-ignite mixture that has a greater composition of exhaust gases, and which is not as dense. It is entirely possible that even with full spark energy available, the mixture may not be able to support combustion at all. This has become more and more of an issue as leaner idle mixtures have been called for and the consequences of misfire (increased emissions and catalytic converter damage) have become more pronounced.

High-load conditions at low engine speeds focus the problem even more; timing must be retarded to prevent detonation due to the faster flame front travel of the richer mixture with fewer exhaust gas components, but the margin between misfire and detonation becomes almost razor-thin.

So even under conditions we wouldn't usually consider critical in an analysis of best power output, we have a fairly large need to precisely control ignition energy and timing. In fact, the requirement for spark duration goes up at lower engine loads and/or speeds, which is why emissions-sensitive street bikes have driven the advancement of ignition controls in motorcycles, rather than race applications; if you are typically running at or near maximum load, and are not concerned with emissions, older components for spark generation and management are quite adequate.

Connecting the Dots

So we now have a tightly knit web of controls and responses, where things must work in tandem, and with great precision, to maintain reliable ignition over a range of operating conditions, and with leaner and leaner mixtures as time marches onward. How are these ideas applied to varying engine conditions in the real world?

THEORY AND PRACTICE

With the integration of ignition control into an EFI ECU, we now have at our disposal all the sensors (and in many cases, the intermediate calculations from their data as well) at our disposal for calculating spark timing and coil changing duration (dwell). How

do we go about turning that data into something useful? A lot depends on your goals, of course, but since we already established that it's possible to make very close to best power while still having a large impact on emissions, it only makes sense to take advantage of what we have to use. We are long past the time when doing so would increase the cost of an ECU by a substantial amount. So we see these sorts of strategies in pretty much all OEM ECUs today. But what are they? What should we be thinking about, and why?

Problem Areas

A separate ignition control box with TPS was a great step forward for both part-throttle power and emissions (especially at cruise). But meeting emissions regulations has provided some special challenges for those designing engine management components for motorcycles. To achieve the mandated goals, designers have had to clean up many areas of operation that had been left out with previous emissions controls. Perhaps the most important part of this change was the requirement to run leaner, especially at smaller throttle openings. This created some problems with knock that could only be handled by changing the approach to ignition control.

The Increasing Importance of Knock Control

We covered knock (or detonation) in the chapter on how the engine works, and I don't think I need to reiterate how horrible knock is for an engine. It damages structural components of the engine, the catalytic converter (if so equipped), skyrockets NOx emissions, and can reduce an engine to a pile of scrap in a very short period of time, if allowed to continue unchecked. Leaner mixtures have more of a tendency toward knock, so we are faced with two options when dealing with lean mixtures (as we increasingly must due to regulatory pressures): Either stick with a 2D ignition map and simply retard timing across the board so that we avoid knock throughout the range of engine speeds and alpha, or gather more data to use in determining correct spark timing combining spark control with EFI has allowed designers to pursue the latter approach.

Special Cases

Just like with fueling, there are a number of special cases with ignition. By and large, they are even the same special conditions that we must accommodate! Coolant temperature and ambient air density are probably the most important ones, because both affect charge density, and coolant temperature has a vast effect on both mixture homogeneity and combustion temperature (since a cold engine will take more heat away from the combustion event as it is occurring, slowing the increase in combustion chamber pressure and slowing the burn). Let's examine some of the special cases and see how they are accommodated by the design and programming of our ignition controller.

Cold Idling

You may recall the problems faced by a motorcycle engine when running cold and how they affected fueling. Most of those problems are caused by fuel vaporization issues and how they tend to leave us with a mixture that is largely leaner than normal. Some areas of the mixture are far richer than normal, though. So we face both detonation and slowed combustion speed under these conditions. On the face of it, these would appear to require opposite strategies for ignition timing.

During cold idling, it is typical to advance ignition timing. Increasing pressure and heat from a combustion event will tend to help in vaporizing larger droplets of fuel that might still be liquid prior to ignition. Further, advancing the ignition will tend to generate more useful power by keeping the PPP nearer an optimal setting. Obviously we don't want to make too much power; if we did, idle speed would climb to dangerous levels very quickly. But we want enough power to be generated to keep the idle speed sufficiently high to keep intake velocity fairly high; this produces a net improvement in fuel vaporization and, accordingly, smoother running and off-idle pickup. Cold idling is therefore a very special case and is usually intercepted and dealt with separately from any other mappings for ignition. By checking for certain ranges of engine speed, throttle position, and coolant temperature, the ECU can determine whether it is dealing with a cold idle condition, and can advance timing to accommodate these needs.

Cold Running

At engine speeds above idle, there is generally some improvement in fuel vaporization due to increased intake velocity. Since the engine is likely under load when above idle (this can be confirmed with road speed sensors), it is producing more power and therefore generating more heat. This is desirable under cold running conditions. We want the engine to warm up as quickly as is practically possible, since fuel vaporization will improve, and more heat energy will go to producing horsepower (instead of being pulled out of the combustion chamber by cold metal engine components). So we want to advance ignition timing as much as possible to facilitate getting all the heat energy we can from the mixture before the exhaust valve opens. However, we are faced with the very problems we are trying to combat: cold combustion chamber walls (which rob a great deal of heat from the combustion process, lowering combustion chamber pressures and slowing the combustion process) and cold engine components (which do the same thing to a lesser degree) invite advancing the ignition timing, but poor fuel vaporization tends to lean the mixture, and thus invites retarding the ignition timing.

Ultimately, a delicate balance is established that varies based on engine design. Several factors tend to make the mixture burn more slowly, dictating an increase in ignition advance. However, the colder the engine, the more likely it is that we will find a somewhat lean homogeneous mixture, which can lead to detonation with excessive spark advance. In the absence of an actual knock sensor, the ignition advance for cold running will be more than for an otherwise identical engine that is fully warmed up, but should be slightly conservative to help avoid detonation.

Often, non-idle cold running conditions can be accounted for by the use of a 1D scaling map; in other words, the base spark advance (read off a 2D table, with engine speed on one axis, and either alpha or MAP [to indicate engine load] on the other) may be multiplied by a certain number based on coolant temperature. The number will start fairly high for a cold engine and will steadily decrease as the engine moves closer to operating temperature. After a certain temperature, the ignition timing will not be affected by increases in coolant temperature at all (except in cases of overheating, as will be covered later in this chapter). In some cases, where the *shape* of the best timing curve might change based on coolant temperature, a 3D table will be used, with one axis each covering engine speed, throttle position, and coolant temperature.

A similar but lesser ignition timing problem can also occur with cold intake air. Since the intake charge is cold, there will be less heat in the intake charge to vaporize the heavier fractions of the fuel. Especially when the engine itself is also cold, we can see the same sorts of problems as with low coolant temperatures, albeit to a lesser degree. Some motorcycles have an additional 1D scaling map for intake air temperature that works on ignition timing identically to one used for coolant temperature.

Overheating

On the other end of the scale, the engine can become too hot. This will also cause detonation, which will very quickly do catastrophic damage to the engine. Therefore, it is very important that we have a way of preventing the detonation that comes with overheating.

One way to do this is to significantly retard the ignition timing once a critical coolant temperature is reached. This is done through the same 1D coolant temperature scaling map as mentioned above. By retarding the timing incrementally as the temperature rises, several benefits are gained. First, detonation is minimized by lowering the peak pressure through a delayed ignition event. As a side effect of this, the second benefit occurs—reduced power output, meaning less heat to be handled by the combustion chamber walls and cooling system. This gives the engine a chance to recover if there is still sufficient cooling ability remaining, and helps prevent cylinder head warping, ring land erosion, or compression ring damage from overheating. And last, the lower power and rougher running encourage the operator of the vehicle to pull over and shut off the engine, probably the best thing he or she could do to help prevent permanent engine damage.

A lesser problem can occur with particularly hot intake air. Since the intake charge is hotter to begin with, combustion chamber surfaces will not have as much chance to shed heat, and an engine can see the same sort of problems as with high coolant temperatures, albeit to a lesser degree. Some motorcycles have an additional 1D ignition scaling map for intake air temperature that works identically to that for coolant temperature.

Starting

As with fueling, we have two major problems when it comes to starting. Low intake velocity and low MAP tend to mean poor volumetric efficiency and poor fuel atomization. Despite the increase in fuel vaporization from low MAP, this means we may not have a very good homogeneous mixture to get things going. In addition, using a large electric motor to spin our engine initially means a significant drop in battery voltage.

Starting generally requires retarding the ignition timing, to ensure that the spark does not occur so soon that it works against the starter motor. However, we need to be very careful how far we retard the timing so as to create enough pressure in the combustion chamber to accelerate the engine and transition from starter motor to being self-powered (in other words, idling).

The other problem with starting is that, much like fuel injectors, ignition coils require a certain amount of electrical energy to be pumped into them in order to build a strong magnetic field inside the coil. When the primary current is cut, the magnetic field collapses, and all the energy stored in the magnetic field discharges through the secondary winding of the coil, into the spark plug, and through the gap between electrodes to create an actual spark. When the voltage feeding the primary side of the coil is reduced (as during starting), the amount of time that voltage must be applied to the coil to create the necessary magnetic field must be increased. The time during which the coil primary is receiving power is called *dwell*, and is typically described in degrees of crank rotation. At higher engine speeds, for instance, dwell must be increased to maintain the same amount of actual time for coil charging. And during starting, dwell must also be increased to insure sufficient time for coil saturation, or the bike may *never* start!.

Idling

Idling is another special case. The engine is under no load except from its own friction. It needs to make only a very small amount of power to maintain a stable idle speed. Any more, and the engine would increase its speed until it blew up. Traditionally, idle speed was kept low with carbs via the use of closed throttles and fairly rich mixtures. The result was a very low charge density, and a slow-burning rich mixture. Combined with the pumping losses (energy lost to trying to pull an entire cylinder's worth of intake charge past a closed throttle plate), these factors kept idle speeds low, with a fairly smooth idle.

As you can imagine, this was pretty unsatisfactory from the standpoint of emissions. A typical carbureted bike's idle mixture will be rich in both unburned HC and CO. To reduce idle emissions, leaner mixtures were needed. But those leaner mixtures did not produce as smooth an idle, so manipulation of spark timing was necessary to regain a smooth idle with the new, leaner mixtures.

In some cases, manufacturers have gone so far as to run closed-loop on idle (like cars have often done from the introduction of closed-loop EFI). This actually makes a certain amount of sense, since particularly on big, narrow-angle V-twin motors, crank speed can vary noticeably between the firing of one cylinder and the next. Running closed-loop can help tame emissions from such engines, but idle speed must then be controlled through IAC solenoids (which control pumping losses and can manipulate power output from each power stroke) and ignition timing. Ignition timing gives a quicker response than an IAC solenoid can, but nothing can make up for a lack of intake charge (which is a significant problem on slow-idling large-displacement-per-cylinder engines, like many V-twins). Timing adjustments can be used in tandem with an IAC solenoid, of course.

In fact, one handy trick many manufacturers use often is to have a cell (or column) in the spark table for an engine speed that is below normal idling speed. This cell has several degrees of ignition advance over the cell (or column) for idle speed. By doing this, the designers try to ensure that should idle speed drop below the correct rpm, an increase in ignition timing will speed the motor back up, keeping it from stalling. This is actually a pretty ingenious strategy, and it works quite well!

Emissions and Spark Control

Well, we've gotten the special cases out of the way. So what about spark timing under normal conditions? The engine is warmed up, we are riding the motorcycle so the engine is under load, and all is well. How does ignition timing really affect us? Why is it increasingly important?

The answer (as you might have surmised) lies mainly in the realm of emissions. Changing the spark timing slightly in either direction from best power timing has very little effect on power output, since the amount of mechanical advantage we get from the burn remains very close to optimal over several degrees of spark timing. But based on the changes in mechanical compression during the burn (due to rotation of the crank), we can have a fairly notable impact on peak pressure (which will also mean temperature and rate of burn). And it's the changes in combustion temperature and burn rate that are the big players in emissions, given a set VE and mixture.

Remember the graphs we looked at for mixture versus exhaust gas emissions, back in the chapter on how the engine works? A good amount of that is determined just by the availability of different atoms in the mixture itself; if you don't have enough oxygen, for instance, you'll get more CO, and less CO_2. But the key here is NO_x, nitrogen oxides. The amount of NO_x found in the exhaust gas is directly related to the combustion temperature.

If we advance the spark (initiate it sooner) by a degree or so, the pressure in the combustion chamber will be higher, and rise more quickly, than a later spark. The burn will be further along at TDC, and thus the pressure will be higher in the combustion chamber. Higher pressure equals higher heat, and thus more nitrogen oxides in the exhaust. Since some of the available oxygen is now going to making NO_x, we also have less available for complete combustion of the fuel, leading to slightly higher CO and HC emissions, and less CO_2. On the other hand, we may have a slightly more complete burn from this advance, and we may make slightly more power as well. The more complete burn will further alter exhaust gases, leading to lower residual O_2 and HC levels.

Now, if we have a three-way catalytic converter in the mix, we can cut down on HC, NO_x, and CO emissions by using the residual O_2, and the oxygen trapped in NO_x, to form CO_2 and N_2. But a catalytic converter will only work once it has heated up internally, and then only within a fairly narrow range of AFR. So this may be a partial solution, and in some cases, it is good enough to get a bike to pass the emissions testing required by the government. But we can manipulate the balance of exhaust gases under pretty much the entire range of engine operating conditions through finessing the spark timing.

You can see why manufacturers are so keen on having tight control over spark timing. In fact, the same reasoning that is moving the industry to EFI is also moving it toward tighter and tighter spark control. And since many of the same factors that determine best fueling are also used to determine best spark timing (for a given set of goals!), it makes perfect sense to integrate everything into one package, using the same sensor data in tandem. Engineers are having to think more about the combustion process as an integrated whole (VE, charge density, mixture composition and homogeneity, and ignition timing all contributing to burn rate and combustion temperature), and that thinking is what allows us to have excellent power and low emissions in one package.

Other Neat Tricks

There are a number of other things we can do with spark control to make motorcycles more controllable and last longer. Since we've already integrated spark control with the powerful hardware inside the ECU, it becomes fairly trivial to manage these additional bits without adding cost to the package. Many of these goodies are advantageous on a number of fronts, to racers and street riders alike.

Top Speed Control and Rev Limiting

One of the worst things you can do to most high-performance motors is to rev them well past redline, or the maximum recommended engine speed. As compression ratios rise and cam timing becomes more radical, there is an increasing chance of having a valve hit a piston, with catastrophic results. For years, drag racers have used rev limiters to help prevent engine damage from accidental overrevs. And while rev limiting has been possible for many years with analog ignition controllers, it's entered a new realm with the addition of road speed and gear position sensors.

Aftermarket applications often show the largest number of available ignition features. This CDI-8 box from MoTeC Systems USA is actually a multiplexer; it can be configured to drive as many different spark events as you might need, using up to eight individual coils. It can also work as a standalone unit with full ignition control and mapping. It has built-in diagnostics for itself and all the coils and igniters and has more features than you are likely to find on any OEM ECU. MoTeC Systems USA

At its most basic, a rev limiter operates in one of two ways, a soft limiter or a hard limiter. A hard limiter operates by simply removing fueling or ignition events entirely once a certain engine speed has been reached. This will result in a very sudden drop in power right near the peak of engine power. So you can see why it might not be such a good idea for use on a motorcycle. Visions of violent highsides come to mind. Still, some forms of hard limiting still see some use. For instance, some limiters will cut spark or fuel in individual cylinders progressively, one at a time, to drop engine power output and keep engine speed from becoming critical. This practice results in the traditional intermittent engine sound that many of us are quite familiar with during wheelies and burnouts. And it reduces power gradually enough to keep the chassis from becoming upset at high speeds. Typically this function is performed by cutting the injector(s) to one or more cylinders in addition to cutting spark, especially when there is a catalytic converter involved (which could be damaged by having entire combustion cycles' worth of unburned fuel and air dumped into them).

When there is sufficient sophistication of the ignition control, a soft limiter is a preferable option, though. A soft rev limiter works by gently but swiftly reducing the power by retarding the timing as the engine passes redline, thus holding engine speed at or near critical without suddenly changing power output. Especially on very powerful bikes with higher compression, it gives a much more gentle roll-off of power output, which helps to maintain riding stability. Although retarding the timing will make the engine run hotter, it's unlikely that the engine will be run in that condition for very long.

The concept can be taken a step further as well. Particularly with ram air, combustion and power output characteristics can change along with changing VE and engine load as road speed changes. Motorcycles with either a gear position switch or a road speed sensor can alter spark timing as well as fueling to prevent overpowering on launches (so you won't wheelie over backwards in first gear), to limit top speed in higher gears (for safety/liability as well as governmental control), and also to help optimize power output in each gear for maximum durability of the drivetrain. While being able to launch your bike with the front wheel 5 feet in the air may be cool, it is decidedly hard on many drivetrain components. Limiting power in lower gears can help prevent costly repairs over the life of the motorcycle.

Knock Control and Flexible Fuel Quality

As compression ratios increase, so must fuel octane increase along with it to prevent detonation. You will recall that higher-octane pump gas requires a hotter ignition temperature to begin to burn, and since raising the compression ratio increases the temperature of mixture, higher octane is required to prevent compression ignition. But in some parts of the world, high-grade fuels are not available. Further, even different brands of the same grade of gasoline can have different detonation limits. So it would be nice for our motorcycles to have some flexibility when it comes to what we put in the tank. With increasing concerns about emissions and leaner mixtures, spark timing must be much more tightly controlled. It is no longer desirable to simply use fairly conservative ignition timing to cover most worst-case scenarios.

One of the best answers here is knock detection, something we are seeing increasingly on motorcycles. Starting with an optimal spark map, knock sensors can detect detonation (and in some cases, misfire) and adjust ignition timing so that detonation does not occur. By being able to balance spark timing between optimal and necessary to prevent detonation, knock-sensor-equipped ECUs allow flexibility in fuel quality without engine damage. Granted, retarding timing to prevent detonation will result in lower power output and a change in emissions, but in a number of cases, this is preferable to limiting the usable fuel types. BMW is notable for using this strategy on motorcycles that are likely to be used in areas where there is question about the reliability of available fuel quality, most notably, their GS models.

Further, with a knock sensor, it becomes possible to adjust ignition timing individually for each cylinder. This allows the ECUs which are so equipped to adjust spark timing to account for variations in charge density and mechanical compression between cylinders, which means you can get the most out of your engine while minimizing emissions even further compared with a timing control method that is consistent between cylinders. Just as no two bikes off the assembly line will make identical power, no two cylinders will see the exact same mixture, homogeneity, and charge density in a given combustion cycle. So controlling ignition timing on a per-cylinder basis allows us to compensate for variations between cylinders.

While I am unaware of any motorcycle manufacturer currently using such a strategy, it is already in widespread use in the automotive world. Thus we are likely to see it appear in the future, as the costs of knock sensors and more complex ECUs continues to drop.

Wrapping It Up

So there you have it. Spark timing was a lot more complex than you thought it was, wasn't it? But since there are benefits to controlling timing based on many of the same principles that are used for fueling, it shouldn't have been too difficult to understand. And as we saw with fueling control, a variety of different factors are at play, and system designers have a set of goals mapped out while developing the components and tuning of the ignition section of the drivetrain. As always, things end up being a compromise between power, reliability, liability, and government control. And it is important to spend some time thinking about what the design goals were when a system was being designed, if we seek to understand how and why it operates the way it does.

WHY EFI, INDEED?

Hopefully, I have impressed upon you the fact that fuel injection is not a single thing with given capabilities and goals and all systems working the same way to deliver the same results. Nothing could be further from the truth. Like with any mass-produced system, there are capabilities that can be designed into a system. Just because something can be done doesn't mean it will be done in any given example, though. The early fuel injection systems found on motorcycles were primitive, even by the standards of today's carburetors. Carbs today can easily outperform most any of the fuel injection systems used on motorcycles through the late 1980s.

So keeping this in mind, what are the relative benefits and drawbacks of past, current, and future fuel injection systems, when compared with the alternatives? Certainly, the one thing we have seen so far in our explorations of EFI is that getting more out of a fuel injection system generally takes more investment in cubic dollars. But there's a lot more to it than that. Let's quantify some of the ways in which fuel injection can be better (and in some cases, worse) than carburetors and look at the prices we may have to pay to achieve superior results.

Different Parts

Obviously, carburetors and EFI use radically different parts to perform essentially the same function. In some ways, changing these parts can give some advantages to the design and construction of a motorcycle. And in some ways, these changes can decrease reliability and increase cost. Let's explore some of the main differences between carbs and EFI, and how they might be evaluated.

Throttle Bodies

One of the biggest differences in terms of construction is the use of throttle bodies instead of carburetor assemblies. Because EFI does not depend on intake velocity to provide fuel metering (as opposed to carburetors), it is possible to use a larger diameter bore than with carburetors, allowing for more top-end power in many instances. Carburetors often require smaller throat diameters to ensure that there is enough intake air velocity at idle to deliver fuel for good idle and off-idle performance. As an example, the maximum practical size for a carburetor throat (not the venturi, but the widest part of the throat) is around 38–40 mm. Some experimental CV carbs have been made in larger sizes, but they can't cover all the bases as well as the smaller carbs, and with increasing emissions regulations, 40 mm is pretty much the absolute cap for a production motorcycle. But several 1,000-cc V-twin sporting motorcycles come stock with 50-mm throttle bodies, and some racing Ducatis have been seen with throttle bodies as large as 60 mm. Fuel injection allows the designers to use throttle bodies that provide enough air to generate the power they want to make in each cylinder, rather than having to work within the limits of the fuel delivery mechanism (in the case of carburetors, that would be air velocity, and thus the differential in pressure between AAP and MAP). And with idle mixture metering separated to a fair degree from variations in manifold pressure and intake velocity, it's possible to meter idle mixture much more precisely, and to afford much lower emissions in the bargain.

What's more, carburetors require an additional narrowing of the bore where the main jet feeds in fuel—a venturi. By removing the need for this (with throttle bodies), we have again increased our maximum airflow, this time without causing a drop in intake velocity in other parts of the intake tract. This helps keep port velocity high, which aids in keeping the sprayed fuel in suspension, rather than wetting down the port walls (which, as we have discussed, will raise emissions, and lower power and fuel economy, in addition to making for poor running, particularly while the engine is cold). Further, it helps induce some turbulence, or swirl, in the intake charge once it passes the intake valve. This can be a big factor in improving both power and emissions.

Another advantage with many throttle bodies is their compactness. CV carburetors (as used in most modern carbureted motorcycles) require both a float bowl and an area above the carb bore into which the slide may retract during operation. Although they have been made very compact in recent years, the space taken up by these ancillaries has a huge effect on the design of the intake tract and airbox, especially in sporting motorcycles. By eliminating them through the use of throttle bodies, designers can further steepen the angle of the intake ports, improving breathing and reducing intake wall wetting from unevaporated fuel. Since side-draft intake ports have intake charge moving perpendicular to

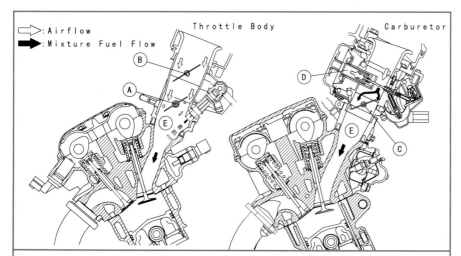

Port fuel injection allows a larger throttle bore and a shorter, steeper intake tract. Combined with a simpler and more compact package, EFI throttle bodies offer some clear advantages over carburetors. Kawasaki Motor Corporation USA

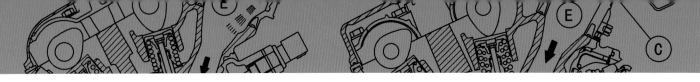

the action of gravity, the heavier droplets of fuel are more likely to fall out of suspension. Steepening the angle of the intake port allows the intake charge to work *with* gravity. Gravity not only assists in pulling the intake charge into the cylinder, but also keeps fuel droplets in the mixture, so they make it to the hot surface of the intake valve head and into the combustion chamber where they belong. The smaller size of the throttle bodies also allows more room for increased airbox volume (remember that the airbox acts as a plenum, or holding tank for air, and that bigger is almost always better). The larger the volume, the more power will be available on demand from the engine. Having less hardware in, on, and around the throttle bodies (as compared with carburetors) also shows a weight savings when compared with carbs. And even better, by steepening the angle of the intake ports, the weight of the throttle bodies is moved incrementally toward the front wheel (especially on inline-twin and -four engines), which helps improve handling.

Elimination of the float bowl (as well as pressure-feeding the fuel at a constant relative pressure) means that the motorcycle will be able to reliably inject fuel at any angle or attitude. Fuel starvation from hard cornering, acceleration, or braking becomes a thing of the past. However, this means that a motorcycle equipped with modern EFI will be perfectly happy to run indefinitely while lying on its side with the engine unable to lubricate itself. Until it seizes its motor, that is. For this reason, all current fuel-injected motorcycles (and most older ones as well) contain a tip-over switch, which senses when the bike has fallen over and shuts off the injection system. This switch, however, can be a failure point as well (especially the older mechanical switches), and under certain conditions, they have been known to accidentally shut off the injection system under hard acceleration (as was discovered by a number of racers in the late 1990s).

The downside of EFI throttle bodies is actually the amazing responsiveness that can be achieved with quick throttle action. Like flat-slide carburetors, it is possible to open the throttle plates too quickly, resulting in a stumble during acceleration. CV carbs use the slide as a self-limiting throttle plate; as the engine can handle increased airflow, the slide raises based on changes in fuel-injected intake air pressure. Some machines just do their best to accommodate rapid changes through fancy acceleration (delta alpha) mapping. But many have some manner of device to perform this function for the injection system; these tend to be the bikes with better off-idle and throttle transition performance, not coincidentally.

Suzuki (and now Kawasaki as well on certain models) uses an ingenious solution on all of its injected sport models. They include a second set of throttle butterflies controlled by a stepper motor. The ECU operates the secondary throttle plates to essentially duplicate the function of a vacuum-operated slide. This retains the compact profile of the throttle bodies, but adds to their length, as well as adding more mechanical and electromechanical components that can suffer failures of various kinds. They also add to the complexity of programming and building the ECU, since it must have complex throttle servo maps to accommodate a variety of operating conditions, as well as an output driver that can run the stepper motor, and additional monitoring hardware (and possibly software) to ensure the stepper motor is positioned properly.

Yamaha goes one step further (or back, depending on how you look at it), and actually has regular vacuum-operated slides installed on some of its sportbike throttle bodies! This obviously negates a major benefit of using throttle bodies, which is to allow a straighter, steeper intake port, but in exchange it greatly simplifies the EFI hardware over, say, the dual-butterfly setup.

Each cylinder has a plastic slide and a rubber diaphragm, just like those found on a CV carburetor. These components are generally reliable and durable and need next to no maintenance to assure precise operation for a long time. No additional computer hardware or software is required; they merely obey the laws of physics.

There are still limitations on the size of the throttle body. If the most restrictive point in the intake tract is not the throat of the throttle body (where the throttle plate is located), then there may be a range of throttle positions at or near wide-open where increasing the throttle angle will *not* result in an increase in airflow to the engine. And of course, there are space and layout limitations, as with any other component on a motorcycle.

Intake Manifolds and Ports

We've already made some discussion above of some improvements that can be made in intake porting and manifolds with the use of throttle bodies. But these same techniques can be used with carburetors, just not to the same degree. Indeed, there are some areas where the design of the area between throttle plate and intake valve can be improved with EFI in ways that they cannot be when using carbs.

Very quickly, I'd like to touch on injector placement. Injectors have a few things on fuel jets in carburetors. First, they typically have a pattern of very tiny holes out of which the fuel is forced under pressure; quite a bit more pressure than is forcing fuel through carb jets. The fuel is in much finer and more evenly sized droplets in spray from a port injector, and the injectors fire directly at the back of the intake valve in most cases, as opposed to the jets in carburetors. Carb jets usually deliver fuel into the intake air stream at the point of highest airspeed, and perpendicular to the flow of air, both of which work against delivering the bulk of the fuel to the combustion chamber as vapor. Instead, fuel from a carburetor jet comes out in fairly unevenly-sized droplets, and at least part of the fuel ends up smeared along the walls of the intake tract, where it evaporates at an uncontrolled rate, which tends to alter the mixture unpredictably. So the commonly used strategy of placing the injectors in the intake manifold as near the intake valve as possible, and the very operation and design of the injectors themselves, makes them superior in most ways to carb jets. The only place where carb jets have a real edge is in their utter simplicity (of design, maintenance, and adjustment/replacement).

The primary differences in design philosophy for intake tracts between carbureted and fuel-injected designs have a great deal to do with the improvements that fuel injectors can offer over carb jets. While intake manifolds with gentle curves and pebbled walls promote the best airflow into the cylinder (and therefore can make the most power), ones with sharper curves and smooth walls help promote turbulence in the intake runner and port itself. Turbulence in the intake runner might seem all bad, until we remember that carbs tend not to deliver fuel to the cylinder as well as we might hope them to. Increasing turbulence in the intake runner will tend to evaporate fuel from the manifold/port walls more quickly. In addition, it will help atomize larger droplets of fuel and speed up vaporization of atomized fuel before entering the combustion chamber. So with carbureted designs, adding some turbulence to the intake tract can improve both power and economy, especially at low engine speeds (when the intake velocity will tend to be at its lowest). Since port fuel injection requires no extra turbulence to help with quick and even vaporization of the fuel charge, the manifolds and ports can be designed to maximize the amount of air getting to the cylinder. This gives

Port EFI allows very short intake manifolds and a shorter, straighter path for fuel entering the combustion chamber. Note the extremely short intake runner and the injector placement seen on this Moto Guzzi.

us more power, especially at the top end, and nicely complements the other improvements in power, economy, and emissions that we can obtain with EFI.

Sensors and Their Data

This is a pretty broad category, but there is one important point to remember. Carburetors only deal with two measurable quantities: atmospheric pressure and intake manifold pressure. The more we think about carburetors, the more amazed we should be that they work as well as they do with such incredible simplicity.

Fuel injection, on the other hand, can measure as many or as few things as we wish it to. We can choose what will best meet our needs, whatever they may be—ease of design, ability to use the same parts across many models (thus cutting development and production costs significantly), and, of course, the big three: power, economy, and emissions. The most obvious advantage here over carbs is that we can much more precisely determine the conditions under which we are operating, and compensate for them. Things like ambient air temperature and engine temperature are far outside the realm of carburetors, but are easily factored into operation with fuel injection. We can measure and quantify atmospheric air density, something we cannot do with carburetors. This is one of the great limits of carbs and is why you need to rejet a carbed bike for best operation when you have a drastic change in altitude (and accordingly, air density). This can be of crucial importance where emissions are a concern—carbs cannot really tell the difference between operating conditions very well, and therefore often run well rich of ideal under many circumstances, to the detriment of overall emissions. Recall that this is one of the big reasons we see manufacturers moving to EFI over the past five years or so.

But the most telling difference of EFI, with our extra sensors and data, is that we can now subdivide operating conditions based on the inputs of a number of different sensors; this allows us to pick out different sets of operating conditions so we can adapt our injection to best meet our needs under much more specific conditions. As an example, a carburetor cannot tell much difference between engine braking (closing the throttle at higher rpms to decelerate the motorcycle) and cruise (steady running on nearly closed throttle) at the same rpm. The only difference a CV carb

will see is lower manifold pressure with engine braking, and so will keep the slide (and the attached needle) lower, providing a bit leaner mixture.

EFI, however, can look at trends in incoming data from its sensors. It can watch how a variety of sensors change over time, which allows the ECU to react differently to different sorts of operating conditions beyond the single dimension of "right now". If the ECU detects low manifold pressure and sees engine rpms dropping over the last few samples, it can "say" to itself that it knows the engine is now engine braking and respond accordingly. A number of motorcycles will turn off the fuel entirely under engine braking, which lowers emissions greatly and provides improved fuel economy without any change in rideability. And this is just one of many examples. Others include determining when the motorcycle is in cruise mode (fairly steady speed, fairly steady almost-closed throttle position) so it can shift into lean or closed-loop operation, knowing how much acceleration is being called for and adjusting fuel and spark according to rider demand, and many more.

The disadvantage to having all this extra data is that, to make it useful, you have to devote time and processing power to it. And most MCUs can really only do one thing at a time. So more sensors, and more tasks, mean more load for the microcontroller inside the ECU. Right? Well, not exactly. We already talked about ASICs and some of how they help us do more in a shorter time without needing a microcontroller that runs very fast (and very hot). Let's look a little closer at how some of this is tackled, and how it affects the drawback of additional processing requirements.

Computers of all sorts use a number of clever hardware and software tricks to operate much more quickly than if the CPU did all the work itself. One of the big ones is called pipelining. Pipelining is taking data and doing work on it outside of the CPU itself. In most home computers, for instance, there is a special chip for controlling DMA, or direct memory access. Programs and devices can read from or write to memory directly, without having to get the attention of the CPU and using up processor time to send data to and from memory. This creates a pipeline between a device (whether it be a hard drive, an I/O card, or what have you) and certain memory locations. The CPU is one of the clients of the chip that controls DMA; if the CPU needs access to memory, it goes through the DMA controller just like any other device. The CPU, however, generally has priority over many other devices in the system, as far as the DMA controller is concerned. Slowing down the CPU is generally the thing that slows down a computer the most, so it tends to get first crack at most things where the DMA controller is concerned.

In most ECUs, this is where ASICs come in. They are often designed to handle common and time-consuming pre-processing of sensor data so the microcontroller doesn't have to worry about it. They can also be made to process several sensors to get an intermediate value from a certain combination of data, and then make that intermediate value available for the microcontroller to use at any time. Not only does this mean we can work with slower (which means cheaper and cooler-running) microcontrollers, it also helps the microcontroller stick to its deadlines. While a home computer tends to be really flexible when it comes to the timing of particular events, an ECU for fuel injection has to meet a lot of very rigid deadlines for working out ignition and injection timing. While you or I can wait an extra half-second for a window to pop up on our screen, the engine cannot wait to receive fuel or spark, especially if we are concerned about emissions (which tend to dictate when we inject the fuel, and definitely dictate when we create a spark event). So taking as much workload off the

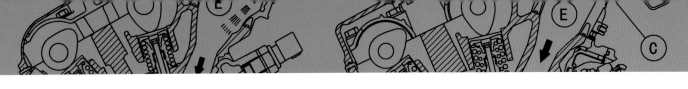

Advancements in the field of integrated circuit design have given us smaller, faster, and cheaper computing power than ever before. This has allowed affordable and sophisticated EFI, as with the Mitsubishi ECU seen on this Vulcan 1500 Mean Streak. The arrow indicates where it is installed in the chassis. Kawasaki Motor Corporation USA

processor as we can is of crucial importance when designing an ECU to meet cost and durability requirements. Remember that our home computers have lots of fans and heat sinks to get rid of heat from processors and dedicated controller chips. An ECU generally has few or no heat sinks, and no fans, so keeping the heat down is a very big deal when it comes to making an ECU work day in and day out for many years without failing.

So when designing an ECU, a manufacturer has to look at a large variety of factors and balance them all against each other to get a product that does the job to their specifications. The more we ask of the ECU in terms of differentiating between different running conditions (and this is of primary importance when it comes to meeting emissions requirements), the more delicate this balance becomes, and the more tricky it is to design and develop a good product. This is one of the reasons why high-quality, fairly flexible ECUs are often seen not only on different models, but among different brands as well. If a design is proven and can be made to fit a given application with little to no modification, there is a great savings in cost of manufacture and development for the motorcycle manufacturer. What's more, it also tends to minimize teething troubles with rideability that are sometimes seen with fuel injection systems on a newly introduced model. But it can be a delicate balance between cost, reliability, flexibility, and the big three (power, emissions, and economy). In fact, not only are motorcycle ECUs often used between different OEMs, but some motorcycle ECUs are actually lightly-modified automotive ECUs. This provides lower costs (since development costs were paid for years ago, and the overall volume of production is much higher), as well as removing some of the difficulty and expense in making the ECU work well within the boundaries of the OEM's goals for the system (since manufacturers can draw from an extensive body of previous automotive development experience).

The cost of manufacturing ASICs has dropped dramatically over the past 15 years or so, and it is now possible to create very small production runs of highly specialized, very fast ASICs for a fraction of what slower mass-produced chips cost just a decade ago. Reliability of both processing hardware and sensors has increased dramatically as well. These factors have made EFI a much more cost-effective proposition, which has provided additional incentive for its use by OEMs.

Different Philosophies

Working with carburetors was originally a separate concept from other parts of the power delivery system. Designers and engineers thought of fuel delivery as being a separate piece of the puzzle from ignition. After all, why not? Spark was electrical, and fuel delivery was mechanical. Combining them was nearly impossible for a long time, and certainly not very practical. Only when emissions considerations entered the picture did motorcycle engineers start looking at altering ignition timing based on other criteria besides engine rpm. Prior to that point, straight mechanical advance strategies were used. As engine rpm increased, the spark triggering was done earlier and earlier to produce the best power output at full throttle for a given engine rpm. And regardless of any other considerations, the spark advance was always the same at a given engine speed. This works pretty well when you want best power at full throttle but it doesn't do much for emissions.

Furthermore, carburetors were favored for a long time because of their simplicity of design and construction. Because the operation of many of the fueling circuits overlapped, CV carbs gained a reputation for being difficult to tune, but for a motorcycle manufacturer, it was quite simple. A four-gas analyzer and an eddy-current dynamometer capable of step testing were all the hardware that was required to get the best power out of a given engine through carb tuning. They operated on simple principles, were reliable over the long haul, and were very easy to diagnose and repair (if you knew what to look for).

It was awfully hard for motorcycle manufacturers to find much fault with modern CV carburetors, or the strategy of mechanical-style ignition advance, as long as all that mattered was halfway-decent fuel economy, drivability, and raw power. But the times were changing. During the golden era of CV carbs, automobile manufacturers were going ballistic trying to make economical cars that could meet rapidly tightening emissions restrictions. A number of different ideas were tried, starting with adding all kinds of compensation circuits on car carburetors. These resulted in a mechanical nightmare; there was more plumbing in the carburetor than in an oil refinery, it seemed. Diagnosis and repair became a lost cause as the number of overlapping fuel circuits skyrocketed. Drivability problems became epidemic as the number of things that could go wrong with carbs escalated. Clearly, this was not the answer.

During these automotive experiments, car manufacturers were learning a lot more about the combustion process. They had to, or they would not be able to make cars that they could sell. They started to discover some of the intricate relationships between intake tuning, exhaust tuning, plenum volume, combustion chamber shape, ignition timing, and a host of other factors. As they learned about how all these pieces of the puzzle fit together, they realized that there were a lot of measurable quantities that, alone or combined, could correspond to needed changes in fueling and spark timing required to meet certain objectives. That's how we came down the road to where motorcycle fuel injection is today, and even beyond (in the case of the automotive world).

So modern motorcycle fuel injection systems look at the complete package in terms of quantity and timing of both spark and fueling, and take an approach that is less a direct relationship between a few simple measurements (engine speed for spark and manifold pressure and atmospheric pressure for fueling) and a more complex relationship between many different dynamic elements. How the system is changing is often of more interest than the exact state of the system at any discrete point in time (but not always!). Using their knowledge of digital electronics and engine dynamics, it was possible for researches and engineers to develop ECUs that could respond to the kinds of changes that were actually going on within the combustion chamber by combining measurements and trends from a variety of sensors with maps that were developed by trial and error (and sometimes with the aid of computer models).

Because exhaust emissions are so closely tied to the sorts of changes that EFI is now designed to provide for, motorcycle EFI systems are able to do a significantly better job of reducing emissions, with minimal impact on both power and drivability. The increased precision of fuel delivery and atomization when compared against carburetors can often increase both power and fuel economy, while simultaneously reducing emissions. The philosophy behind carburetion could not keep up with the demands placed on motorcycle manufacturers today, especially when power was still a significant goal for a particular model. This is one of the reasons we are seeing fuel injection on the most sporting models at the forefront, with large-displacement cruiser engines (which generally have an innate handicap with regard to emissions and fuel economy due to the relatively huge bore of each cylinder) catching a ride into the world of EFI as well.

The Case For and Against EFI

We've already touched on the increased cost of design and development of an EFI system, and then the further cost and time involved in tuning and altering the system (which can lead to rewriting large chunks of the program running the ECU, or even changes in the hardware contained inside it) so that it meet power, emissions, and fuel consumption targets set by regulators and the motorcycle manufacturer. But we've also seen ways in which those costs can be cut; using a flexible ECU in many models cuts production and design costs for the hardware. Suzuki and Kawasaki have entered into a strategic alliance recently, selling each other's off-road models and sharing parts and parts suppliers. This becomes even more obvious when you look at the very similar systems used on both companies' sporting machines. Designed by Denso, both use very similar Keihin throttle bodies with secondary, servo-controlled butterflies. By sharing system design and mass-production costs, Kawasaki and Suzuki have been able to make motorcycles with good power, drivability, and emissions, while shaving prices and still maximizing profits. Another example is the JCAE (formerly SAGEM) MC1000 ECU, which is used on models from Aprilia and Triumph, as well as Excelsior-Henderson and Cannondale, both now defunct. Systems can also be developed for a particular set of needs—vehicles with lower power and emissions demands, for instance—saving on design and development costs.

We've also covered the fact that EFI, in even fairly crude forms, usually blows carburetors right out of the water when it comes to emissions. Included in this package is trend tracking by the ECU to determine what state the engine is operating in, integrated spark control, improvements in intake tract design, and improvements in introducing fuel into the intake airstream. Because of the possibility of building extremely high resolution into an EFI system as a whole, it is often possible to very finely control drivability without much change in power, or even emissions. Marc Salvisberg of Factory Pro Tuning talks extensively of sculpting maps when tuning fuel-injected motorcycles, since he can often make drastic changes in the feel of a motorcycle when ridden without changing the power output by a measurable amount. And of course, the big benefit in this area for manufacturers is in being able to manipulate emissions without badly affecting either rideability or power output.

This JCAE (formerly SAGEM) MC1000 ECU has been used by a variety of manufacturers on everything from single-cylinder dirtbikes to three-cylinder sporting machines to cruisers. Flexible design is what makes it such a widely used component. This one was taken from an Excelsior-Henderson V-twin cruiser. Tim Marsteiner

What other downsides are there? Well, there is the obvious increase in complexity with an EFI system. The more parts there are, the more potential trouble sources there can be. With some machines, such as Delphi-equipped Harley-Davidson motorcycles, there are electrical, electronic, and sensor linkages between systems as diverse as the alarm system, the turn signal control, and the fuel injection ECU. Nearly the entire wiring harness is involved in multiple, linked systems involving the fuel injection system, which not only means more possible trouble sources, but significantly more difficult fault diagnosis, in some situations. The fact that all the components involved are electrically powered means poor connections, a weak charging system, a bad battery or ground connection, or even strong radio signals can sometimes cause problems with fuel delivery. With carburetors, any problems are limited to the carburetor or other parts of the intake tract. Carburetors have only mechanical parts, and they can be replaced, adjusted, or inspected with relative ease. In some cases the componemets can even be repaired. With EFI, there are a far greater number of interlinked components of all different types, and almost all of them are electrical or electronic, making EFI harder to troubleshoot on the component level (especially if the bike will not run at all). And as so many mechanics will tell you, electrical problems are often intermittent in nature, which vastly increases the time and expense involved in diagnosing and repairing the malfunction.

This increased linkage of systems, as well as the merging of a variety of goals that may vary along with riding conditions, means that it is more possible to make fuel injection that does not work well (from any given observer's standpoint) than it was with carbs. Accordingly, it is even more difficult for an end user to fix the system to better meet particular goals at the expense of others.

And of course, perhaps the most important factor most consumers have to face today is that, compared to the mechanical simplicity and the typical mechanic's long history with carburetors, fuel injection is a vast and confusing unknown. As with carburetors, though, knowledge of and experience with how different parts affect each other when adjusted or altered is enough in most cases to devise a strategy for attacking a trouble source, whether it be a fault in the system or a tuning issue. This book is meant to provide the foundation of understanding with which a mechanic or layperson might consider the operation (or malfunction) of an electronic fuel injection system. Some of you might even use this information as a jumping-off point to tuning, repairing, or replacing EFI systems and components!

CHAPTER 10

HISTORY OF MOTORCYCLE EFI: 1980-1990

Those of you riding fuel-injected bikes today who think of EFI as a relatively new technology for motorcycles have a surprise in store when you open your history books. Manufacturers began using fuel injection on production bikes as early as 1980, and Kawasaki used it for eight years before returning to carburetors as their sole method of fuel delivery. This may seem strange, in light of the fact that Kawasaki has not been at the forefront of the new wave of fuel-injected bikes. Perhaps we might learn a few things in this chapter that will give us some clues as to why that might be.

WHERE DID IT COME FROM?

A number of different cars had begun using fairly simple EFI systems by the early 1980s to help meet emissions standards without harming drivability. In the grand tradition of OEMs everywhere, manufacturers wanted systems that were cheap to develop and build, easy for their mechanics to learn, and just good enough to meet the objectives they had laid out in terms of emissions, mileage, and drivability. In addition, they were pioneering the technology to make more affordable and smaller sensors. The first pressure sensors used in a speed-density system (Bosch D-Jetronic) were each the size of a softball!

By the very early 1980s, motorcycle performance was increasing in ways never dreamed of before. At the same time, regulators were cracking down hard on emissions. Beginning in 1978, motorcycle manufacturers had to meet emissions requirements in the United States for the first time. And the carburetors they had been using could not handle the combination of performance and emissions demands at their then-current state of development.

Motorcycle manufacturers began turning to EFI as a method of making more power and meeting emissions standards. This allowed the turbo wars that some remember fondly from the early 1980s, spawning a wonderful forced-induction model from each of the Japanese "Big Four." Three of these were fuel-injected. European manufacturers also started using fuel injection to meet U.S. emissions standards. And as cars were forced to use fuel injection more and more, the technology began to advance, making it cheaper and easier to fuel inject the smaller, less-emissions-strangled engines of motorcycles.

By the mid 1980s, carburetor development was catching up with available fuel injection technology (at least with what was affordable and necessary for motorcycle use). As carburetors began to offer higher performance and better tenability for emissions, the pendulum swung again back to carburetors (at least in Japan). It would be years before we saw EFI struggle to life again in the world of the Japanese motorcycle. Meanwhile, in Europe, things kept on track toward today's systems, thanks mainly to Fiat, believe it or not. But let's get on to the bikes, and their EFI systems.

The Japanese Companies
Kawasaki

Kawasaki was the first of the "old guard" to incorporate fuel injection, and the last of the Japanese companies to abandon it the first

Tightening emissions standards, along with the turbo wars of the early 1980s, dictated new answers to the old questions and problems of fueling and spark control. Here we see a stunning technological achievement of that era, as we look under the metal heat shields of a 1983 Honda CX650 Turbo at the heart of its performance hardware, the IHI turbocharger itself. Motorcycle courtesy of Greg Goss

time around, largely based on their simplistic but proven designs taken from the automotive world.

Kawasaki spearheaded the entry of motorcycles into the brave new world of fuel injection in 1980, with the KZ1000G. Designated the Z1 Classic, it took advantage of the fact that fuel injection can use large throttle bodies for better top-end power, but still maintain decent cruise and idle. The available carbs at the time could not do what fuel injection could—even primitive EFI systems such as those used by Kawasaki.

The Z1 Classic only lasted a year, but the same EFI system was available the following year on the KZ1100B, better known as the first GPz1100. This system's design and analog ECU were almost identical in execution to the L-Jetronic system from Bosch that was common on air-cooled Volkswagens and Datsun Z-cars from the late 1970s. Individual throttle bodies and the 1000's smaller cylinders actually made some parts of that system unnecessary in a motorcycle application.

This system used a fuel pump external to the fuel tank, as well as an external fuel filter. The tank and petcock were carried over from carbureted models, with the addition of a fuel rail line. Mikuni provided butterfly-style throttle bodies. It used a flapper-type VAF (volumetric airflow) sensor to measure airflow, and it correlated that input against an IAT sensor inside the VAF sensor (or airbox in the case of the GPz) to calculate the actual air mass demands of the engine. Since the VAF was some distance from the throttle bodies, and there was an airbox in between to damp down pulses, this was not very responsive when the throttle angle was suddenly changed. It was a necessary evil, however, as in any other configuration, large variations in flow rate from individual cylinder pulses (found at low rpm) would send wildly varying signals to the ECU.

There was also a throttle position switch that sent data to the ECU about whether the throttle was fully closed, fully open, or somewhere toward the middle. By watching for sudden large changes in throttle position, it would modify the fuel delivery to compensate until the airbox pressure stabilized, at which point the

VAF sensor would again be a fairly accurate representation of the engine's air demands. There was also, of course, a CHT sensor to tell the ECU to richen the mixture when the engine was cold.

The ECU did not have a separate engine speed sensor to trigger injector pulse timing and give a coordinate for the base VAF map burned into the PROM (Programmable Read-Only Memory chip). Instead, it took its signal from the igniter box (which also went to the coil primaries). This was convenient because it pulsed at twice actual engine RPM. But as we know, ignition timing (even back then) changes with RPM. This would make the signal rather complicated to use as a crank angle reference. Without crank angle or engine phase data, the Kawasakis used batch fire, the simplest form of port injection, where all four injectors fired at once. (Note that the fact that this was an analog ECU also favored using all the simple signal control and timing we have observed.)

With a setup like this, injector timing is far less critical than it would be for a port injection system, so allowing the trigger point for the injection to change with rpm was acceptable. As we can surmise from the primitive air measurement methods, getting the best mixture as often as possible was not the design engineers' primary consideration. Emissions were not yet high on the list, and "better" was perfectly fine for them. They got a boost in performance, acceptable throttle response, and better gas mileage over the available carburetors, and did so at a price they considered acceptable.

The drawbacks of the system are obvious. A flapper-type VAF obstructs airflow, thus restricting the intake to some degree. VAF is slow to respond to changes in airflow at the intake valve, and a simple throttle switch gave only the grossest measure of the difference between airflow at the valve and airflow at the flapper. And the loose air-cooled engines of the day almost needed to be run rich of best power, just to keep engine temperatures down. Since the change in power output for a given change in fuel/air ratio is smaller on the rich side of ? = 1, erring in this direction gave smoother throttle response up to the point of rich misfire.

Almost immediately, people began to notice unpredictable throttle response with these bikes. Sometimes they would go lean with rapid opening of the throttle. A common fix was to stretch out the return spring in the VAF flapper, which allowed it to travel farther for a given airflow, fooling the ECU into thinking there was more air coming in than there actually was, thus richening the mixture. But this was not a very good answer. The precision of response to changes in throttle angle was still very poor, and the modification did nothing to increase maximum fueling.

So in 1982, Kawasaki went to both the most basic of systems and a more advanced ECU, while obtaining more throttle response in the bargain. Hitachi developed an alpha-n system for them. Introduced on the 1982 GPz1100, this system remained in use through 1988, and was found on all three of their fuel-injected models during those years: the GPz1100, the Voyager 1300, and the GPz750 Turbo.

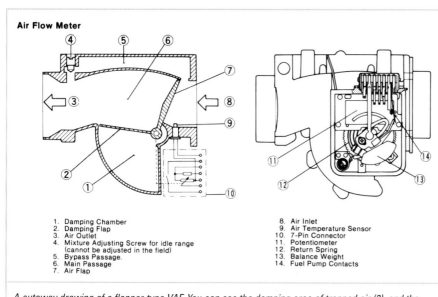

Air Flow Meter

1. Damping Chamber
2. Damping Flap
3. Air Outlet
4. Mixture Adjusting Screw for idle range (cannot be adjusted in the field)
5. Bypass Passage
6. Main Passage
7. Air Flap
8. Air Inlet
9. Air Temperature Sensor
10. 7-Pin Connector
11. Potentiometer
12. Return Spring
13. Balance Weight
14. Fuel Pump Contacts

A cutaway drawing of a flapper-type VAF. You can see the damping area of trapped air (2), and the potentiometer (12) used to measure airflow volume. This method of determining airflow to the engine was not well suited to motorcycles and was quickly abandoned. Kawasaki Motor Corporation USA

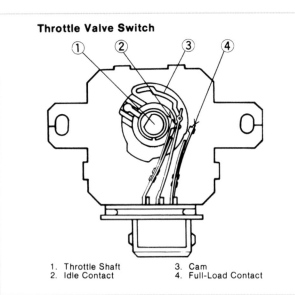

Throttle Valve Switch

1. Throttle Shaft
2. Idle Contact
3. Cam
4. Full-Load Contact

To assist early Kawasaki VAF-based systems in choosing correct fueling for operating conditions, a throttle position switch was added to the throttle bodies. This one, from a KZ1000G, indicated closed-throttle idle/engine braking, as well as full-throttle operation. It was later replaced with a potentiometer-based TPS, which remains with us in today's designs. Kawasaki Motor Corporation USA

Kawasaki's all-digital 6801-based ECU was a large step toward the future. The large chip slightly to the right of center is the 6801 MCU. The small-lighter-green circuit board in the upper right corner contains the ambient air pressure sensor (the square black box attached). Note the power transistors on the lower left and right, bolted to the metal case for use as a heat sink. This unit is from a 1982 GPz1100. Sid Young

This system was all-new. Since delta alpha gives a much better representation of airflow at the intake valve, this system cured the responsiveness problems of the previous one. Using many of the same parts as the older system, it now incorporated a Hitachi 6801 8-bit microcontroller, which had 4k of internal EEPROM and 128 bytes of RAM. In fact, this was the first real microcontroller (a single chip with ROM, RAM, and a microprocessor) used in a motorcycle. For its day, it was pretty capable. A 1 MHz clock speed gave it plenty of power to run the system. A 16-bit timer allowed plenty of precision. And four I/O ports with external interrupt gave the flexibility and data-handling capacity necessary for what Kawasaki called Digital Fuel Injection, or D.F.I. It even had a diagnostic mode that would flash an error code on a built-in LED when it received out-of-range (or no) signals from a sensor. Because it was an alpha-n system, it required fairly precise calibration of the TPS for proper idle and off-idle cruise performance, as well as off-the-line throttle response (tip-in). Kawasaki's answer was to offer a factory calibration tool that would give a "go/no-go" indication while the sensor was rotated relative to the throttle shaft at a fixed throttle position. While easy to use, these devices have become hard to find, and Kawasaki never offered a resistance or voltage specification that could be measured with a multimeter, making the calibration of these TPS sensors very difficult today.

The 1982 GPz1100 had a TPS, as you would expect, and an idle position switch from the older system. AAP (inside the ECU) and IAT sensors determined air density. CHT was again used for cold-start purposes. And engine rpm signal was derived from the coil primaries, thus relegating this system to batch-fire mode. In addition, this meant having separate spark control via an igniter (in those days that meant strictly rpm-controlled advance).

The details of its physical layout, including tank and fuel pump, were nearly identical to those on the earlier system. In fact,

the CHT sensor used on the 1981 GPz1100 was carried through on all models until 1988 (including the water-cooled 1300s, which used it as a CT sensor). The IAT sensor first used on the 1982 GPz was used on all EFI Kawasakis through 1988 except for the Turbo 750 (which needed a wider range), the fuel injectors were identical on all the 1100s, and the TPS was common to all the bikes with alpha-n systems.

The GPz750 Turbo model of 1984–1985 had to make some changes to accommodate the turbocharging, but otherwise its EFI system is basically identical (but for mapping) to the alpha-n system used on all EFI Kawasakis from 1982–1988. It used different injectors, a different IAT sensor and, of course, a TIP (throttle inlet pressure) sensor in the plenum/surge tank to measure boost, in addition to the standard TPS, AAP, and CHT sensors. For air density measurement, the ECU primarily used the plenum-mounted IAT and TIP sensors and operated in regular alpha-n mode. Like the other systems discussed here, it was fairly crude by comparison to modern systems and tended to err on the side of richness, important on the turbo model since ignition timing was not retarded under high boost levels.

Since the Turbo was theoretically intended for racing, Kawasaki released a four-page bulletin on how to put the ECU into what it referred to as "race mode". On the turbo, there were two signal return lines to the ECU from the IAT sensor, and disconnecting one of them switched the system into "race mode." The ECU would flash a consistent trouble code of "33" (three long flashes followed by three short flashes) to indicate that it was in "race mode." Race mode was never documented in the USA, probably for liability and emissions reasons. It is used in conjunction with the removal of the stock turbo intake and air filter, which allows the turbo to build boost more quickly, and deliver higher terminal boost. The conversion actually switches to

To help keep costs low and maintenance simple, most of the early fuel-injected Kawasakis shared many EFI components. Pictured here is a 1984 GPz1100, square in the middle of the year range for Kawasaki's first experiments with production EFI. David Vastag

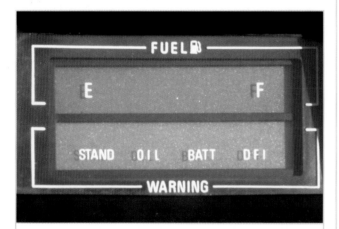

Most of the early ECUs had some method of signaling problems to the operator. In Kawasaki's case, a lamp lit on the dash to indicate trouble, and a code of flashes indicated where the problem might be. This is the instrument panel from a 1984 GPz1100. You can see the DFI lamp on the lower right of the LCD panel. It was here that the trouble code of 33 would be visible on a motorcycle set to race mode. David Vastag

another, rather different bit of mapping; among other things, the fuel cut-off on overrun was eliminated (presumably to help keep the turbo "spooled up" while engine braking), despite this being bad for economy and emissions. It also removed the overboost fuel cutoff, which would protect a stock bike in the event of a failed wastegate; on a modified bike, this would also allow for modification of the wastegate to make more peak boost. Kawasaki claimed this would only work on non-U.S. model motorcycles so as not to get into trouble with the EPA, but the fact was that it would work on any 750 Turbo.

Last of the line was the ZN1300 Voyager 1300, a full-dress touring derivative of the old KZ1300 inline six-cylinder muscle

bike. Using the alpha-n D.F.I. system over the KZ's carbs gave not only more power, but better fuel economy, and it remained with the bike from 1983 until the end of the model run in 1988.

The design philosophy behind the two types of systems used on early EFI Kawasakis was the same, despite using two different methods of calculating ingested air mass, and two different methods of creating injector pulses: They were both designed to replace carburetors, but be standalone systems. Ignition was handled by an independent control unit (the igniter), which made it easy to add EFI on to an existing bike. Kawasaki was not yet concerned with integrating systems, and this was by far the more expedient engineering approach.

Suzuki

Suzuki jumped on both the turbo and EFI bandwagons in 1983 with the release of the XN85 Turbo. The "85" in the name supposedly referred to the horsepower output of its two-valve air-cooled 673-cc motor.

The system used on this turbo bike was the same design as the early Kawasaki system—the Bosch L-Jetronic pattern, with flapper-type VAF sensor. As with the Kawasaki systems, the Suzuki system ran in batch-fire mode, with all injectors firing at the same time. One advance was the use of a MAP sensor to run a boost gauge, as well as to retard ignition timing at high boost levels. The MAP sensor is only used by the ignition system in this machine, however.

Despite its similarities with the early Kawasaki system, the Suzuki system was digital and was made by Nippondenso (eventually to become Denso, supplier of current fuel injection computers and other electronics to most Japanese manufacturers). According to Suzuki, half of each engine revolution is devoted to calculating the fuel injector pulse width, at which point the injector pulse is delivered to the injectors. In addition, at higher rpms, the ECU switches from one injector event per engine revolution to one injector event per two revolutions. Since there is greater airflow and less time between intake valve opening events, this does not adversely affect fuel vaporization. But it does offer one important advantage: The injectors are only required to open and close once per complete four-stroke cycle, which allows for greater fuel delivery by effectively removing one set of injector ramping events. In other words, it increases the maximum usable duty cycle for all practical purposes (and thus expands the dynamic range of the injectors). In addition, the Nippondenso system had the advantage of using peak-and-hold injectors, which allowed them to gain better idling control with a higher peak flow rate.

The AAP sensor on this machine is a bit different from the one used in almost all other applications. Here it is a simple barometric switch, which when activated indicates a significant reduction in AAP over sea level atmospheric. Apparently Nippondenso and Suzuki found that the flapper VAF sensor was good enough at reading airflow within certain parameters, and only needed modification once air pressure got too far from the "target zone" of the ECU map's calibration. It switches on at approximately 3,200 feet above sea level. Keep in mind, though, that this system was very crude in metering fuel with anything approaching repeatable precision, so this approach was tolerable.

Again the engine temperature sensor (in this case, an oil temperature sensor) is used for cold start enrichment, and the AAT sensor is used in conjunction with the VAF sensor to calculate air mass. The throttle switch adds the ability for the ECU to completely stop injection events upon closing of the throttle above 3,500 rpm, thus saving fuel during engine braking. There is also a cranking/start enrichment protocol based on engine temperature that helps with cold starts—the extra fuel being added is ramped down between 5 and 30 seconds after starting, depending on engine temperature.

The ability to switch between two different batch-fire modes (every revolution and every second revolution), as well as using closed-throttle engine-braking leanout to reduce emissions, confirm that this is indeed a digital ECU instead of analog. These features would be nearly impossible to duplicate in a cost-effective manner with an analog ECU.

Even the separate ignition module was more advanced than Kawasaki's. In addition to boost-driven timing retard to prevent detonation at high boost levels, the Nippondenso-designed unit also had a rev limiter to prevent engine damage, and a cutout in case of waste-gate failure to prevent engine damage from too much boost pressure. Dwell (the amount of time charge is applied to the coil primary, thus controlling spark voltage) was varied based on engine rpm, allowing more precise spark timing at low rpms, while ensuring sufficient time for a magnetic field to build in the coil secondary at higher rpms to ensure a healthy spark. This was all pretty sophisticated stuff at the time. But still, the EFI design was standalone, and not well-integrated with ignition.

After the very brief "turbo wars," however, Suzuki reverted to carburetors until the 1990s. Even the XN85 itself lasted just one year, and was gone before the GPz750 Turbo was released.

Suzuki had a short-lived turbo bike of their own, in the form of the 1983 XN85. Its EFI system was very similar to the first Kawasaki systems. The long, convoluted path from the exhaust ports to the turbocharger compromised power output. Robert Mitchell

Honda

I saved Honda for last in the Japanese manufacturers section, and for a reason. Not only did they start the turbo wars in 1982 with the release of the CX500 Turbo, they also created with it a technical tour de force. In many ways, this motorcycle (and its spawn, the 1983 CX650 Turbo) proved to the world that Honda was a step and a half ahead of anyone else. At a time when BMW was still building only air-cooled boxer motors fed by carburetors, when Ducati had only two-valve air-cooled carbureted twins, Honda released a bike that was better developed, more technologically advanced, and a showcase for its engineering abilities. Beyond all the other technical innovations (such as being the first water-cooled sport machine), it had injection technology that is quite similar in operation to many of today's commonly-used motorcycle EFI systems. As with the Suzuki, this system was manufactured by Nippondenso and became the basis of the Denso EFI systems seen on today's Yamahas and Suzukis, as well as Honda's own PGM-FI.

Honda's C.F.I. (computerized fuel injection) was the first production motorcycle system to use sequential fuel injection (which it actually needed for smooth idle, being a V-twin). It was therefore the first to use a cam position sensor (not strictly necessary for sequential operation, but by far the easiest way to handle things). It had a cast alloy intake manifold (provided by Keihin) that featured integral throttle bodies and fuel rail. It had complex chambering in the intake system to reduce intake noise, and it was the first bike to use a resonance chamber in the intake tube (used to prevent turbo surge based on intake resonance, a similar principle to airbox resonance tuning). Like its contemporaries, it had both the fuel pump and the fuel filter outside the fuel tank, and also had a petcock (as you would find on a carbureted engine, but for the fuel rail return fitting). Unlike any other system at the time, it used an idle air bypass system to raise idle for cold starting, and this was automatic. A valve to allow air bypass and enrichment was attached to a bimetal strip (like that found in a home thermostat), which mechanically opened and closed a bypass passage (enrichment during this time was built into the cold-start mapping of the CT sensor). The ignition system (from Hitachi) was separate from the injection electronics, but used a MAP sensor like the Suzuki to retard timing at higher boost levels.

An interesting note is that this EFI system takes engine speed signals from the cam sensor alone. Two pickups allowed the system to calculate crank angle to properly time injector events for both cylinders. The crank sensor was only used for the ignition system, and no signal was transmitted from the coil primaries or igniter to the ECU. In this, it had something in common with some early Ducatis.

Like with many of today's motorcycles, the ECU ran using speed-density mapping at small throttle openings, and alpha-n mapping at larger throttle openings, so it had a TPS as well as a MAP sensor and a TIP (throttle inlet pressure) sensor measuring surge tank pressure (post-turbo). It also incorporated an AAP sensor in the intake for good measure. The acceleration enrichment on this bike was done with a separate map based off of delta alpha, and it actually added an additional, separate injection event for acceleration fueling.

Honda even specifies using this feature in their diagnostic injector testing. With the key on and the engine not running, a rapid opening of the throttle actually triggers an injection event, and you are instructed to listen for the sound of the injectors cycling to confirm proper injector operation!

Honda trumped the rest of the motorcycle world by turbocharging one of the least-likely engines in their inventory, the pushrod-operated, four-valve V-twin CX500 motor. Here we see the author's own 1982 CX500 Turbo, resplendent in VFR red. Motorcycle courtesy of Greg Goss

The EFI system on the 1982 CX500 Turbo was the most advanced ever used on a motorcycle at the time of its introduction. In 1983, the CX650 Turbo took things a step further and is the basis for today's PGM-FI systems from Honda. Here we see a CX650 Turbo with the bodywork removed; above it is the entire fuel injection system from a CX500 Turbo. You can see just how complicated it is from the sheer mass of sensors, hoses, and wires. Motorcycle and EFI courtesy of Greg Goss

Whenever possible, Honda implemented a limp-home mode for sensor failure. This would ignore missing or questionable sensor inputs, and would substitute a standardized value that would allow the motorcycle to continue running in many cases, although at reduced efficiency. Limp-home capability was built into the ECU for faults with the IAT sensor, the CT sensor, all three pressure sensors (the fourth was for ignition retard alone), either of the two cam position sensors, and the TPS. This meant the bike kept running in nearly any possible condition short of multiple severe electrical failures. The ECU also had a series of LEDs to indicate the source of a trouble code. It was also the first production motorcycle to be equipped with a tipover switch that would kill the fuel pump and stop the motor in the event of a drop or crash.

Honda did themselves one better in 1983, modifying the upgraded CX650 motor for better turbocharged performance and both developing and simplifying the injection system. The 650 benefited from larger valves, more intake valve lift, and higher compression (with a corresponding decrease in maximum boost), all of which allowed for a smoother transition when the turbo kicked in and stronger running throughout the rev range. The turbo itself was revamped with a larger compressor wheel, and the resonance chamber was removed from the surge tank. The cold start idle air bypass was also removed.

But the big changes were in the black box in the tail. In fact, the CX650 Turbo system was the basis for the Honda PGM-FI system, which is still used today. First, ignition was handled from inside the ECU. This was the first production motorcycle with a true engine management system (by comparison, the high-tech BMW K-bike would have to wait until the 1990 K1 to integrate ignition and fueling). Since ignition was integrated, there was no longer a reason to have a separate boost sensor for

Honda's Nippondenso ECU was a triumph of digital electronics and allowed the bike to limp home in many cases if one or more sensors became inoperable or unreliable. This ECU, from a CX500 Turbo Custom, was encased in a sealed metal box, with a high-quality AMP connector. The inset shows the LEDs that read out the various trouble codes if the system is malfunctioning. ECU courtesy of Greg Goss

the ignition system alone, and it was deleted. Also removed was the AAP sensor located in the inlet pipe; a reading of ambient air pressure was taken before starting the bike (which could necessitate the need to shut off and restart the bike after large changes in altitude). With a TIP (surge tank) sensor and a MAP sensor, as well as a TPS, it was quite possible to easily and accurately compute the air mass entering the engine, on boost or off. To assist in preventing detonation when the engine was cold, ignition timing factored coolant temperature into the mix (another production first, and used again in future systems). In fact, ignition timing was now done by two overlaid 2D maps,

one for alpha-n and one for MAP-n, which allowed a more complex method of mapping timing based on boost pressure than was available on the 500, in addition to allowing more advance at part throttle. And last, there was now also a crank position sensor for the EFI. Thanks to this addition, Honda was able now to run both ignition and injection with any one of the three engine speed/position sensors inoperable. Previously, if the crank sensor had malfunctioned, there would be no spark.

Sadly, after completing this technical masterpiece and being king of the motorcycle playground hill, Honda took its ball and

The CX650 Turbo was introduced in 1983 and has many detail improvements to make the bike smoother and easier to ride. Perhaps the biggest (although the least visible) is the integration of ignition control into the ECU, a first for the motorcycle world. This is a beautiful example of an all-original 1983 CX650 Turbo, wearing its original factory paint. Its EFI technology was not tested until well into the 1990s. Motorcycle courtesy of Greg Goss

what Kawasaki intended, they could be easily fitted to motorcycles without removing anything but the carbs, and they used the same basic system on a number of different machines for nearly a decade (thus spreading out development costs significantly).

Honda had wanted to show the world their engineering and technology was years ahead of anything else available, and that they would stop at no cost to make showpiece machines that were polished, perfect, and would take any competing machine to the cleaners (as they have so often shown with their racing outings, from Formula 1 to CART to, well, motorcycle racing). They would seem to have achieved that aim in spades.

Ultimately, improvements in carburetor technology, combined with increasing emissions regulations, are what did in the early Japanese OEM foray into EFI. When one or more of the injectors went bad (which was not uncommon when these bikes were still fairly new), most mechanics believed they could more easily and cheaply repair the problem by removing the EFI entirely and replacing it with carburetors. In later years, as carburetor technology improved, you could actually get better mileage and more performance from the naturally aspirated Kawasakis with carbs than you could with the original stock EFI system.

The European Companies

While Japan was making small, light cars for the United States, and capitalizing on the technology developed to produce turbocharged motorcycles, European companies were hard at work making their motorcycles more powerful and fuel efficient, in addition to meeting the increasingly strict EPA regulations in the United States. Before 1990, though, only Ducati and BMW took the plunge. And in both cases, the technology was available due to automotive technological developments.

went home. Fuel injection would not appear on another Honda-badged motorcycle until 1998.

The End of the First Generation in Japan

As has been noted, all these systems (except for Honda's) were crude by comparison with today's systems, but they got the job done. Kawasaki's systems are a prime example. They worked well enough for

BMW

BMW wasn't sitting still in the technology department. They realized that their boxer twin, with two valves and big Bing carburetors, was getting a little long in the tooth for the coming days of emissions controls and longer vehicle life. Thus they drew heavily on their car manufacturing and design experience and released something that was in most ways entirely new for the motorcycle world.

Possibly in response to Honda's technical prowess with the CX500 Turbo, in 1983 BMW released a design that was revolutionary in the motorcycle world: the K100. BMW already had plenty of experience with Bosch injection systems, and adopted the LE-Jetronic systems on their 3-series cars at the same time they were releasing the system on the K100. Two years later, BMW released the second in the K series: the K75, with three cylinders and a counter-rotating balance shaft to make it the smoothest of all the K bikes, then and now. This was also equipped with Bosch LE-Jetronic injection.

The LE-Jetronic system used on the K bikes in those days was very similar to the system used by Kawasaki and Suzuki in their early systems. A flapper-type VAF was augmented with a throttle switch to measure air and throttle demands. Bosch is a little vague on how the LE-Jetronic system differs from the L-Jetronic, but they appear to be very close to identical in terms of operation and design. The LE-Jetronic was capable of running in closed-loop mode with a catalyst, if so desired by the vehicle manufacturer. Since this was not yet required to meet motorcycle emissions standards, however, BMW opted not to take advantage of this feature for either the K100 or the K75 models.

A schematic reveals a relatively simple analog design, using but four integrated circuits, a handful of diodes and capacitors, a few crystals, and four transistors. Like the Kawasaki system, an analog computer was sufficient to deliver a reasonable fuel mixture with only a few sensors, but it had similar limitations to the Kawasaki system. The BMW K engine layout afforded more room for intake components, making the volumetric airflow system a better match to the character of the engine. And despite the relatively high output from its water-cooled powerplant, it was relatively sedate in its air demands, much like a small car engine. This good match in EFI system design and engine demands allowed BMW to continue using the system on K bikes well into the mid-1990s. In fact, only when the K100 series went to four valves per cylinder (the K1 in 1990 and the K100RS in 1991) did Bosch Motronic system, with integrated ignition control, appear on a K bike. BMW opted not to add fuel injection to the R model line (horizontally opposed twins) until much later.

BMW had thus capitalized on its automotive experience in manufacturing, economy, and emissions control in the design of the K bikes. And it was able to use the LE-Jetronic system for many years. BMW has continued in the tradition of increasing economy and lower emissions to this day, as we will see in upcoming chapters.

Ducati

Ducati, too, was feeling the pinch of the 1980s, both on the track and at the EPA's offices. But through the 1980s, a new concept was being developed. And it came, at last, in the form of the legendary 851 that returned Ducati to racing greatness in World Superbike (in the hands of 500-cc World Champion Marco Lucchinelli). With water cooling, four valve heads, a dry clutch, and a trellis frame, it was the first Ducati in the lineage that remains at the top of their lineup today.

Ducati turned to two companies that had worked together for years providing fuel injection components for everything from basic Fiats to racing Ferraris. Weber (famed for their racing carburetors) and Magneti Marelli teamed up once again to bring us the Weber-Marelli P7. This particular design had actually been used for some time on various high-performance and racing cars with great success.

The P7 had some neat tricks up its sleeve, but many of those are looked upon as quaint and archaic by today's standards. You could trim the stock map as long as the ignition was left on, thus allowing you to tune the bike without changing or adding any hardware. The drawback, of course, was that all your changes were lost when you switched the ignition off. The P7 stored them all in RAM. At the very least, though, you could burn a new PROM once you knew what parameters in the maps needed changing. Since it, like all the Weber-Marelli systems found on Ducati motorcycles up to today, was a strict alpha-n system, TPS calibration was very important. So it recalibrated its internal "zero point" for the TPS every time the throttle was closed. While this meant you never had to calibrate the TPS by hand (something that was necessary with annoying frequency on most alpha-n systems), neither could you cheat the system and force it to richen the mixture by intentionally setting the TPS to indicate more alpha than actually existed.

It was, however, a true digital ECU, like those of Honda and the second-generation system from Kawasaki. And what set it apart from anything seen in the motorcycle world thus far, besides its real-time trim capacity, was the fact that its maps were in the form of a socketed PROM. This meant you could burn a new PROM with different maps, and replace the one on the mainboard. Further, Weber-Marelli offered a daughterboard that could be added to the mainboard that added the capability of persistent trackside mapping changes. Instead of being written to onboard RAM, these changes would be flashed to the daughterboard, thus allowing complete trackside tuning without requiring a new PROM to be burned. From a racing standpoint, this ECU was the very thing!

Alpha-n mapping gave it four very real advantages for racing purposes. First, it was very responsive, which meant less of a demand on the resources of the microcontroller. By contrast, VAF-based systems were hard to tune for good throttle response, especially when constant remapping would be required (as in racing). Second, it required no special packaging of the intake system for proper operation. Third, the maps made sense in terms that tuners could understand. Instead of trying to modify map settings that were not intuitive, the main maps that were adjusted by tuners were simple tables that corresponded to engine speed and throttle position. And last, the mapping points for alpha could be arbitrary, and therefore set so that there was more map resolution in areas where it would be most useful for the application. A racing chip would have more resolution near wide-open throttle, where a racer would spend most of their time, while a street-oriented chip could have more resolution near closed-throttle, to improve cruise, off-idle performance, and other areas of drivability. It also had a trim table that would allow for variations between the front and rear cylinder (the main map was for the front cylinder, and there was a trim table to adjust fueling for the rear cylinder as required; if left empty, both cylinders ran off the front cylinder's map). The 851 motor put out 128 bhp at 11,500 rpm in race trim, and the P7 was up to the task.

Oddly, early in its life with Ducatis, the P7 used separate ECU crank angle sensors for fueling and ignition, and the cam sensor

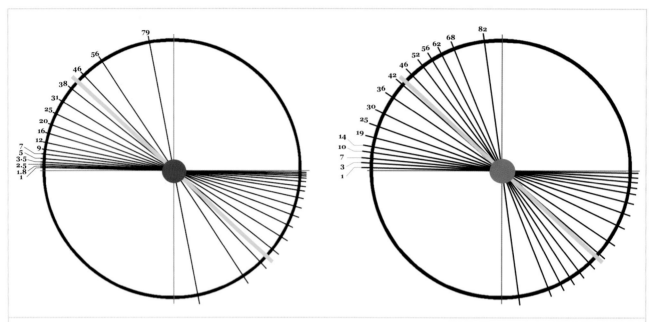

Alpha-n mapping can be enhanced by tuning the TPS map points to favor certain areas over others. This illustration shows the mapping points of a Ducati 748RS TPS on the left, and a Ducati 748R on the right. Since racing motorcycles are mostly concerned with near-full-throttle operation, the 748RS concentrates its calibration points near full throttle (horizontal). Since street bikes spend a lot of their life at idle, cruise, or roll-on from cruise, most of the 748R's calibration points are near closed throttle (vertical). Maya Culbertson

was used strictly for fueling (although the TPS was shared by ignition and fueling systems throughout). This meant a more complex ignition section and implied that ignition and fueling were handled by discrete, unconnected systems within the same box. As has become the trend, they were soon integrated, which made a great deal more sense in terms of reducing sensor complexity and wiring. This kept weight to a minimum, and was made possible through rapid price drops in the manufacturing of integrated circuits.

Clearly, Ducati made the right choice in turning to Weber-Marelli for their injection hardware. The company had a great deal of experience in designing injection systems for racing vehicles, as well as production passenger vehicles, and had ready-made components that could be adapted with very low development costs.

The 851 was continued right into the early 1990s, when its displacement grew, and a new ECU appeared on the scene. The late 1980s were just the beginning for Weber-Marelli's association with Ducati.

The End of the 1980s

As we rolled into the 1990s, almost all cars were fuel injected with complex, multi-map systems that included closed-loop operation. Yet only two major motorcycle manufacturers were using fuel injection: one was using an analog computer system with a flapper-type VAF (a design that had been abandoned half a decade ago by most automakers), and one was using a fast but simple alpha-n system. Automotive systems were far more sophisticated by this point in time, and all new cars were fuel injected. In contrast, only three ranges of motorcycles (the BMW K75 and K100 series and the Ducati 851 series) had EFI!

If it were not for the EPA, we'd likely still be using carburetors. Carbs are well developed, they are well understood by engineers and tuners, and they are cheap and easy to make, tune, and repair. Had it not been for increasingly stringent emissions regulations, fuel injection would have been little more than a curiosity, relegated to racing or special vehicles (in the automotive *and* the motorcycle worlds). But because of the need to meet those standards, we have struggled through the developmental phase, and are coming to the dawn of a new day, where engines are not only more fuel efficient, but make more power, as well. And as a happy side effect, they have far lower emissions levels than ever before in history.

Some of you may have noticed that several of the motorcycle manufacturers that jumped into fuel injection headfirst (one with a complex and precise system, and one with the commitment to a whole range of new bikes) also manufacture automobiles. The ones that don't were most successful when they adapted systems used on cars, or better yet, worked with companies that had much experience with fuel injection courtesy of automotive research and development.

That's right. As much as many of us may bridle at those metal boxes we call "cages", if it were not for the stringent emissions standards levied on them in the late 1970s, we would probably be seeing the first fuel injection systems on bikes only now, nearly 25 years later. So before you shake your fist at the next car that passes you too closely on the road, think about what's under their hoods for just a moment, and how what's under that hood has benefited our machines, and will do so even more in the future. Then you can mutter under your breath into your helmet lining about those "darned cagers."

HARDWARE OUT OF THE BOX

We've pretty exhaustively covered the behavior of the engine and its intake and exhaust systems, as well as the various methods of determining base fueling—which is the main (multidimensional) fuel map being used—and what those methods do well. We've talked about the hardware needed to provide data, process data, and deliver fuel and spark. In fact, we have all the basic information we need to understand the major part of what fuel injection does, how it does it, and why it does it. So what's left?

The first practical application of all our new knowledge will be to understand what has come installed on motorcycles since 1990 and what mapping strategies they use. Once you can identify the parts on your own bike, or a bike you are servicing, you can tell a great deal about how fueling is determined. This information can be critical in troubleshooting, and is absolutely necessary for any plans you may have for tuning the bike.

There are a fair number of different ECUs in use today, and sometimes even different mapping strategies used by different bikes that share a common ECU. Since most of the information about these machines can be found in factory shop manuals and even dealership brochures, it would be redundant to go into great detail on each and every machine with fuel injection that has been made to date. Further, when different makes use the same ECU (possibly with different mapping and utilization), they commonly will use very similar mapping strategies and ancillary components. So in terms of organizing information for the purposes of this chapter, I will break down the available systems by ECU manufacturer, then a further division if there are different possible mapping strategies, and last I will give a number of details unique to particular models. If you know what brand of ECU is in the machine you are working on, you can immediately go to the appropriate section of this chapter; alternately, you can read it all the way through and learn about all of them.

Please note that this chapter is meant to be a general overview. While my attempt is to be as comprehensive as possible, I cannot list every detail of every system. Even if a particular motorcycle is not

Denso ECUs from the mid-1990s onward have a characteristic pair of high-density pin connectors, one with 34 pins, the other with 26 pins. This example is from a Kawasaki ZX-12R. Kawasaki Motor Corporation USA

listed, you should be able to determine a great deal about the system it uses by reading about other models with the same ECU, and checking the sensors seen on the motorcycle. If you have a bike with no MAP sensor, you can be sure it won't use speed-density mapping!

DENSO

Perhaps the most commonly seen EFI systems on today's motorcycles are variations of the Denso ECU, typically with Keihin throttle bodies. Kawasaki, Suzuki, and Yamaha use Denso systems on just about all of their fuel-injected sportbikes. Triumph's much-maligned inline four-cylinder TT600 sport model ended the EFI troubles that had plagued it by replacing the original system with the now-standard dual-butterfly Denso system found on so many Japanese bikes. And Aprilia switched very recently from their old Weber-Marelli unit to a Denso system for their RSV1000 Mille.

Characteristically, Denso ECUs are sequential-injection systems, with control for individual, sequentially fired stick-type coil-on-plug coils. Injectors are saturated-mode (with a variety of pintle/rod configurations), as one would expect on a production fuel injection system. The ECU's program is permanently burned into some form of ROM, and thus the same ECU cannot simply be moved to another model or type of motorcycle. There are almost always limp-home default values that can be substituted for a faulty sensor input.

A number of these systems have user-adjustable trim for the main fuel map, and many have individual cylinder idle trim adjustments. On most bikes, this is in onboard EEPROM; for the Yamaha GTS1000, tiny potentiometers were used instead. Most include a tipover switch to kill the engine when the bike has fallen; newer units replace the older, somewhat trouble-prone mechanical switch with a Hall-effect sensor. Now let's take a look at some of the individual components you might find in a Denso system, and how they differ between manufacturers and models.

Throttle Bodies

With the exception of Suzuki's TL, SV, and V-Strom models and the Aprilia Mille, all the Denso systems you're likely to encounter are made for inline four-cylinder bikes. Development of the Keihin throttle bodies progressed along those lines as well. Early Suzuki GSX-R models were plagued with throttle "feel" issues, with off-idle performance being abrupt and hand to control. Keihin and Suzuki solved this problem by creating the dual-butterfly system, where a secondary throttle plate was opened in stages by an ECU-controlled stepper motor. This allowed nearly all the advantages of having throttle bodies over carburetors, and greatly improved rideability. Such dual-butterfly throttle bodies can now be found on nearly all of the fuel-injected Kawasaki and Suzuki sportbikes, as well as the sole Triumph model with a Denso ECU.

Additionally, Suzuki has saved weight and lowered maintenance requirements by switching to a pair of dual-throat throttle bodies on the 2004 GSX-R1000, rather than four individual throttle bodies. Instead of three synchronization adjustments, there is now only one, and by eliminating the heavy steel bracket that holds the throttle bodies together into a rack, precious ounces can be saved.

Yamaha went a different route, choosing instead to use Mikuni-built throttle bodies with simple vacuum-operated

Keihin dual-butterfly throttle bodies are extremely common on Denso-equipped motorcycles. Seen here on a Kawasaki Z1000, a servomotor and second TPS are used to allow the ECU to control changes in intake airflow. This prevents throttle application from being too abrupt, as can happen with flat-slide carburetors. Note the small dual TPS sensors, one gray and one black.

but also helping curb emissions and fuel consumption.

All inline-four Denso systems (and the Suzuki V-twin sport machines) utilize a gear position sensor with only a handful of exceptions (those generally use a road speed sensor on the sprocket cover that doubles as a feed for the speedometer). They all have a tipover switch to shut off the engine in case the bike is dropped, which has come to be *de rigueur* on today's fuel-injected bikes. And importantly for the world of emissions, ignition timing is alpha-n based (throttle opening and engine speed in a 2D map), but also has a 1D map for coolant temperature, which allows for smoother idle when cold, quicker warm-up, and allows less conservative ignition mapping (since the ignition is now being controlled by a larger number of environmental inputs). In this, Denso is again paralleling the automotive world, where mapping based on such factors has been the norm for many years.

diaphragm and slide assemblies, just like those used in CV carbs! While reducing the overall advantage of throttle bodies over carbs, they are both lighter and simpler than equivalent dual-butterfly throttle bodies, so they do have the edge in some areas. They never need stepper motor calibration and tend to work well for a very long time without service. They also had the R7 that, not requiring smooth off-idle response, used throttle bodies similar to the original Suzuki type, with a huge 46-mm throat to accommodate tuning up to 140 bhp. It should be noted that the R7 also utilized shower injectors, as befit a full-on race machine.

An additional feature found on fuel-injected R1 and R6 models is the diagnostic dash panel. Used to run all EFI diagnostic tests, it eliminates the need for separate dealer tools to diagnose EFI troubles, and would be a welcome addition to future models from other manufacturers.

For the V-twin Suzukis, Mikuni took care of throttle body construction. By all appearances, they have more experience and expertise at making throttle bodies for twin-cylinder motorcycles, which is where you will typically see them.

ECU and Mapping

The Denso ECU is very similar in mapping strategy to that used by most EFI cars on the road today. At or near closed-throttle, the system operates on a speed density basis, and at larger throttle openings it will operate with an alpha-n base map. This allows us the advantages of speed density in areas where it shines, and likewise alpha-n. It's a great way of not only taming throttle response,

In addition, many of the Denso ECUs have capacity to trim the internal maps in a varying number of load/speed zones. This mapping can be done in any number of ways. The Yamaha R7, for instance, used a plug-in controller with three buttons, allowing switching between several built-in base maps, as well as providing four zones of trim (closed throttle/light load, closed throttle/heavy load, open throttle/light load, and open throttle/heavy load), and trimming the idle mixture on each cylinder individually. The control unit could also be used to set engine speeds for a shift light/rev limiter, and even to change ignition timing curves.

All of the Suzukis that I know come with internally trimmable ECUs that can be adjusted either by a tuning box from Yoshimura (commonly referred to as a "Yosh box") or a handheld unit from Factory Pro (called a Teka SFI). We'll cover them both in more detail in the chapter on aftermarket EFI products.

Unfortunately, neither Kawasaki nor Yamaha appear to offer this capability in their Denso ECUs. Perhaps the capability is there, but needs to be accessed in a different way from the Suzukis. If there is a way to remap the boxes internally, you can be sure there will be a product available for that purpose in the future. At this point, however, no one in the aftermarket has been able to discover such a capability.

All the Denso ECUs have some manner of fault-code warning. Most utilize a blinking LED to indicate fault codes. Yamaha goes a different route, using the dashboard of the R1 and R6 motorcycles as a miniature diagnostic unit. By setting the dash to dealer mode, one can conduct testing of all the sensors, injectors, coils, switches, relays, and even the ECU itself through the dash readout. The ECU will even hold stored fault codes, so should the problem be intermittent, one can still work toward finding the fault (this is similar to how most automotive ECUs operate).

A Well-Developed Entry

The Denso system, as it is currently being designed and built, clearly offers some significant advantages for inline four-cylinder motorcycles. It has a long development history, and has been used on a variety of machines with cylinders both large and small. Now it is firmly established and well developed, and you can be relatively sure when buying a new motorcycle with a Denso system that it will tend to have good throttle response and power output right out of the box.

MITSUBISHI

So far, only Kawasaki cruisers use a Mitsubishi ECU. Kawasaki uses this system on most of its VN1500 and VN1600 Vulcan V-twin cruisers. As with all V-twin injection systems, you will find air bypass screws and idle air bypass solenoids on the throttle body/bodies to provide sufficient idle speed with a closed throttle. Keihin sources its dual-throat throttle body assembly, and it takes advantage of a road speed sensor for both mapping changes and speedometer drive duties. The system is speed-density mapped at or near closed throttle, and utilizes alpha-n at wider throttle openings. Mitsubishi systems are typically found with saturated-drive injectors, as we have come to expect. As more cruisers from Japanese manufacturers appear with fuel injection, expect to see this system grow in popularity.

PGM-FI

Honda, being a manufacturer of automobiles as well as motorcycles, opted to take the early Denso design from the CX650 Turbo and expand it into what has become the PGM-FI line. These are designed and built in-house by Honda, and vary depending on application. Like the systems discussed previously, PGM-FI utilizes speed density mapping at or near closed throttle, and alpha-n mapping as the throttle opens farther. It has been used mostly on their V-four and V-twin sporting machines, but is now making solid inroads in their four-cylinder machines.

Because of vapor lock and heat soak issues on the V-four fuel rails, idle speed for the V-four bikes is generally controlled via idle air bypass solenoids rather than through fueling alone. In addition, starting with their racing RC-45 RVF750, the V-fours have used separate mapping for the front and rear cylinder banks to accommodate differences in cooling efficiency. In some cases, each individual cylinder can be trimmed in a similar fashion. On the engine's first revolution, all the injectors fire together until such time as the cam sensor delivers a signal to the ECU, allowing it to know engine phase. And like the RC-45 and RC211V (the

The Kawasaki Vulcan 1500 Mean Streak is one of a growing number of V-twin cruisers with fuel injection. The system used on Kawasaki cruisers is made by Mitsubishi. Kawasaki Motor Corporation USA

Honda is producing more and more motorcycles with EFI. The RC-51 combines power, grace, style, and efficiency. A key element of the package is Honda's PGM-FI fuel injection.

new five-cylinder four-stroke GP motor), the CBR600RR and CBR1000RR use "DSFI," Honda's dual-stage injection (a port and a shower injector for each cylinder), giving greater dynamic range for fuel flow, as well as greater fuel delivery in a short time period (such as at full throttle near redline).

The first VFR800i sport-touring bike was equipped with one O2 sensor for each cylinder, but this was later cut back to a single sensor in the exhaust. Some Honda models have ECU-controlled air injection into the exhaust for emissions control, as well as ECU-controlled variable intake geometry that allows intake resonances to be changed for maximum benefit at both high and low engine speeds. And there are even "race" ECUs available for some models, providing different ignition curves as well as the same sort of limited "trim" adjustment as that found on many of the Denso ECUs. Some newer models feature "EXUP"-style exhaust flappers that can change the tuned length and restriction of the exhaust system. All this adds up to flexibility and additional power with reduced emissions, especially important in small-displacement street machines.

Aside from having additional accessory functionality and more sophisticated tunability (especially on racing models), the function of these systems is fairly similar to most of the other speed density plus alpha-n systems we've covered. Honda has capitalized on their

automotive experience by adding these extra features and being noted for a very good throttle response feel on their injected motorcycles. As some professional tuners have noticed, a fairly wide window of throttle response can be had with minimal impact on emissions. Honda knows how to achieve excellence in both.

BOSCH

Bosch has been involved in manufacturing electronic fuel injection systems from their advent in commercial use. Because they have always developed and manufactured cutting-edge technology, they have a wealth of experience and ideas on which to capitalize. Their motorcycle products, available through BMW, are no exception.

Both Bosch and BMW are very secretive about the design and operation of their motorcycle EFI systems. In fact, technicians do not even perform diagnostic testing on any part of the EFI system! Instead, dealers plug the motorcycle being diagnosed into a special rolling computer cart, called MoDiTeC by BMW. This machine performs diagnostic tests on the EFI components, charging system, and starter motor and relay, and then simply tells the tech what components to check or replace. As a result, there are no shop manuals on the EFI systems from which to glean information.

While the LE-Jetronic system mentioned in the history chapter lived on through 1996 in the K75 series, and 1992 in the K100 series, BMW began introducing Bosch Motronic systems on its motorcycle product range starting in 1991 with models that had four valves per cylinder. Both the LE-Jetronic and all Motronic units up to present have a socketed integrated circuit containing all the maps—and most Motronic EPROMs contain multiple map sets.

There have been three different versions of the Motronic system found on BMW motorcycles. They are known as MA 2.0, MA 2.2, and MA 2.4. The differences between the systems are not clear, although the Motronic designation implies integrated fueling and ignition control. Oddly enough, the Motronic 2.4 system found on four-cylinder motorcycles appears to operate in batch-fire mode, which would not be what one might expect. Spark control is of the waste-fire variety, as well, rather than firing individual cylinders independently.

BMW was the first manufacturer to incorporate catalytic converters throughout their entire production range, starting in 1995. Along with the catalytic converters came O_2 sensors. Note that some catalyst-equipped models were available in certain markets without a catalyst, but not too often.

Idle is typically controlled by a servomotor which acts on the throttle stop by raising it in discrete "steps," which forces the throttle plates to open a certain amount to achieve desired idling speed. On touring bikes, with their heavy electrical loads, the ECU will insure proper charging at idle under heavy electrical demands by raising the isle speed to 1350 rpm! And on those touring models with a "reverse" gear for parking (which is actually the starter motor running geared to the back wheel), the idle is increased to 1500 rpm to offset the drain! The ECU also controls electric cooling fans via relay.

To accommodate differences in regulations between different countries (as well as differing fuel quality in some cases), a method was developed to allow a single ECU with a single removable PROM to be easily configured for a number of different characteristics or regulations. Bosch did this by combining a number of different maps on a single chip, with selection being controlled by

Even the police are taking advantage of the fine handling, ABS, and fuel injection found in BMW motorcycles. Here we see two California Highway Patrol examples of the R1150RT-P Police model, equipped with Bosch Motronic fuel injection.

a series of jumpers inside a small plastic module that looks very much like a relay. This is known as a "cat code plug," and changing the wiring of it can give access to different built-in maps. On a very limited number of machines with catalytic converters, there will be an available map on the stock chip that does not rely on closed-loop fueling at cruise.

Bosch fuel injection systems for cars are among the most sophisticated in the world. So it's fairly safe to bet that some models out there have knock detection, in addition to O_2 sensor feedback. A similar system made by Hella for the BMW F650 (called the BMS-C, for the German equivalent of BMW Compact Controller) has been confirmed as a learning system, with semi-permanent trim adjustments made automatically by comparing O_2 sensor values against target values under different operating conditions. Only by disconnecting the battery are the trims reset to 0.

MAGNETI MARELLI

Perhaps the fuel injection system most used on European motorcycles throughout the 1990s has been the Magneti Marelli line. Even Harley-Davidson used it for a number of years, starting with their first systems in the mid 1990s. Even though models and capabilities have changed, one thing has not: Magneti Marelli (sometimes called Weber-Marelli to denote the Weber-sourced throttle bodies) has always used straight alpha-n mapping, with or without closed-loop augmentation (with a single exception: certain Ducati 851s were equipped with a hot-wire MAF sensor, but this was found to give poor throttle response and was done away with rather quickly). A clever trick is used by Marelli to avoid the issues with TPS calibration that can plague alpha-n systems. When the ignition is first switched on, the ECU checks the TPS voltage and sets this as the "zero point". This prevents the user from fooling the system into richening the mixture by deliberately misadjusting the TPS, but it does make for extremely consistent throttle response, even if the TPS is in need of calibration.

Ducati has the longest history with Marelli. Starting in 1988 with its Desmoquattro line, Ducati adopted Marelli's race-based EFI system, called P7. The P7 ECU, which was discussed in more detail in the history chapter, was used until 1993 on various models, mainly SP and SPS homologation variants of the four-valved race bikes.

After the P7 came the P8, nicknamed "the big brain" because of the rather large case for the ECU. Very similar to the P7, the main difference was the ability to fire injectors separately in dual-injector per cylinder setups. This allowed the use of both shower

Above, a Marelli 1.5 M ECU installed in a Ducati Monster; on the left, a Marelli 1.6 M little brain installed in a Desmoquattro. Note the round black rubber plug to allow access for replacing the EPROM, as well as the Power Commander fitted to the bike. Images courtesy of the author; Motorcycles courtesy of GP Motorcycles

injectors and port injectors together, while still retaining the same computer and sensors. Also new for the P8 was the use of trimming potentiometers inside the ECU for setting idle mixture, which was increasingly important for meeting emissions regulations. The P8 was replaced on regular street bikes in 1995, but lived on in SP and SPS homologation bikes until 2000. It should be noted that some P7 and P8 boxes, especially early in their production run, had separate crank triggers for rpm signaling to the EFI system and spark generation. This would imply that the ignition timing system was merely in the same case as the EFI control system, and not truly integrated.

Replacing the P8 was the 1.6 M ECU, which has found a broad following among many makes. For Ducati, it was the main staple on their fuel-injected bikes between 1995 and 2000. It has seen frequent use with Aprilia, Moto Guzzi, Laverda, Cagiva, MV Agusta, and Bimota in addition to Ducati. There was even a Gas-Gas 400-cc four-stroke dirtbike equipped with a Marelli 1.6M injection system! With Ducati, it was nicknamed "the little

brain," since it was substantially smaller than the P8. This was to be the last of the Marelli systems to feature a socketed PROM, allowing a simple chip replacement to alter mapping. Using a 68HC11 processor running at 16 MHz, it was more than powerful enough for simple alpha-n mapping, and was often asked to run as many as four injectors off of four separate maps (for instance, the 996 street range, which had a pair each of shower and manifold-mounted injectors).

A further development of the Marelli ECUs started showing up on Ducati's air-cooled bikes in the late 1990s: the 1.5M. Eventually added to most of their line of air-cooled two-valve bikes before being supplanted by the new 5.9M ECU, the 1.5M had a flash-loadable map. For someone with the proper software, this meant quick changes could be made to the map with nothing more than a laptop. However, Ducati has kept the entry code for access to the flash map a closely guarded secret, and only a very few tuners have discovered how to remap these boxes. Even Ducati simply offered a replacement computer with a new map

The Ducati Multistrada is their entry into the growing big "trailie" market segment. Powered by a 1,000-cc air-cooled 2-valve twin, it shares the Marelli 5.9 M ECU with most of the rest of the current Ducati product range. Motorcycle courtesy of GP Motorcycles

installed along with its racing exhaust systems, available through dealers. A number of Moto Guzzi models also used the 1.5M, and Harley-Davidson even offers a Marelli race-only ECU with data acquisition!

Starting in 2001, a much smaller and more sophisticated unit showed up on the scene. Also a modification of a car ECU found in some Fiats, the 5.9M is the state of the art for Ducati. Running at 20MHz, containing twice as many mapping points as the 1.6M, and being closed-loop ready, this unit is better suited for increasingly stringent emissions regulations. First appearing on the four-valve Desmoquattro models, the 5.9M ECU can now be found throughout the Ducati model line. Expect to see it appear on other small-volume European motorcycles in the future.

The Ducati factory rarely took advantage of the ability of Marelli ECUs to be programmed with a trim table for the rear cylinder; its first appearances on factory ECUs occurred with the 1998 996

Biposto, followed in 1999 by the ST4, and in 2000 by the 748R. Only one aftermarket chip manufacturer takes advantage of this capacity: UltiMap, in Australia. In fact, they take advantage of the fact that the stock PROM also contains the runtime code for the MCU and allows further trimming of the maps by utilizing unused areas of their EEPROM for extra trim maps. This gives UltiMap chips the same sort of end-user tunability (with use of software or a remapping stand-alone handheld unit) as you find with the Suzuki sportbikes, a very handy addition for serious street riders and racers alike.

Further, all makes that had Marelli systems including a diagnostic port could be evaluated statically and while running by using a diagnostic computer (Marelli's MATHESIS unit, which can be used on a variety of different makes) or software. This would give access to all sensors in real time, as well as injector pulse width, and the MATHESIS unit could be used to run diagnostics on any component of the fuel injection system, in

Throttle body for the Delphi system for the Harley-Davidson V-Rod. The finned area above the bore is the mount for the IAC valve. Note the TPS to the left of the throttle body. A single split intake runner allows for a gentler curve for the air to follow when compared to a dual-port throttle body. Motorcycle courtesy of San Diego Harley-Davidson

conjunction with a special manual and the assistance of a technician. On some models, the cylinder offset trim tables could be adjusted using one of these methods as well.

VDO/WALBRO

Although little more than a footnote in the history of Harley-Davidson, Buell motorcycles used an EFI system from an unexpected source. VDO is probably best known as the company that manufactures gauges for German cars, and Walbro is best known for making snowmobile carburetors, but both have come up to speed with today's motor vehicle market.

Called DDFI (for Dynamic Digital Fuel Injection), it was a closed-loop system utilizing a waste spark ignition system and a 16-bit ECU. As you would expect with a two-cylinder bike, injection was sequential. It appears that most, if not all, motorcycles equipped with this system had narrow-band O_2 sensors and oper-

ated in closed-loop mode. There is an indication that this system will soon be supplanted by the Delphi system now in wide use on most Harley-Davidson-branded motorcycles.

DELPHI

You may find it hard to believe, but the most sophisticated EFI system found to date on any production bike is being fitted to only one make: Harley-Davidson.

The Delphi system first appeared on Harleys in 1999 and has been added to the groundbreaking Buell XB9R for 2003. Featuring the ability to store intermittent trouble codes, ion-sensing technology, and closed-loop operation, they even save costs by utilizing the same coil pack that has been used since the mid-1990s on the Marelli-equipped Harley-Davidson models. It even interfaces with an optional alarm module to function as an immobilizer in case of theft!

This shining Harley-Davidson V-Rod represents the pinnacle of motorcycle engineering today. With an engine co-designed by Porsche and a Delphi EFI system that exceeds the capabilities of most current automotive EFI systems, it shows that Harley has invested in the future.

Like most other systems available, the Delphi unit operates in speed-density mode at smaller throttle openings and switches to alpha-n running at heavier loads. It is also equipped with an O_2 sensor and can operate in closed-loop mode. But by far the most interesting feature is the aforementioned ion sensing. As discussed in more depth in the chapter on future developments, ion sensing allows the ECU to observe the results of combustion using a small current passed through the spark plug to act as a sensor. Not only can it detect misfire (which could damage the catalytic converter in addition to causing lower fuel economy and poorer running) and detonation, but the ECU can then take corrective measures to eliminate the cause of the problem. This puts Harley on the cutting edge of *any* production EFI technology, and their system should be adaptable to emissions regulations for years to come.

Like the more advanced of the Marelli systems, the Delphi system allows diagnostics via software that can be run on a computer or laptop. It can also store sophisticated diagnostic information internally, assisting technicians in discovering the true nature of any

problems with the EFI system. The Delphi system was introduced on the 2001 Twin-Cam models, and continued on with the 2002 introduction of the V-Rod, another technological innovation from Harley-Davidson. This system will surely continue in usage for many years with Harley-Davidson, and we may even see it being adopted by other manufacturers when the pressure of emissions regulations turns up the heat on their current EFI systems.

SAGEM

Even though SAGEM of France has been bought by Johnson Controls (JCAE to be specific), the MC2000 and MC1000 ECUs are still commonly referred to as "SAGEM" systems. Like the Marelli systems, they are strictly alpha-n, but due to the amazing flexibility built into their ECUs, they can be adapted to a wide variety of motorcycles with nothing more than a flashing of the runtime code. This makes the SAGEM ECUs well-suited to a wide variety of motorcycles, from Triumph's three- and four-cylinder motorcycles to Excelsior-Henderson's big twins to Cannondale's single-cylinder off-road bikes and ATVs.

All SAGEM-based systems have some commonality: They all include (or can at least drive) an idle air bypass stepper solenoid, and they all operate in alpha-n as their sole open-loop mapping mode. Like Marelli ECUs, SAGEM systems seem to work best on one- or two-cylinder motorcycles. The more throttle plates you add for a given displacement, the more sensitive an alpha-n system becomes to small changes in throttle opening near closed throttle. This would account for the difficulty in providing smooth throttle response on three-cylinder, and especially four-cylinder, motorcycles equipped with SAGEM systems. Triumph debuted their TT600 four-cylinder motorcycle with this system, but has since switched to using a Denso system for improved throttle response smoothness off-idle.

The IAC valve has several functions on Triumph models, some of which are found on other SAGEM-equipped motorcycles as well. In addition to controlling idle speed, the IAC valve is also used to add extra air on closed-throttle engine braking (which helps prevent unburned fuel from building up in the exhaust, causing backfiring and possible catalyst damage), and it also functions as part of the purge system on California models, allowing fuel vapors from the fuel tank to be burned off in the engine rather than escaping to the atmosphere. And it can even assist in part-throttle power compensation when the machine is run at high altitudes. If the AAP sensor shows the pressure to be below a certain point, the IAC stepper allows extra air past the throttle plate, helping make up for the less dense air at higher altitudes.

Triumph

Triumph was the first to adopt the SAGEM system in the motorcycle world, and, by and large, the system has served them well. Early machines were equipped with the MC2000 ECU and had cam position and road speed sensors as you would find on most modern EFI machines. These were both eliminated on later models. It is very likely that the ECU determines engine phase by watching for the slight slowing of the engine during cranking as the #1 cylinder reaches the top of its compression stroke.

The Triumph line is the only one I have found that used the MC2000 system, which was SAGEM's first to see motorcycle use. Triumph went to the improved MC1000 system in 2000, in an interesting quirk. The primary differences are the improved connectors and the integration of the AAP sensor into the ECU case (it connects to the airbox by a length of tubing in most cases).

Since adopting fuel injection in the late 1990s, Triumph has almost always used the alpha-n SAGEM system. Ideal for low-volume producers, the hardware offers capabilities that make it very attractive to automotive and motorcycle constructors alike.

The Futura is one of only two Aprilia models using the SAGEM ECU. The Capo Nord is the other. They represent a more touring-oriented nature than the Marelli-equipped Aprilias. Motorcycle courtesy of GP Motorcycles

Another short-lived low-volume make, Excelsior-Henderson had a very brief day in the sun. However, using the SAGEM system confers an advantage to those who now own orphaned bikes. A slight modification in aftermarket software for Triumphs allows owners to remap and diagnose their Super-X motorcycles far into the future. Tim Marsteiner

With the demise of Cannondale, it has become exceedingly difficult to find the off-road motorcycles they manufactured. I was only able to find one of their ATVs to photograph, but the drivetrain is nearly identical to that of the motorcycle, and they share all their SAGEM EFI hardware. ATV courtesy of Alba Action Sports

Other Manufacturers

In addition to Triumph, which has been using SAGEM systems almost exclusively since the introduction of EFI to their product line in 1997, SAGEM systems have also been used by Excelsior-Henderson on their large-displacement V-twin cruiser, as well as Aprilia (with their Futura and Capo Nord sport-touring models, as well as their Pegaso 650ie single-cylinder machine) and Cannondale (on both their off-road motorcycle and ATV, sharing a common single-cylinder engine between them). As you can see, the strictly alpha-n fueling strategy has been easier to work with on larger-displacement single- and twin-cylinder motorcycles.

Excelsior-Henderson

The Excelsior-Henderson iteration, found on the 99-00 Super-X model, is actually set up almost identically to the Triumph layout, leading to speedy development and tuning for the now-defunct company. They used a similar handheld diagnostic and tuning tool (called "The Examinator") through their dealerships, and in fact had pretty much identical sensor setups and long-term trim mapping strategies, differing mainly in that the E-H had a road speed sensor and could not self-calibrate its TPS. Like most of the Triumphs, though, they are closed-loop enabled as well. The Super-X uses a dual-butterfly throttle body, with a separate intake runner for each cylinder. And the trouble codes are just as detailed for this machine as for the Triumphs, all of which shows that there are only the most minor of differences between the two systems.

Cannondale

Cannondale motorcycles were a sight to behold. Completely new, they featured a backwards cylinder head, with the intake manifold incorporating part of the frame and steering head, and the exhaust exiting where a carburetor would usually live on a traditional four-stroke dirtbike.

Cannondale went a slightly different route with their SAGEM system (tuned for them by Optimum Power Technology), but kept the same basics in terms of mapping architecture. It is an alpha-n system at heart, like the other SAGEM applications, and that suits a single-cylinder engine mainly used for performance quite well. And like the others, it uses an IAC valve to control idle at a variety of engine temperatures. It also featured an ECU-controlled radiator fan, same as our other examples. And like the others, new maps could be flashed via connection to a computer, although the connection here is somewhat different.

One of the most exciting things about the Cannondale was that it was the first consumer motorcycle to offer multiple maps that were user-selectable on the fly. A switch on the handlebars allowed the rider to choose from three separate maps, and apparently to add trims as well. Thus, a rider could change the character and throttle response of the bike with the flick of a switch, alleviating the time-consuming jetting changes that were necessary in the past for best response and performance at a motocross race.

The OPT/SAGEM system offered much greater flexibility in tuning than its brethren, both for ease of factory setup and potential future tuning. While the software gave the usual diagnostic and calibration tools (like verifying the TPS setting), it also had variables that were usually set at the factory: "throttle body leakage" (which is essentially the amount of air that bleeds past a closed throttle plate), injector flow rate, and injector offset (which is actually the dead time between an injector event signal reaching the injector, and the time where the injector is actually open and delivering fuel). The flow rate setting allows fine calibration of fuel delivery to the stock injectors (essential for proper throttle response in a single-cylinder dirtbike), but potentially also offered the possibility of fitting larger injectors at some point. And if the throttle body or fuel injectors were ever in need of replacement, the replacement parts came packaged with new values to enter into the ECU, so the bike would require little or no adjustment after the installation of new components. And, of course, one could monitor the sensor values and IAC valve position with the software while the engine was running, making diagnostics that much easier for the dealership mechanic.

THE ODDBALL: DITECH AND THE APRILIA SR50

Of course, there has to be an "odd man out" in everything in life. In the case of motorcycle OEM fuel injection systems, it is Aprilia's little SR50 scooter that takes the honors. It's not equipped with just any old two-stroke motor—it has a low-emissions two-stroke designed by Orbital Technologies. Orbital got together with a big name in automotive electronics, Siemens, and formed a joint venture called Synerject, which, among other things, designed and developed the electronic GDI (gasoline direct injection) system for the DITECH.

What makes Orbital's engine so different from other two-strokes is that it does not burn oil in the combustion chamber. Instead of using crankcase compression like traditional reed-valve two-stroke motors, it uses a centrifugal supercharger to fill the combustion chamber, with the crankcase being sealed off from the combustion chamber entirely. The supercharger develops an amazing 5 bar of boost (1 bar = atmospheric pressure, or 14.7 psi), or 74.5 psi. And what's more, it's not a port-injection system like the vast majority we have discussed so far; it's a direct injection system. Fuel is injected at very high pressure directly into the combustion chamber.

To get exemplary fuel economy and low emissions from a two-stroke, a stratified-charge system is used. Similar to the lean-burn prechamber seen first in late-1970s Honda CVCC automobiles, a rich mixture is held in a small prechamber and ignited there, and this raises pressure (and thus temperature) in the main, much leaner area of mixture, allowing very lean operating mixtures without misfire. In addition, the use of the prechamber means that the fuel can be injected into the prechamber over a much longer period of time than is available with port injection, further enhancing fuel vaporization.

The upshot of all this technology is that the SR50 lowers oil consumption by 60% and fuel consumption by 40% over similar reed-valve two-stroke motors. This adds up to an 80% reduction in pollutants in the exhaust gases, allowing the SR50 to meet the newer Euro 2 European emissions standards without the use of a catalytic converter. A simple alpha-n system is responsible for not only fuel and spark, but for oil delivery as well.

The DITECH uses a fairly simple and basic form of GDI, with a fairly simple fueling strategy. This allows for improvements in cold starting, fuel economy, emissions, and power output without incurring great expense. We will definitely be seeing more of such systems on two- and four-stroke motorcycles in the years to come.

HOW DO WE CHANGE IT?

We've come a long way in this book. We started out with a thorough evaluation of how an engine works, what we need to measure to determine fueling, what we measure it with, and what we do with the data. We've dealt with the theory and practice of turning a pile of hardware into a calibrated system for the delivery of fuel, and we've seen some details of the systems that come installed on our bikes and how they evolved.

But if you're reading this book, chances are pretty good that you're not satisfied with the compromises embraced by the manufacturers. You might be a mechanic interested in understanding enough about a system to diagnose and repair it, but more likely, you're someone who wants to tune a system to your own ends—a race mechanic, a performance tuner, or just someone who wants their own bike to be something special. And to achieve your ends, you will need to modify, or possibly even replace, the stock EFI. If you're a real tinkerer, you might even be inclined to build a system from scratch for a bike that came equipped with carbs from the factory.

Since most factory systems offer little if any ability to change the stock settings, we have to turn to the aftermarket to achieve those aims. We can use a variety of different methods. And as we have discussed in other areas of fuel injection, your choices in the aftermarket world will depend on which compromises you want to make, and which you don't.

The purpose of this chapter is not to be a comprehensive listing of every available aftermarket option for every motorcycle ever built. Rather, I will explain the various classes of aftermarket products and illustrate each class with a few examples. I'll discuss the pros and cons of each, so you can make an educated choice when it comes to making up your own mind about how to best suit your particular needs and wants.

To Answer, We Must Evaluate

It may seem obvious to some, but the first step in tuning your fuel injection system to suit your own needs and wants is to sit down with the factory service manual, this book, a pad of paper, and a pencil. You'll want to have read this book thoroughly, especially the sections on how the engine works and modeling strategy.

Start by charting the advantages and shortcomings of your current system. Moving on from there, map out briefly on your pad what it is you hope to accomplish. What are your goals? Are you a drag racer interested mainly in full-throttle high-rpm running? Are you a road racer, requiring the smoothest possible throttle response to keep traction while cornering? Are you a street rider who wants to maintain throttle response and get some extra power without too much investment or difficulty? Knowing what you are trying to accomplish is an important part of deciding how to achieve your goals! Slapping on some component or other because all your buddies have one is as likely to make things worse as it is to make them better. And most of the aftermarket EFI hardware out there is anything but cheap. Think first, and spend your money wisely!

And last, consider other possible ways of achieving your goals, and list their benefits and drawbacks. In some cases, an improvement in exhaust tone and a bit of extra power can be gained from a simple exhaust change, without any modification to the EFI system itself. Knowledge is power when it comes to reaching any goal, and making power with a motorcycle is definitely in this class.

At this point, you're ready for the rest of this chapter.

Remapping Tools

Obviously, the simplest way to effectively change the tune of an EFI system is to change the maps used by the ECU. This is not always simple, though. Let's look at the various products that fall into this category and see if we can sort out the benefits and limitations.

Replacement PROMs

If you have an EFI-equipped bike more than a few years old, there is a good chance that the maps are stored in a socketed, removable PROM. Before the explosion of affordable flashable EEPROMs, using a DIP (dual inline package) socketed PROM was the best way to allow for alteration of the stock map. ECUs with socketed PROMs include the Marelli P7, P8, and 1.6 M ECUs, as well as the Bosch ECUs.

Commonly referred to as "chips," these aftermarket PROMs come in a variety of forms and with a variety of capabilities. The most basic chips will simply replace the base 2D fuel map, and leave ignition timing, delta alpha (accelerator pump or transient), and coolant temperature maps alone. This is fine if you are looking for a little extra power or somewhat smoother running, but it will generally not do much for overall performance. Slightly more advanced chips will change the transient mapping to smooth out throttle response. Some chips for the Aprilia Mille, for instance, have small tweaks to the base fueling map and somewhat larger adjustments to the transient (acceleration) mapping, giving a smoother throttle response without offering any other real benefit. They certainly feel better while riding the bike, but they don't go "all the way." The most advanced chips will usually alter most of the 1D fueling maps as well as the base map and the ignition map. And some very special ones, like the FIM UltiMap chips for Ducatis, unlock capabilities in the stock ECU that were unused even by the factory.

An example of a well-done chip would be the Factory Pro RSVZ1413 chip for the 1998–2001 Aprilia RSV1000 Mille/Mille R and 1998–2002 Aprilia SL1000 Falco. This chip

The RSVZ1413 EPROM for Aprilias from Factory Pro Tuning. This chip replaces the stock EPROM inside the ECU and offers both new mapping (with two user-selectable maps) and some additional functionality for the ECU. Chip courtesy of Factory Pro Tuning

| T1 | T2 | T3 | T4 | T5 | T6 | T7 | T8 | T9 | T10 |

AP BThr
OP
G Lat
StrAng
SPos FB

6000
5000
4000

not only bests the stock chip by a wide margin, but it is the only chip that significantly alters the stock (and very poor) ignition timing maps. Like the stock chip (and most other aftermarket offerings), it contains two maps that are user-selectable, but an addition to the functionality of the stock chip (and most of the aftermarket ones, as well) is the activation of the trim potentiometers on the ECU. They allow one to tune the closed-throttle mixture in each cylinder independently for optimal idle and transitional throttle behavior.

To develop proper maps for the machine, a device called an emulator was used. This plugs into the stock ECU in place of the PROM and allows real-time alteration of the map values cell by cell. The emulator connects to a computer, which displays the map or maps of your choice on the monitor, and allows you to see which cells of the map are being accessed in real time. By running the motorcycle on an eddy current dynamometer (or dyno) with a four-gas exhaust analyzer, it was possible to tune the base fueling and ignition maps for best power at all engine speeds and loads (and this includes things like cylinder offsets where applicable!). Some trial-and-error testing leads to the best possible transient and coolant temperature mapping, and final tweaks were done by road testing. As I've noted before, very small changes in the fueling and ignition maps can make fairly dramatic changes in the throttle response and feel of the bike during throttle transitions, so this is an important part of chipmaking, and is where much of the "craftsmanship" aspect comes into play.

Once final values are determined using the emulator, the actual values contained in the map are burned to the PROM by a software-driven programming box. PROMs can be written to only once, and once burned, cannot be altered, much like a CD-R recordable disc. EPROMs can be erased (thus the "E" in the name) by exposing them to ultraviolet light and then re-burned (more like a hard drive, because they can have new data burned to them). Since the actual instructions (the program run by the MCU) remain the same, most of the contents of the chip will be the same as with the original factory chip; typically, only the values contained in the map areas will differ. In the case of the RSVZ1413 chip, there is one significant difference in the program area from the stock chip. A section of code that allows use of the idle mixture trim potentiometers (pots) on the ECU itself has been added, thus giving some additional end-user tunability.

The final result, when installed in the motorcycle, improves greatly on the factory chip (which was clearly developed to help meet noise and emissions standards), especially in the area of ignition timing. In fact, the bleed screw allowing air bypass at idle must be closed substantially after fitting the RSVZ1413 chip, because the bike makes so much more power even at idle that the idle speed goes up over 500 rpm! Many other chips on the market for this application have completely stock ignition maps, thus losing out on much of what is gained with Factory Pro's offering.

It is very difficult to substantiate the various claims made by chipmakers near and far. Without a chip reader and access to a number of different chips, usually enhanced by an emulator program (which will be able to sift out the map data, since it can be located anywhere on the chip), there is no real way to know exactly how one chip differs from another. Your best bets are usually to ask around and see what other people are using on your particular bike, to contact the manufacturer of the chip and ask pertinent questions, and to find knowledgeable tuners who have experience with your make and model of motorcycle. Some facilities will have an emulator and programmer and can burn a custom chip for your

particular motorcycle. As with carburetor jetting, there is never a substitute for a custom tune. When done properly, it ensures that you have the optimum mapping to achieve your goals, whatever they may be. A generic chip will usually be very close, but cannot account for wear, calibration, and adjustment of the various components in the drivetrain that might affect tuning.

There are few other disadvantages to using an aftermarket chip. The stock injectors, fuel pump, and mapping strategy are ultimate limitations. Typically, the injectors and fuel pump are sized in excess of what is needed by the engine to allow for wear over time, so unless you have a very modified engine, they should not be an issue. The mapping strategy is typically not much of a problem, except in certain cases (which I will cover in more detail in the aftermarket ECU section). And one significant advantage to replacement PROMs is that, like the stock mapping, ignition timing is separated from injector event triggering, meaning the ignition timing can be altered with no adverse consequences caused to fueling.

In short, an aftermarket PROM is a good option for most bikes that can use them, especially when the engine is not highly modified, but it can be hard to tell the difference between a well-designed set of maps and those that are just adequate without expensive tools or knowledge. And of course, only a limited number of ECUs have socketed PROMs. If yours isn't one of them, you'll have to find another way. Most PROMs only carry a single set of maps, meaning that if the tune is not adequate for your needs, you'll need to eat your losses and find another one (BMW chips usually contain multiple maps, and some FIM UltiMap chips can be trimmed, but they are the exception rather than the rule).

Flash Mapping Software/Hardware

Newer ECUs often take advantage of affordable, compact flashable RAM. Flash RAM is actually a bit of a misnomer, since all other RAM (or random-access memory) is volatile. That is, it requires electrical power to retain its data. Flash RAM is actually an EEPROM (the two Es stand for electronically erasable). With a certain command fed in through a data channel, the contents of the RAM can be deleted, and new data can be flashed (or written) to the ECU. The interface between tuner and ECU can either be through a dedicated electronic device or via software run on a computer. In each case, a cable connects the ECU through a diagnostic or tuning port. Software solutions available today include TuneBoy and TuneEdit from Wayne MacDonald for SAGEM-equipped Aprilias and Triumphs, its adaptation for Excelsior-Henderson motorcycles from X-Man and Screamin' Eagle software for Delphi-equipped Harley-Davidsons (which features not only fueling adjustment and real-time sensor readings, but can data-log a selection of 28 engine variables for up to an hour, as well as allowing mapping in speed-density mode for street, or alpha-n mode for track). Hardware solutions include the Game Boy from Triumph Motorcycles USA, "The Examinator" from the now-defunct Excelsior-Henderson, and a similar diagnostic tool from Harley-Davidson, as well as Suzuki remapping tools from Yoshimura (the famous "Yosh box") and Factory Pro Tuning (the TEKA SFI, offering such features as individual cylinder idle trim, five load ranges, and on-the-fly tuning available nowhere else).

On the one hand, flashable RAM has distinct advantages over a socketed PROM. There are no pins to bend while inserting a new chip, no chance of static electricity destroying delicate electronics in the ECU, and no seal to break on the ECU's case (voiding the warranty on this rather expensive component). And it provides a great deal more flexibility for the user. You can load multiple maps

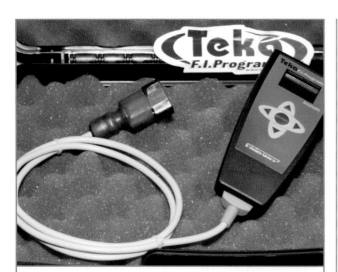

The TEKA SFI tuning tool allows quick and easy access to the broad trim tables in Suzuki's Denso ECUs. Boasting individual idle trims, five load ranges, and twice the adjustment range of its famous "Yosh box" predecessor from Yoshimura, its big advantage over other tuning tools is its real-time alteration of fueling, allowing brave tuners to remap the machine while riding it! TEKA SFI courtesy of Factory Pro Tuning

until you find the one you like best, or in some cases even design your own map (or trim) to suit your tastes and goals. A single hardware mapping tool can tune an unlimited number of bikes, making this a good choice for a dealership or tuning shop. However, most of the software-based remapping tools are keyed to the serial number of the motorcycle, preventing use on multiple bikes unless you buy an expensive site license. And in cases where the stock ECU has unused capabilities, software solutions can sometimes add functionality not available on the stock machine (like the addition of an ECU-controlled radiator fan or removal of the rev limiter on the Excelsior-Henderson with the use of TuneBoy software).

But the disadvantages are fairly large compared to a PROM. For one thing, either a dedicated piece of hardware (like the Factory Pro Tuning TEKA SFI remapping tool for Suzukis) or a software package with cable (like Wayne MacDonald's TuneEdit software for SAGEM-equipped Aprilias and Triumphs) is required in order to change the mapping. Either is costly, and in the case of software, you must use a computer as well. Some bikes, such as the Suzukis, do not allow any remapping of ignition timing, which may be a disadvantage for some users. Most ECUs use elaborate "handshaking" routines of communication between computer/remap tool and ECU that are hard to crack, making aftermarket solutions less plentiful and more expensive. And as mentioned, most of the software packages will only remap a single motorcycle, although it will typically allow it to be remapped an unlimited number of times. Those who wish for data-logging capacity will be disappointed to know that most software-based solutions do not provide this either. And of course, to tune for best effect in most cases will require an eddy-current dyno (and the odd man out here is the TEKA SFI, which can tune a fuel-injected Suzuki very well based solely on road testing, when following the instructions supplied by Factory Pro Tuning).

Because remapping tools vary widely in their ease of use, flexibility, and options, it pays to take a very close look at what you will be getting before you buy. Race tuners and shops will prob-

ably be more interested in hardware remapping tools where available due to their reusability. For them, the tool is essentially another shop tool, able to perform the same function on an unlimited number of bikes. However, a software-based solution is more likely to be the preferred choice for individual riders. They usually cost a bit less and can remap a single motorcycle an unlimited number of times, allowing for future modifications to the bike.

Add-On Boxes

Many consumers are not comfortable with the idea of tuning a fuel injection system themselves. Even more are not comfortable with actually replacing a PROM or altering the tune of the stock system directly. Thus the market for add-on boxes was born.

A staple of the automotive world in the early days of EFI, add-on boxes have some distinct advantages—and disadvantages. Since there are a number of different boxes that operate under a number of different philosophies, I will divide them into classes to better explain their operation.

Techlusion "Fuel Nanny"/TFI

Three devices actually fall under this description: The analog 83i, a digital replacement for the original (called the TFI 1030i/1030, with and without OEM connectors), and a new version for BMWs with O_2 sensors called the R259. I lump them all together here because the principle is the same in all of the boxes, regardless of internal electronics. They all use the same methods for tuning, and all attach to the stock EFI in the same manner. In addition, both the RevTech DFO and the Horsepower, Inc., boxes for Harley-Davidson motorcycles are simply repackaged FN devices. The Terry Components Terminal Velocity box appears to be a repackaged FN as well.

The FN, developed by the people who produced the original DynoJet Power Commander, is incredibly simple in its user interface and manner of operation. Most units have only one set of connections to the motorcycle, combining a ground wire and two other wires per cylinder that splice into the fuel injector wiring (the TFI 1030i, and possibly the R259, have OEM connectors already installed, so that it simply plugs into the original injector harness). The device takes its power and engine speed signals from the injector harness, which is fed with constant vBatt (+12v) to power the injectors. By measuring the injector pulse rate and changes in the pulse rate over time, the unit can determine both engine speed and acceleration. The R259 model also interfaces through the O_2 sensor, but I have not seen installation instructions for this model yet. It appears that the device richens the mixture by lengthening the stock injector pulse width by grounding the injector for longer than the "stock" ECU orders. The amount of additional pulse width can be controlled (to a degree) by the end user.

The user interface is ingenious and remarkably simple. A total of three potentiometers control fueling, one each for low-load and high-load fueling, and a third that selects the crossover between the two. Changing the settings will alter the amount of additional pulse width. The unit also has an accelerator pump feature that is preset and not user-adjustable.

The idea is that at cruise or other low-load condition, fueling will be richened by an amount determined by the first pot. Under heavy acceleration or high-speed running, fueling will be richened by an amount determined by the second pot. The crossover is to be set to deliver as smooth a transition as possible between the two adjustment ranges.

THE AFTERMARKET

T1 T2 T3 T4 T5 T6 T7 T8 T9 T10

ET
AP BThr
OP
G Lat
StrAng
SPos FB

6000
5000
4000
3000

The advantages are obvious. It requires no computer to use, is simple to tune, and does not change anything in the stock system until after the ECU. And thus far, the R259 is the only device that will change oxygen sensor signals to richen closed-loop operation. While richening closed-loop defeats some of the emissions controls, it can often smooth out transitions between open- and closed-loop running, which can result in surging and unstable idle (this is especially prominent on BMW twins, and can be seen on other motorcycles operating on strict alpha-n mapping in the stock ECU). In fact, the current FN for BMW applications has a "fooler" function for the O_2 sensor, which helps greatly with the surging problem when switching between closed- and open-loop modes. Unfortunately, this feature raises emissions and will actually end up damaging the catalytic converter, although it definitely makes stubborn BMWs more livable (it should be noted that careful throttle body calibration and idle air bypass adjustment alone can get rid of most of the surging in many cases).

The disadvantages, however, are numerous. First, on most models you are required to splice into the stock injector harness. As I have mentioned earlier in the book, connector resistance and wiring harness issues can be a key factor in losing power from that delivered by optimal fueling, as well as long-term rideability issues resulting from corrosion or high resistance. By cutting open the insulation on the injector wiring, you pretty much guarantee that there will be eventual problems with the harness, if none are created during installation. And even if you remove the device for warranty service, you may find that a fuel injection problem on your bike will no longer be covered under warranty due to your modifications. A short in the device could seriously damage your electrical system, wiring harness, or ECU.

But the big problem, in my eyes, is that the device is just too coarse and crude. While it is terribly easy to adjust, that very simplicity works against the fine tuning of the existing ECU. Because it has no way to measure throttle opening, it can only determine engine rpm; and since you can accelerate hard at low engine speeds, or cruise at high engine speeds, the device cannot really "see" load. In addition, with only two ranges and no sensors, there is a very wide variety of operating conditions under which it will alter the injector's on time by the same amount. The very simplicity of the system is its biggest drawback. Each setting covers a very great number of different operating conditions, and the device can only add fuel. It cannot change the ignition timing, and maximum fueling is still limited to what the stock injectors can deliver with stock fuel pressure.

The Fuel Nanny and its offspring operate under the principle that a slightly rich mixture will lose a little power but provide good drivability. In addition, a bike that is relatively leaner (as with closed-loop mode) will idle and closed-throttle cruise poorly when throttle bodies or TPS are out of sync/calibration, but will idle much more smoothly if richened (even if it becomes slightly too rich in one or more cylinders). If your main aim is to cure rideability issues, and you are not concerned about emissions, a slight drop in gas mileage, or precision in throttle transitions, the Fuel Nanny can be a useful option for unmodified or lightly modified bikes. Still, a careful calibration of the TPS and synchronization of the throttle bodies may cure some or all drivability issues, especially in closed-loop and alpha-n EFI systems. However, it would make a great deal of sense to stick with models equipped with OEM connectors. Splicing into the EFI harness is a dangerous game to play, and it can cause significant and expensive problems down the road.

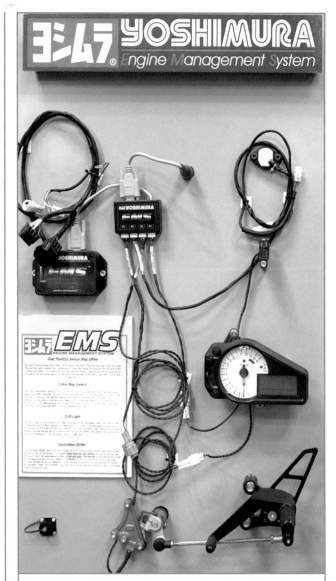

The Yoshimura EMS system has many useful racing add-ons, but under the hood, it is really a Power Commander with a daughterboard. Such boxes are the only way to remap some systems today, but they are not perfect.

68HC11-Based Add-Ons

The predominant class of add-on boxes in use today is essentially a small ECU, similar in function to the stock ECU. It either conditions input signals to the stock ECU, fooling it into offering different fueling and ignition, or changes the pulse width being delivered to the stock injectors. Programs and "canned" (prepackaged) maps are available for a wide variety of motorcycles. Depending on how the device is programmed, it can be an effective tool in changing the fueling for a stock or lightly modified bike, and it offers several distinct advantages over the FN. But it is not without its own issues as well.

"Fooler" Boxes

The original DynoJet Power Commander, Power Commander II, and PC IIr, as well as the Yoshimura EMS, are in this category.

Also included is the forthcoming Factory Pro Tuning TEKA EMS, which works under the same principles. Using a 68HC11 MCU, these devices read a number of sensor inputs and alter the sensor signals before passing them on to the stock ECU. This allows alteration of fueling as well as ignition timing, again with a ceiling based on the amount of fuel that can be delivered by the stock injectors using stock fuel pressure.

Similar to many OEM EFI systems, these "fooler" boxes use a 2D alpha-n map as a base map for fueling alteration. In most cases, they will richen or lean the mixture by altering the coolant temperature signal to the ECU, thus utilizing the built-in 1D CT map within the stock ECU. Because the stock ECU will richen the mixture when engine coolant is colder, manipulating this signal will "fake out" the stock ECU into delivering a different mixture than it was originally programmed to. The "fooler" boxes that offer ignition mapping typically offer a 2D alpha-n map for that as well. The Power Commander-based units also allow global trims for three different load ranges from pushbuttons on the unit itself. This can be handy if you are riding and a sudden change in altitude causes running problems, and you need to adjust the EFI but don't have a laptop with you.

It should be noted that while the Yoshimura EMS system offers a lot of extra functionality (shift lights, ignition shifter kill, and more), it is actually a Power Commander with an additional daughterboard attached to control the extra accessories. Power Commander maps can be used in a Yosh EMS, and vice versa (and this can be a very good thing, since the Yosh EMS maps are generally acknowledged as being somewhat superior to the provided DynoJet maps). The upcoming Factory Pro TEKA EMS will offer such things as closed-loop remapping on bikes equipped with an O_2 sensor, the ability to send the unit back to the factory to be rewired for use on a different motorcycle (so you don't have to buy a new one every time you replace your current bike with a new one), and the ability to add on individual race-type components (instead of having to buy an entire package, as is the case with the Yosh EMS system).

Because these boxes use a very flexible Motorola 68HC11 MCU, they can be programmed in any number of different ways. The throttle position mapping can be tuned by the box's manufacturer in the same way as Ducati's Marelli systems. The map points can be assigned to any throttle position desired, allowing fine-tuning in areas where precision is most needed. And the same MCU and support hardware can be wired and programmed to work with any motorcycle EFI system available (as long as it has a TPS), allowing economies of scale in production (and hopefully, lower cost). You can create your own maps with the software provided by the manufacturer, and you can also download and use many maps created by other people. These are often sold or traded over the Internet, allowing a broad ability to tune and experiment by tuner, repair facility, and consumer alike.

Because of the flexibility in terms of number of inputs and how they are handled, it is possible to do things like map the gear position sensor so that, for instance, you can get the extra low-end power of the Hayabusa in sixth gear, but can switch back to fifth gear mapping when approaching the soft limit imposed by the factory in sixth gear (currently, this functionality is only available in the Yoshimura EMS). As has been mentioned, the manufacturer can also alter the target point for closed-loop mode, helping control throttle response and prevent lean surging (this is not currently available, either). And theoretically, you can also modify EXUP-style or variable-length intake valve operation to gain additional power, another planned development for the near future. The forthcoming Factory Pro offering promises to do all of these things on models so equipped, as well as offering a service where you can mail your unit back to the factory to be rewired and reprogrammed to work with a different motorcycle.

There are some significant disadvantages with this design, especially as certain manufacturers have developed it. First, most EFI systems operate at least some of the time in speed-density mode. The "fooler" boxes only operate in alpha-n mode, and in cases where the stock ECU is in speed-density mode, it is probable that there will be several running conditions that provide different fueling from the stock ECU, but get the same fueling modification from the add-on box. This may or may not be a problem for you; as with carburetors, you may need to pick the best compromise between those running conditions that are linked by the action of the add-on box, sacrificing in one area to gain in another. Second, the response of stock ECUs to changes in coolant temperature is not linear. This means that on some motorcycles, it may be extremely difficult to get enough precision in richening the mixture, especially when the bike is cold. In addition, ignition timing is also often altered by the stock ECU as coolant temperature changes; this means that the add-on box is unable to avoid changing ignition timing when changing the coolant temperature signal to the ECU. In some cases, this can be compensated for in the base map for ignition, but for add-on boxes without ignition control in particular, this is not possible. In some other cases, ignition timing cannot be kept precisely at factory mappings regardless.

While we are on the subject of ignition timing, several other factors come into play as well. First, the boxes that alter ignition timing do it by changing the timing of the crank position sensor signal to the ECU. However, the ECU also uses that timing to determine when to fire the injectors! Altering the ignition timing will therefore alter the injector firing time. Going more than a few degrees in either direction can significantly impact the vaporization of the fuel, and the lambda of the resulting mixture. While some of this can be compensated for by changing fueling, changing ignition timing, and then re-tuning the fueling afterwards, it is really not a very good idea to change the injection event trigger point. And one last timing issue to be aware of in the existing generation of boxes is in their handling of the actual crank position signal. As noted in the chapters on sensors, the analog signal from the CPS can vary from half a volt during cranking to over 80v at redline—a really wide range of signal for most analog conditioning circuits to handle. At high engine speeds, the hardware in the current crop of "fooler" boxes cannot handle finding with precision the leading edge of the spike caused by the rotor's tooth passing the CPS. This results in high-rpm ignition "scatter", where the signal passed from the "fooler" to the ECU can vary by as much as +/-3 degrees of advance, with the amount constantly and randomly changing over time. This automatically costs several horsepower over what could be attained with a stable signal.

"Fooler" boxes are widely available and generally offer a wide variety of maps to choose from. However, the boxes are limited in their precision due to the difference in mapping methods between many stock systems and the add-on box, not to mention issues with the capability of the hardware to handle the signals (in the cases of current boxes that alter ignition timing). The TEKA EMS, now in development, has learned from the shortcomings of other boxes and has sophisticated circuitry to pre-process the crank trigger signal, actually improving ignition precision during cranking by raising the sensor output voltage, which should offer easier starting than stock in some conditions.

THE AFTERMARKET

	T1	T2	T3	T4	T5	T6	T7	T8	T9	T10	ET

6000
5000
4000

AP BThr
OP
G Lat
StrAng
SPos FB

Add-on pulse width modification boxes, like the DynoJet Power Commander IIIr shown here mounted in a Honda CBR600F4i, alter the injector pulse width coming from the ECU. Such boxes are currently the favored method for altering the tuning of stock EFI, but they are not without their faults. Motorcycle courtesy of Matt Keebler

THE AFTERMARKET

The broad availability of maps can be a disadvantage as well. With no reliable method for determining the utility of a given map, users are presented with a bewildering variety of claims and options, many of which are not as good as they could be. Like most flexible mapping options, it requires knowledge, skill, and an eddy current dyno to build your own map from scratch, or perfect a given map for your particular bike (it's actually possible to do through trial and error and riding the bike between changes, but this is not practical). Current boxes, while having OEM connectors and being removable, cannot be taken from one machine to another. They are model-specific, and buying a new bike means buying a new module. And they all require a computer to load and alter the maps. Still, they are the only available option for many machines, and they are tunable (whereas replacement PROMs have limited, if any, tunability).

Also roughly included in this class are the gear position "foolers" like Ivan's TRE. They work because machines with gear position sensors generally have different ignition and fueling maps for each gear. Some fool the ECU into thinking the bike is in second gear when it is really in first, some fool the ECU into thinking the bike is in fifth gear when it is really in sixth, and some do both. The biggest problem with these devices is that they don't really get you any closer to ideal ignition timing or fueling than when the bike is all stock. There is usually some form of traction control for first gear, implemented by reducing power. Defeating this makes you wheelie much more easily in first gear (which is fine if that is what you want to do, but it makes for more danger on the street and slower launches when drag racing or starting a road race, and greatly increases wear and tear on drivetrain components, including the clutch, cush drive, wheel bearings, chain and sprockets), and/or removes the soft speed limiter in sixth gear that is implemented by progressively retarding the timing. The problem with the sixth gear "fooler" is that bikes like the GSX-R1000 and Hayabusa actually make *more* power up to about 8,000 rpm with the sixth gear map than the fifth gear, due mainly to there being more ram air pressure at sixth-gear speeds

(and that means more fuel to take advantage of the extra air). So while you might have a slightly higher top speed with a gear position "fooler", you're going to take somewhat longer to get there.

Injector Pulse Modification Boxes

The other major class of programmable add-on boxes modifies the actual injector pulse, leaving the sensor signals to the ECU untouched. These have the challenge of having to handle high-current pulses in and out, but they can be as precise in altering the pulse width as the designer wishes them to be. Currently, the only product line in this class is the line of Power Commander III boxes: the PC III, the PC IIIr (with ignition timing control), the PC III USB (with both a USB interface port and an expansion port for future modular add-ons similar to those found with the Yosh EMS), and the PC IIIr USB (same as the previous model, only with ignition mapping control). Like the PC II-class of add-on boxes, these use an alpha-n map for fueling, as well as spark (where appropriate).

Because of the high currents involved, and how they need to be handled, cooling becomes more of a concern. In addition, more expensive components are typically needed, leading to higher costs for the unit. And all the same disadvantages hold true as for the "fooler" boxes, except for the issues with non-linearity of the CTS map (since there is no alteration of the CTS signal). Concerns with high-rpm ignition scatter are as valid here as they are with the PC II-class devices. The advantages are the same as those for the PC II-class devices as well, with the addition of the elimination of the previously mentioned disadvantage.

Complete EFI Systems

In some cases, tuning alone just will not do. Perhaps you have highly modified your engine, and are making much more than stock power. In this case, you will likely need larger injectors at a minimum, and if you have a big V-twin with stock injection, you may find that you are unable to get an acceptable idle (from the large fluctuations in intake vacuum caused by larger displacement and more aggressive cams). Or you may have a motorcycle that

WhiTek produces an EFI system for Evo and Shovelhead carbureted Harley-Davidson motorcycles. It can be operated in a number of modes on many different engines and is easy to program and install. Here you can see the intake manifold, air filter housing, upper fuel injector, and pressure regulator, along with the chrome cover and display unit. WhiTek is currently developing a replacement for this unit. WhiTek

T1   T2   T3   T4   T5   T6   T7   T8   T9   T10

ET
AP BThr
OP
G Lat
StrAng
SPos FB

6000
5000
4000
3000

was never equipped with fuel injection at all. You may even be a racer, who needs vast data-logging capacity to help refine and focus his riding, tuning, and performance. All of these cases lend themselves in one way or another to a replacement ECU, which, as you will see, is the likely future direction for most aftermarket fuel injection and tuning tools.

I could write a small book on just the currently available aftermarket systems. They are as varied as the numerous OEM systems now available, and soon will be as plentiful. They run the gamut in terms of mapping method and strategy, interchangeability, and extra functionality. Some, like the Daytona Twin Tec for Delphi-equipped Harley-Davidsons, have a wideband O_2 sensor and use it to "learn" the engine's response and help fine-tune the system for your particular modified engine without so much as a dyno run to help (or confuse) you. And some, like the MoTeC M800 and its sisters, allow an amazing flexibility of sensors, actuators, and data logging capabilities, making it adaptable to almost any vehicle and any use. And there is everything in between, including the WhiTek EFI system that replaces the stock carburetor on older Harley-Davidsons. Let's take a look at the details of a few systems so you can get an idea of what is possible. If you can imagine it, someone can design and build it, and you can install it on a motorcycle. There are even do-it-yourself kits like the Megasquirt and Megasquirt AVR, designed to be built and tuned for under $300. Let's take a look at some of the wide range of available products.

WhiTek EFI for Harley-Davidsons

This is one of the more interesting aftermarket systems I have encountered. It is designed as a bolt-on system for Harley-Davidson Evo and Shovelhead engines (with 46-mm throttle body), as well as Sportster motors (with 42-mm throttle body) and their clones, from stock to heavily modified. It is designed to be self-contained and easily adaptable to machines previously equipped with a carburetor. It can be easily tuned in a variety of ways by almost anyone and can be installed in just a few hours by someone of average mechanical skill. It fills a unique niche, and I feel it deserves mention for its ingenuity.

The system is composed of two main units. One is a display unit, finished in a nice chrome housing, to be mounted in the traditional dash area of a Harley. The other is the business end—a complex unit composed of intake manifold with injectors mounted that is attached to a throttle and an air filter housing. To one side of the manifold is a small electric fuel pump, to the other is a mechanical fuel pressure regulator. On the top of the air filter housing, beneath a chrome cover, is the actual ECU circuitry. This makes for a simple, compact installation that requires little of the special plumbing and sensor mounting that might be found with other aftermarket complete EFI systems.

The display unit is backlit for night use and has built-in temperature compensation to keep the LCD display easily readable, regardless of ambient temperature. It allows diagnosis, tuning, and full mapping of the EFI at the touch of a button.

Fueling

Fuel is injected immediately behind the throttle body, in what WhiTek refers to as "Sequential Throttle-Body Injection." It does not actually have one injector per cylinder as might be expected; instead it operates the injectors in a staged fashion, as some racing motorcycles do with one port-mounted and one shower injector. When a small amount of fuel is required, only one injector will deliver fuel, but when more fuel is required, both injectors will operate. As was

noted earlier in the book, this greatly increases the dynamic range of usable fuel delivery and works well in this application.

The WhiTek system runs on a 68HC11 MCU, and has a fairly large number of built-in, user-selectable, base maps that can be altered in two different ways. In one mode, each cell can be mapped individually, allowing ultimate control over the mapping when eddy-current dyno tuning is available. Alternately, a second mode applies broader adjustments and is designed to be tuned in a manner more familiar to those who have a lot of experience with carburetors. This flexibility covers the needs of the vast majority of end users without introducing undue complexity into the act of programming itself. In addition, you can set a redline for the built-in rev limiter, which will cut out fueling entirely at a predetermined engine rpm, thus preventing over-revving the motor.

The unit also has an auto-prime "choke" function, which can be disabled. It will automatically richen the mixture for starting, leaning it incrementally until there is no additional enrichment to the main map after one minute of operation. Disabling for dyno tuning and drag racing is the order of the day, but it is a nice, handy feature for normal street riding and requires no rider intervention.

On the other side of the scale, there is also a feature that will automatically lean out the mixture for part-throttle cruise, based on constancy of engine speed and throttle position. This can aid in fuel economy on long hauls without causing the lean surging ordinarily associated with enleanment at cruise (as in closed-loop modes on some motorcycles).

There are also toggles for the acceleration enrichment function (which should normally be left on, to help deliver appropriate fueling when the throttle is suddenly opened), and a deceleration fuel cut (which, like most stock Harley-Davidson EFI systems, will cease delivering fuel when in a closed-throttle engine-braking condition). The latter increases engine braking, decreases backfiring on a closed throttle, and improves both fuel mileage and emissions.

Ignition

The WhiTek EFI can run a single-fire or dual-fire ignition system (older Harley designs fire both plugs off the same coil, in a style similar to waste fire systems. Many aftermarket systems use individual spark triggering for each cylinder), and has full 2D alpha-n ignition mapping. As with fueling, there are a large number of base spark maps to choose from, and tuning of the spark timing is done in a single broad section, much like general tuning for fueling. This helps prevent the unwary from accidentally causing engine-damaging detonation through radical changes in ignition timing.

There is an optional "shift-kill" function, which will temporarily kill the engine when it reaches a shift point. This is used with an air shifter to facilitate a smooth shift when drag racing. The amount of rpm drop before firing the engine once more is user-adjustable, allowing enough time for a shift, but ensuring the motor is under power again when the shift is completed, regardless of gearing or redline. A very handy feature for those drag racing with a Harley-engined motorcycle.

Options

In addition to the components that are required to install and operate the system, WhiTek provides the option for additional components as well. An optional shift light, programmable from the display unit, can be mounted in the dash area. In addition to functioning as a regular shift light, it can also be toggled from the display unit so it will flash if a predetermined cruise speed is

THE AFTERMARKET

exceeded—the next best thing to cruise control! There are also optional oil temperature and oil pressure sensors, which will read out on the display unit on command and can be used to kill the engine in the event of a loss of oil pressure. Either is a useful addition to the air-cooled Big Twin motor, and they are almost necessities for those who wish to drag race with such an engine. Also optional are adapters for electronic speed sensors. While these do not affect ignition or injection, road speed can be very accurately displayed on machines so equipped.

Perhaps more important is the option of adding an AAP sensor. This can give a direct readout on the dash, and of course can be used to adjust mixture to suit changes in air density. Personally, I would recommend adding this option for anyone who wants the WhiTek unit for regular street use. The WhiTek will also offer utility to racers, but street-ridden bikes are more likely to experience a wider variety of weather conditions and altitudes. In lieu of the sensor, the display unit has a function in which the rider can enter the current altitude for a cruder, but still effective, method of adapting to changing conditions.

Installation

Because of the compact arrangement, the system installs in much the same way as a performance carburetor would. WhiTek provides specific instructions as to what pieces are required for installation and how to go about installing them, right down to Harley-Davidson part numbers to simplify sourcing. WhiTek also offers optional mounting brackets for the display unit to accommodate a number of traditional Harley-Davidson handlebar/ instrument dash layouts. Such attention to detail makes life incredibly easy for the end user. Installation is as simple as reading down the instruction manual, purchasing the proper pieces, and installing them as one would a carburetor or aftermarket handlebar clamp.

The manual is very descriptive, giving specific instructions for a variety of models over a fairly wide range of years. No matter what sort of Harley you have, you should be able to find your step-by-step section. Numerous pictures and diagrams ease installation to the point where it is very simple indeed.

Tuning

A comprehensive set of instructions for tuning, whether in the general tuning or dyno tuning modes, is included with the unit. This takes you through step-by-step, and gives you symptoms and their likely causes along with suggested cures. The front and rear cylinders can be adjusted independently through the use of a trim map for the rear cylinder. In general tuning mode, the idle, cruise, and overall mixture are user-adjustable, all adding to or detracting from the pre-selected base map (of the several that come with the system). Spark can only be advanced or retarded across the board, after choosing one of several base maps.

For the average end user, the instructions are thorough, and the options should be suitable to get acceptable results on almost any naturally aspirated Big Twin engine. For the more advanced tuner, or the drag racer (or their team), the flexibility and near-total tunability of this unit make it an excellent choice where there is no question that the engine has a constructive and proven combination of components.

Summary

This unit is truly amazing. It has been thought out so well that I have trouble finding fault with any part of it. While the state of tune achievable using the general tuning section may not be as precise as one might like, it will be more than adequate for most users and can be made to equal or better most carburetor setups. Adding ignition curve control gives it a decisive advantage over carburetors as well, as big-bore air-cooled engines tend to be very sensitive to ignition timing. It is easy to install, easy to use, and does a good job of what it sets out to do. WhiTek even has an overnight parts delivery service in case of failure while on a road trip!

The only disadvantage for most users is that it is no longer in production! WhiTek has promised that a new model is on the way; presumably they will be tackling the twin-cam market with their new design. No matter what they come out with, if it is as good as this model, it is sure to be a winner. While it does not offer data-logging or closed-loop operation, I do not consider these to be disadvantages considering the machines and market the unit is designed for. If this product were to be used with a modern sportbike engine, its design philosophy would not be nearly as good a fit for the hardware, but for Harley-Davidson engines (even high-performance ones), it is a superb piece of kit.

Daytona Twin Tec TCFI for Twin Cam Harley-Davidsons
The Delphi ECU that comes stock with newer twin-cam Harley-Davidsons is a very sophisticated unit. It is also integrated heavily with other electronic systems on the motorcycle. But the more sophisticated a unit becomes, the harder it is for an end user to adapt it to their own needs. Building a highly modified twin-cam engine is a situation where the stock system cannot be adapted well enough to deliver very good results. Since building stroker motors with big cams has long been a tradition for Harley owners, there was a vacuum waiting to be filled.

Along came Chris Schroeder and Daytona Twin Tec. Those from the Harley world probably recognize the Daytona Twin Tec name. They have been building sophisticated programmable ignition control units for a variety of Harley-Davidson models, mostly as direct plug-in stock replacement units. Utilizing state-of-the-art MCUs, Twin Tec has become the Rolls-Royce of aftermarket ignition controllers. And now they bring the same engineering savvy and tuning knowledge to fuel injection. The TCFI unit they build is a highly tunable drop-in replacement for the Delphi ECU, right down to using the stock data port connector, and interfacing correctly with the stock turn signal and anti-theft units!

Daytona Twin Tec has been a little tight-lipped about the exact architecture of their ECU, but there are indications they may be using the very powerful and flexible ATMEGA MCU. This is many steps beyond the 68HC family that has become an industry standard for MCUs. It offers much faster data processing, as well as more numerous (and more flexible) I/O channels. And the TCFI puts them to good use.

As those who have put big cams in carbureted engines know all too well, large cam overlap produces very poor and irregular intake vacuum at idle. This is why all those 1960s muscle cars have lumpy idle sounds when equipped with a big cam—the carburetor(s) worked poorly without much metering vacuum, and reversion pushes most of the fuel/air mixture back out into the intake. What's worse, how much of the fuel/air mixture it pushes back out is not predictable. So getting a machine with a lot of cam overlap to idle at all is a significant chore. Port injection improves upon carburetion as it injects fuel directly against the back of the intake valve head(s), and, subsequently, does not depend on intake vacuum to meter fuel delivery. However, the Delphi system functions as a speed-density system on closed

	T1		T2		T3	T4		T5		T6		T7		T8	T9		T10		ET

6000
5000
4000
3000

ET
AP BThr
OP
G Lat
StrAng
SPos FR

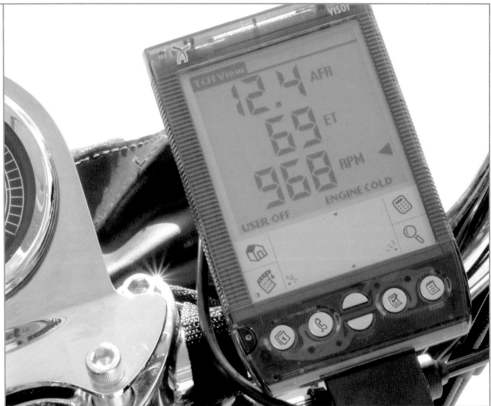

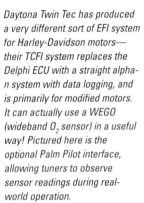

Daytona Twin Tec has produced a very different sort of EFI system for Harley-Davidson motors— their TCFI system replaces the Delphi ECU with a straight alpha-n system with data logging, and is primarily for modified motors. It can actually use a WEGO (wideband O_2 sensor) in a useful way! Pictured here is the optional Palm Pilot interface, allowing tuners to observe sensor readings during real-world operation.

throttle—and that *does* depend on intake vacuum. The only reasonable solution is a straight alpha-n system, so that is what the TCFI delivers: A drop-in alpha-n solution!

Dropping in as a straight replacement for the stock ECU and interfacing correctly with the rest of the bike's electronics, actuators, and sensors is impressive enough. But the TCFI goes several steps further: It data-logs the last 15 minutes of operation (which can be extremely handy when trying to troubleshoot an odd reading or a running problem), it can be quickly and easily tuned via excellent computer software, and, best of all, it can (with certain limitations) self-tune using a wideband O_2 sensor!

Tuning

For many users, the software will compose the core of their tuning experience with the TCFI. Twin Tec's supplied software is called PC Link, and your computer can plug directly into the wiring harness on the motorcycle, or link to the ECU directly on the bench with an optional power supply and cable. In this way, it is possible to program your ECU without having to take a laptop out to the motorcycle. It's also possible for an aftermarket motor builder to program a number of ECUs with a pre-developed map for a motor they might produce. PC Link offers full access and tunability for all the maps and parameters in the TCFI ECU, as well as downloading the data log data.

Tuning for a given engine is simplified by some of the base values being computed for you by the software. Starting with one of the "canned" data sets, you enter the displacement of the engine, redline, injector flow rate, and some other parameters specific to the engine, and a rough base map is fleshed out for you automatically. This should be enough to get you up and running and allow you to tune the engine (either on the road or on the dyno).

Mapping is comprehensive and thorough, allowing user access to every possible setting. There are a total of eight 1D maps, five 2D maps, and over 20 individual parameters, covering very fine levels of tuning (especially for idle control). Everything— from engine temperature compensation tables to cold-cranking tables to IAC throttle compensation tables—is tunable by the advanced user to get the smoothest starting, running, and throttle response from their high-dollar motor. Of course, there is a rear cylinder trim table as well.

Daytona Twin Tec now offers a palmtop computer adapter that allows you to monitor any three parameters of the system while you ride. This can be invaluable for tuners with transient problems that only occur on the road. These guys thought of darned near everything!

The Star: WEGO

But the real star of the show is the optional WEGO sensor and what it can do. You may recall that in the chapters on sensors, I discussed what oxygen sensors could and could not do. I also discussed how wideband oxygen sensors gave more data, but you needed to have a target to make that data truly useful. Unless you already knew what the target AFR was at a given load point, the data from the sensor would only be ballpark at best. Well, Chris Schroeder knows this, too. And this is the key to the TCFI's unique and very effective "learning" WEGO interface.

The trick with the WEGO is that you have to have some idea of the target AFR you want under various load/speed conditions. You must have a 2D map of target values for the WEGO tuning to function properly. However, it is not difficult to get ballpark figures for this. What it really requires is an understanding of where the engine makes its torque—all other things being equal, more torque means better volumetric efficiency. And better VE generally means more efficient and complete combustion. You can aim slightly leaner here for a given amount of air. With only one exhaust gas being measured, it is difficult to get a precise reading as a percentage of exhaust gas volume (since the sensor doesn't know how much exhaust gas is passing over it, or how fast, there will be some variation based on the design of the exhaust and the power output of the engine at that point in time), but erring slightly on the side of caution, you can set some pretty decent target values with a solid understanding of load and VE (although it should be noted that you cannot get a true picture of VE for a given engine anywhere but on the dyno, and dyno testing should really be done with at least one example of the engine setup that one wishes to tune). Once the target AFR table is filled (ideally through dyno testing with four-gas analysis)and you have a rough alpha-n map hashed out, the next step is to go ride the motorcycle for several hours, taking care to hit as many cells in the alpha-n (load/speed) table as possible.

What happens during these rides is that the ECU is busy recording the values read by the WBO_2 sensor at these map points and is comparing the measured AFR against the target AFR in the 2D map you created. From these comparisons, it builds what Twin Tec calls a BLM (Block Learn Multiplier) table. This table shows whether the EFI was delivering more, less, or on-target fueling levels. With the BLM table filled with values, the PC Link software allows you to simply apply the BLM table to the alpha-n table, in essence improving your base fueling map automatically! By repeating this process several times, until the BLM shows small or no values in most of its cells, the system is automatically altering the base map until it is actually delivering target AFR values! This self-tuning feature will be very important to those who need a high state of tune, but cannot afford the extensive dyno time on and eddy current dyno with four-gas analyzer that would be necessary to create such finely tuned maps otherwise. It's perfectly tailored to small-value motorcycle manufacturers, who need to quickly and easily tune each newly-built engine to match the target values they have obtained, for perfect continuity between different examples of the same engine.

Once maps are created, the ECU can still use an O_2 sensor for closed-loop idling and cruise. Especially with big cams, closed-loop idle may be a very effective way of ensuring reliable fueling at idle. This is further enhanced by the extremely high degree of control provided for idle and starting parameters. The amount of tunability actually exceeds a number of OEM systems, and this can be put to good use in capable hands.

Summary

This system is not for the faint of heart. It is only for someone who is familiar with the operating principles of both the stock Delphi system and internal combustion engines in general. And the price of entry, while excellent for what you get, is not exactly cheap. For a full kit with WEGO and WEGO monitor, expect to pay over $1,000.

However, Chris Schroeder and the staff of Daytona Twin Tec are extremely knowledgeable, and can provide helpful support as required. There is an extensive help file with the PC Link software, which goes a long way toward getting you started on tuning for your engine. And of course, the unique WEGO "self-tuning" system is the best possible way for a knowledgeable tuner to dial in a precise set of maps for an engine without having to dyno each example. For the small company that builds engines or complete

The MoTeC M4 has been their flagship ECU for all kinds of motorcycles in racing. It offers flexibility, great support, and is designed with racing in mind. It can interface with the ADL data-logger dash, as well as a wideband O_2 sensor. Because of the commonality between the MoTeC ECUs, it is quick and easy to upgrade without losing time, and in many cases, money as well. MoTeC USA

motorcycles, this system provides most of what you could get from a $100,000 R&D lab in terms of end results at a much lower cost, and with much less required training. And for the tinkerer, or the person who just has to have the very best, this is the cream of the crop. It is also the only current drop-in Delphi replacement ECU I am aware of. This alone makes it valuable to those who want to modify a late-model Harley motor.

Other motorcycle manufacturers will follow suit and begin offering more sophisticated ECUs that meet steepening emissions standards. This will make life harder and harder for the racer and tuner alike. Daytona Twin Tec is leading the way in what will turn from a trickle to a tidal wave; stock replacement ECUs, geared to the desired precision and knowledge level of the target audience, be they small-scale manufacturers/builders or simply very savvy retail customer. The future is here today, and it comes from Daytona Twin Tec.

MoTeC ECUs and Components

MoTeC has one of the most interesting and ingenious series of ECUs on the planet. Not only can they be easily interchanged while using the same tuning software, they were designed for racing as well. This allows many capabilities that most other ECUs can't even touch. They can replace stock ECUs or be used as a base for creating a system from scratch. And they can interface with other devices, like their electronic dash with built-in data logger or telemetry radios, which further increase their usefulness for top-level racing teams. Their systems can be found in racing powerboats, off-road buggies that challenge Baja and the deserts of Africa, Formula One and Champ cars, World Rally and American Le Mans Series cars and, of course, motorcycles.

The core of the system is a 32-bit CPU running at 33 MHz. MoTeC combines this with an advanced ASIC that they refer to as a "time processor." The newer units (those with a three-digit model number) have a more advanced processor that can handle more tasks with greater precision, allowing for more cylinders and/or higher redlines. All of the ECUs in the MoTeC lineup have the same MCU, and all are accessed the same way, with the same soft-

THE AFTERMARKET

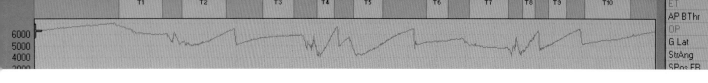

The MoTeC M800 ECU is the latest generation of their ECU line. Adding a wider range of sensor inputs as well as offering control of variable valve timing systems, along with additional data-logging capability, this is the new flagship of their ECU line. Note the use of connectors identical to those used on most Denso ECUs. MoTeC USA

ware. This makes upgrading to a new box a snap and means that once you are familiar with the features of one ECU, you need only learn a little bit about the differences to be proficient with other models. One can see where that would be a great advantage for a race team in the long run; even if a new vehicle is acquired that needs a different ECU, the team specialist is already familiar with most of the setup and operation of the new unit. Additional capabilities (like data logging, traction control, staged injection, and more) can be added to ECUs already installed by unlocking the features with additional software from MoTeC. This allows nearly any racing budget to get in on the ground floor and still preserve the investment in hardware and programming as the team grows. Combined with excellent software, data-logging, presets for most common sensors, and many race-ready features, you can understand why the top race teams in the world often turn to MoTeC.

M4/M48

The M4 is the older series of MoTeC ECUs, which includes the M48. Using the same MCU and ASIC, the main difference is that the M48 can fire eight injectors separately (making it ideal for four-cylinder machines with two-stage injector setups), while the M4 handles only four injectors. A further difference is that the M4 can have four individual ignition outputs, while the M48 has but two (this is not a real problem, however, as MoTeC has a special ignition multiplexer box called an expander that data-links to any of their ECUs, allowing a wide range of spark control outputs). Since one or more of the ignition outputs is shared with other actuators (like an air shifter, IAC solenoid, or fuel pump relay), this is usually moot; for most uses, the multiplexer is required anyhow. Still, for simple systems, the M4 can often suffice with nothing but a pair of outboard ignitors. This made it the primary choice by MoTeC for road racing motorcycles until the introduction of the new M400 unit this year.

M400/600/800

The new generation of ECUs from MoTeC started with the M800, their flagship ECU, and its M880 derivative. In addition to driving eight separate injector outputs (or as many as 12 when

used with high-impedance injectors), it boasts eight auxiliary outputs and 10 auxiliary inputs, allowing for things like temperature monitoring of multiple fluids, controlling pumps and fans, and much more. The M880 is basically identical to the M800, with the main differences being a mil-spec connector and the addition of more data-logging memory onboard. Due to the mil-spec connector, the M880 requires the purchase of a custom wiring harness from MoTeC. The M600 is the version made primarily for six-cylinder engines, with six injector and six ignition drivers. The M400 follows this trend, with four of each.

As I mentioned before, the M400/600/800 series ECUs have a more precise and more powerful ASIC, which allows all these additional inputs and outputs to be managed while still offering more precision in timing output events as compared with the M4 series. They also have CAN (controller area network) controllers, allowing them to receive sensor data or transmit parameters and sensor data to CAN-equipped devices, including MoTeC's ADL (advanced data logging) dash unit (more details of the CAN bus can be found in the future developments chapter). Whereas the M4-series ECUs can handle at best one wideband O_2 sensor, the M600 and M800/880 ECUs allow two, which can be helpful when tuning multi-cylinder engines. These ECUs can hold up to 512 KB of data logging memory, which can be set to record data from whatever sensors or ECU data the user requires at a user-defined sampling rate. Up to six temperature inputs and eight voltage-based inputs (which would cover most common EFI sensors like TPS and MAP, as well as gear position switches) can be used, along with the two WBO_2 sensor inputs (M600/800), eight sequential injector outputs (M800, and as described above for the others in the family), six ignition outputs (which double as auxiliary outputs if they are not being used, or if an expander or CDI-8 eight-channel capacitive discharge ignition unit is used), eight auxiliary outputs (used for IAC valves, fuel pump relays, driver warning lamps, turbo waste gates, or nearly anything else you can imagine), and four digital inputs (wheel speed or Hall-effect CPS) make this family of ECUs one of the most flexible available to the end user. It's part of the reason these units are so popular in racing circles—if it has an internal combustion engine and spark plugs, a MoTeC ECU can be fitted to it.

Mapping

All MoTeC ECUs share a common mapping philosophy. Designed as they are for racing, they are primarily alpha-n based (although they can be programmed to use a MAP sensor, generally as backup). The main fueling table (load/speed) features 40 rpm sites and 21 load sites, allowing for excellent control of fueling over a wide range of engine operating conditions. As you would expect, these sites can be mapped to whatever range you wish, allowing the user to customize their behavior based on the engine they will be managing. A 2D injector crossover map switches in a secondary injector for machines with staged injectors, and this is a 20 rpm site by 11 load site map. Individual cylinders can be trimmed globally or one can use additional 20x11 maps for each cylinder (with separate sets of maps for primary and secondary injectors in staged systems). This allows tailoring of fuel delivery for small variations in injectors, engine wear, and even valve adjustment! If you know how to tune, you can really squeeze the most out of an engine with this kind of control. There is the usual range of 1D maps to compensate for air temperature, coolant temperature, and delta alpha, as well as 1D maps for gear position, fuel pressure, and more. There is also a 20x11 2D map for boost control on turbocharged applications. For engines that

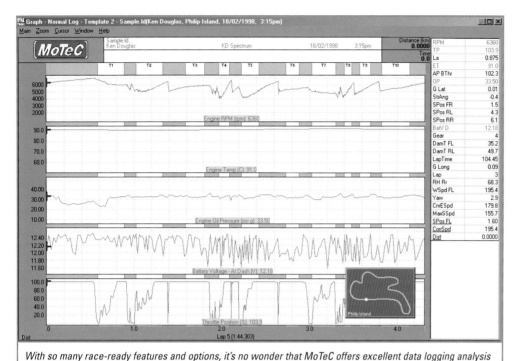

With so many race-ready features and options, it's no wonder that MoTeC offers excellent data logging analysis software. With it, engine and suspension tuning can be improved. Riders can even learn how to improve their lap times from what the data logging shows them. And with optional telemetry radios, crews can keep track of just about every sensor you could squeeze onto a motorcycle, in real time. MoTeC USA

can not only detect open or shorted sensors, injectors, and ignition coils, but can also detect partial failures like high resistance in an injector connector, excessive noise on sensor lines, or even problems inside the ECU itself. This saves valuable time at trackside, which is worth a great deal to most racers.

Race-Specific Features

All the flexibility and ease of use discussed so far would be of great benefit to racers all on its own. But it's the extra features provided by these units that really make them stand out. There is fully programmable cam timing control for most major variable valve timing schemes (which is important now in the car world, and is likely to become increasingly important in motorcycles of the near future), regular O_2-sensor closed-loop control (for vehicles that must pass emissions testing), a variety of programmable driver alerts (which are programmable in complex ways, combining timing, various sensors, and other factors to be extremely sophisticated indications of developing problems), speed limiting (essential for racing where pit lane speed limits are in place), control of turbo waste gates and nitrous oxide (and the fueling demands of either or both), programmable rev limiting (hard or soft, fuel or spark or both), fuel pressure control, traction control, gear change ignition cutout (for air or electronic shifters), turbo anti-lag systems, launch control, even drive-by-wire throttle! In fact, just about any feature you could think of; if it can be done, MoTeC can help you do it!

Other MoTeC Features and Products

While not strictly directly related to fuel injection alone, MoTeC makes a number of other products that interface with their ECUs that deserve mention here.

I already spoke briefly about their ignition expander and CDI-8 ignition box (which can be run as a standalone unit on carbureted vehicles). The CDI-8 can perform the same function as the expander and whatever igniters one attaches to it taking a coded signal from an ECU and creating up to eight individual ignition events on separate channels.

Also briefly mentioned was the ADL data logger, which not only functions as a multifunction dash display with up to eight programmable actuator outputs (which can be programmed with the same complex logic as can the ECUs), but also contains advanced data-logging capabilities. This can be used as a standalone, or with any of their ECUs, and it is one of the more popular components among racing teams around the world. It's great for giving drivers the information they need quickly and clearly, and race engineers love its ability to log or display up to

are not inline or horizontally opposed (such as V-twins), there is an "odd fire" table that is set to the crank angle in degrees between the cylinder banks, removing the need for multiple sensors

Sensor Calibration and Type

One of the greatest flexibilities of the MoTeC ECUs is their unique method of handling sensors. Since many people fit these ECUs to production vehicles or engines, there is the need to accommodate stock sensors and injectors, not to mention interfacing with a wide variety of stock ignition systems. MoTeC handles these variables by having a 1D response map for each sensors, which allows the ECU to "understand" the signals from many different brands and types of sensors.

There is a large stock library of sensors from which one can choose. If you have a sensor that is in the calibration catalog, you simply tell the ECU which sensor you are using, and the ECU does the rest. MoTeC can also write a calibration file for any sensor you have, in case you have a non-standard sensor. It's easy to see how this strategy greatly simplifies installation and use of their ECUs, and of course it allows for replacing or upgrading sensors in the future without having to change anything else except the accompanying response map. One can even program in the crank trigger wheel configuration, allowing a single entry in the software to replace the need for a special trigger, or massive reprogramming. Ignition control is handled in a very similar way, making it a snap to interface the ECU with the ignition system in vehicles that were originally carbureted, or with independent ignition systems.

Diagnostics

In racing, it's of critical importance to know just what has gone wrong in the case of a failure. With that in mind, MoTeC ECUs

The ADL data logging dash offers standalone use, or it can be interfaced with any MoTeC ECU, as well as their WBO$_2$ sensor. Combined with its ability to use complex criteria for giving specialized alerts to the rider or driver, the dash unit is used a great deal in the racing world. MoTeC USA

170 separate sensors (including suspension sensors as found on many GP bikes)! It features 28 analog inputs, four digital inputs, four switched inputs, and two WBO$_2$ inputs, as well as the eight switched outputs mentioned above. It can be programmed with alphanumeric warning messages to tell the driver exactly what is going on with the vehicle and what corrective action needs to be taken. Data-logging memory is expandable anywhere from 348 KB up to a full 8 MB of memory. It can be downloaded at up to 68 KB per second, making downloads for data analysis quick and easy. And MoTeC provides data analysis software that allows engineers and tuners to quickly evaluate the gathered data and make useful changes. In the chapters on sensors, I discussed the primary use for WBO$_2$ sensors in tuning (to isolate the load/speed sites where most time was being spent, to help focus the efforts of the tuners), and MoTeC builds this functionality right into their data analysis software, giving a graphical representation of where tuner needs to focus their attentions between track sessions.

The PLM, or professional lambda meter, is far more than just a wideband O$_2$ sensor. It can be programmed with response curves for a wide variety of fuels, something that confuses other sensors that are running on an assumption about the stoichiometric ratio for gasoline. It also has a CAN output, allowing interfacing with the ADL dash or the M400/600/800-series ECUs. In addition, it also has a 0–5v analog output, for those vehicles that already have data logging, but without the means to record wideband lambda data. They can even be linked together (up to 12!) to allow real-time metering of differences between cylinders. It runs on a 68HC-family Motorola MCU, and can be flash programmed with upgrades in the field.

Summary

There is a reason the Vance & Hines drag racing team, Yoshimura Suzuki, Attack Racing, and Annandale Honda turn to MoTeC for their racing solutions. Not only is the hardware, data-logging and telemetry all there, but the amazing support of the staff at MoTeC make problems disappear as fast as they crop up. With the knowledge, experience, and skill to help racers with just what they need, MoTeC is tops in the field. And with the release of their drop-in

kit for the Hayabusa (coming soon), anyone can get in on the ground floor with fully programmable fuel injection, knowing that as their needs grow, their hardware and company will support it. Since the drop-in kits (scheduled for more FI bikes in the future) use the same ECUs as custom setups, all the capability is there for adding nitrous, an air shifter, or even full turbocharging control without losing the investment already made on EFI hardware. The downside here is the high cost of MoTeC hardware. If you're a top racing team, you know that the investment is more than worth it in time and effort saved. If you have the money to get in the door, MoTeC will offer you everything you could ever need in racing fuel and ignition management and data logging.

Other EFI Parts and Services

While alterations involving the ECU are one of the first things that people think of when discussing the tuning of EFI, there is a lot more that can be done. The devil is in the details, they say, and there are a variety of oft-overlooked services, parts, and techniques that can be essential to making the most power for your machine.

Injectors and Injector Servicing

In the car world, nearly everyone into performance tuning recognizes the need for bigger injectors. In the motorcycle world, this is one of the last things that people think of. Stock injectors are designed to be as small as possible and still deliver enough fuel at maximum output. Remember that the smaller the injectors, the better idle metering will be. Major changes to the engine (bigger bore, racing cams, higher redline, and especially turbocharging) will require more fuel; this means larger injectors.

Companies like RC Engineering stock a huge variety of different size, shape, and drive injectors. They can also build their own out of parts, making just the right injector for your application. RC Engineering injectors are guaranteed for one year and get lifetime free inspection and flow testing. If your goal is to make the most horsepower and have your engine run as smoothly as it can, having a balanced set of injectors and making sure they are clean and flow as they should is essential.

RC Engineering also offers a cleaning service, in which injectors are disassembled and cleaned ultrasonically in a special solution. Fuel leaves deposits on the injector pintles or discs, and this can lead to leakage and/or reduced flow. Leakage is one of the biggest culprits for causing major deposit problems. After a ride, the hot engine will combine with leaking fuel and condensation, creating a gummy residue that accelerates the problem in a tightening spiral.

Most people would be surprised to know that stock injectors can vary up to +/-5% in flow rate right out of the box. That's potentially a 10% difference in flow between two injectors! RC Engineering offers a balancing service, in which injectors can be tuned or swapped out for a set that all flow at a uniform rate. If you're interested in getting the most out of your tuning work, this is really step one. No one would ever think of grabbing a random handful of jets when tuning a carburetor—jets are carefully machined to deliver nearly identical flow rates consistently. Remember that injectors should be no different. You could be costing yourself free power and missing out on a smoother idle as well as smoother throttle transitions!

Throttle Bodies

Oversized throttle bodies have long been used by car tuners to derestrict the intake tract of high-performance cars. Thankfully, very few modern engine designs will require a greater flow rate

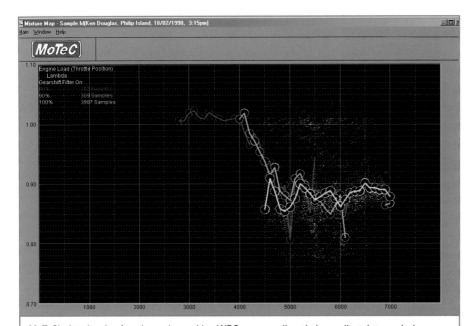

MoTeC's data logging functions, along with a WBO$_2$ sensor, allow their excellent data analysis software to show you a 3D map of engine speed, lambda, and throttle position. This quickly narrows the range of tuning choices to those that are truly useful for the current racetrack and rider, saving a great deal of time and effort. MoTeC USA

than stock throttle bodies can deliver. Still, very large V-twins can often benefit from an increase in throttle body diameter, especially on a modified engine.

Many companies can enlarge stock throttle bodies, among them RC Engineering. However, sometimes there is just not enough metal in a stock throttle body for it to be widened enough. In cases like this, we must turn to aftermarket throttle bodies. RC Engineering can supply some custom throttle bodies to order, and there are companies like Horsepower, Inc., that make oversized throttle bodies for fuel-injected Harley-Davidson motorcycles. These are needed on some powerful machines to provide enough airflow. The drawback to using an oversized throttle body is that only machines using a MAF will be able to bolt one on without mapping changes. Speed density systems will read properly near closed throttle, but will become increasingly lean as the throttle opens. And alpha-n systems will have the same problem, but to a greater degree. So remapping of some sort will be necessary.

In addition, some companies offer aftermarket throttle bodies for systems that never had EFI. Hilborn, long a famous name in mechanical fuel injection, developed a unique throttle body system for inline motorcycles that can be used with either mechanical or electronic fuel injection. A pair of steel rods holds the individual throttle bodies captive, and the spacing between throttle bodies is held constant with set screws. This makes the throttle body set adaptable to any spacing of intake runners and even allows the same throttle body set to be moved to a new motorcycle with different spacing in the future. Being oriented more toward motorcycle drag racing applications, Hilborn offers few other motorcycle pieces at this point, but they do have a very simple and easy to set up EFI controller specifically for full-throttle applications. Unfortunately, it is currently limited to use with Harley-Davidson motors, as the controller can only handle engine speeds of up to 6,000 rpm.

Fuel Pressure Regulators

Another option for delivering more fuel than stock is to modify or replace the fuel pressure regulator to raise the fuel pressure in the rail. Higher pressure means greater flow rate, so this can have an effect similar to increasing injector size. Note that there are limits to the linearity of the change in fuel delivery based on fuel pressure. At very high pressures, the change in delivered fuel mass per unit time decreases for the same increase in pressure, which means that past a certain point of system pressure, the engine will run increasingly lean under higher loads and engine speeds, which is quite bad for the engine, of course.

In the case of Aprilia V-twins with Marelli injection systems, there has been a great variation in fuel pressure between similar units. It is unclear whether this was by design, or whether the quality control on the regulators was in need of improvement. In any case, on machines with a higher than "normal" fuel pressure, aftermarket chips often gave poor results due to the engine being constantly run richer of best power. Evoluzione, a company specializing in performance parts for European V-twin sportbikes, developed an adjustable pressure regulator to allow tailoring the fuel pressure to suit the needs and wants of the owners of these bikes. In the case of too high a stock pressure setting, such a regulator is required to gain acceptable performance from the better aftermarket chips.

Some people also modify stock pressure regulators to raise fuel pressure for better performance or to suit a modified engine. This is generally a bad idea because it richens the entire load/speed matrix and cannot be tuned very well. In some cases it may give overall slightly better performance, but it is a far cry from a proper tuning of the fuel delivery system.

Ignition Advance Rotors

As with carbureted counterparts, there is a wide range of ignition advance rotors for fuel-injected motorcycles. Since it is harder to ignite mixture that is less dense (and therefore not heated as much by compression), starting the spark earlier can often give noticeable increases in power when rolling on from part throttle. Generally, this is at no cost at higher rpms and a wider throttle opening. However, the best compromise setting for an EFI bike is typically with less advance than with a similar carbureted unit. I believe the reason for this is not necessarily improved ignition advance curves, but the fact that when using an ignition advance rotor, injector event timing is offset along with ignition timing. This leads to a reduction in fuel vaporization and even delivery, which robs back the power made by the advanced ignition timing.

The drawbacks here are pretty obvious. Aside from the injection timing issue, there is also no way to change the amount of advance based on engine operating conditions. A far better solution would be a well-designed alpha-n mappable ignition timing control that ran off the coil primary wire(s). Unfortunately, such a solution is not yet available, although Factory ProTuning's TEKA SFI promises to deliver such a solution.

THE AFTERMARKET

139

Flow-testing your injectors is an important part of getting the most out of your machine. Seen here is an injector flow testing machine, which runs the injectors through various timed cycles and allows you to compare flowed volume. The graduated glass tubes hold the fuel passed by each injector. Flow tester courtesy of Factory Pro Tuning

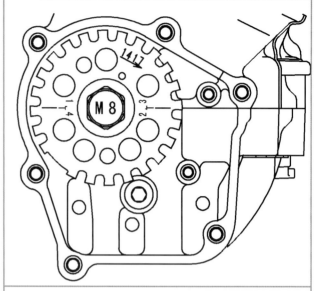

Aftermarket ignition rotors, similar to the one seen here from a ZX-6R, can improve part-throttle acceleration, but may cost in fuel efficiency and top-end power. Kawasaki Motor Corporation USA

SO WHAT IS BEST?

We have weighed the pluses and minuses of a number of products on the market that illustrate various approaches to changing your stock EFI system (or adding one to a bike that came with carbs!). And the answer to "What is best?" is murky, even for people who know exactly what they want. Like all things, there are compromises to be made in choosing your aftermarket solution. Only *you* can say what makes the most sense for your bike, your wallet, and your desired goal.

But beware. The market is still small enough (and consumers are not yet well-informed) that so-so products can hang around for some time as the "next big thing." As OEM fuel injection and their aftermarket solutions become more sophisticated, and consumers start learning more about how the system actually works, we will see products of increasing quality and utility as time goes by. This is exactly what happened in the car world, and I fully expect it to be the standard in the world of motorcycles within five to ten years.

Stuart Hilborn holds an assembled throttle body rack for an inline-four motorcycle. This one is set up for mechanical fuel injection, and has the fuel distributor on the lower right of the assembly. The only difference between this and the EFI unit is the type of injectors and fuel distributor. Note the two rods holding the individual throttle bodies together, and the set screws keeping them in place. Throttle bodies courtesy of Hilborn

GETTING THERE FIRST

Racing has always driven the breed in the world of motor vehicles. And nowhere is this more true than with motorcycles. From their earliest days as commercially available transportation, motorcycle manufacturers have been on dirt circle tracks and salt flats, trying to best each other for advertising and bragging rights. Companies like Indian and Harley-Davidson used to compete for top honors in the highest levels of racing. And today, Japanese and European manufacturers vie for top honors in the fastest and most technologically advanced racing series in the world. Harley-Davidson keeps up the pace on dirt tracks, just as they did nearly a century ago.

Racing often means special components and sometimes re-engineering almost all of the motorcycle. With emissions control being a non-factor and fuel economy often being unimportant, many modifications and even outright component and system replacements have become the norm. This is increasingly true with fuel injection. Manufacturers are under regulatory pressure to make their emissions-related systems more and more resistant to tampering by tuners and customers. As a result, very few systems are easy to tune or modify by a tuner or end user without replacing or modifying at least some part of today's engine management systems.

History

As I mentioned in the chapter on history, early EFI systems were often crude and were more able to ensure good power over a wide range of conditions than reduce emissions. Since they were fairly crude to begin with, it was relatively easy to modify them for the better in racing usage. Things like stretching the spring in flapper-type VAF sensors or replacing the CTS with a fixed resistor were common performance modifications on early motorcycle EFI systems. Very little power was lost in areas that were already rich, and power could often be increased quite nicely by richening areas that were marginal on race-modified bikes.

But EFI systems quickly became too complicated, with too many interrelated sensor values, for such crude fixes to improve power without drastically affecting rideability. Interestingly enough, this period corresponds quite well to the waning use of motorcycle fuel injection between the mid-1980s and the mid-1990s. Most models using EFI during that time were large-displacement touring bikes, if it was used at all. EFI's use on more performance-oriented machines was limited to large-displacement V-twin sportbikes (notably those from Ducati).

Modern Methods, Modern Solutions

When EFI was "reborn" in the motorcycle world in the mid-1990s, much had been learned from automotive use. The newer systems were typically more complex, and their operation usually represented a more delicate balance between complex (and often competing) goals. Finding good power, smooth drivability, good fuel economy, and still passing emissions certification was a vast challenge. As the designs of these systems became more complex, with more integrated priorities, they became harder and harder to modify for the racer. In systems that could not be completely reprogrammed (either through replacing the EPROM or flashing), one had to accept the compromises built into the system and work around them. The introduction of replacement ECUs

in the very late 1990s heralded the motorcycle racing world of the future. Soon, it may be the only way to get good enough results on a dedicated racing bike to get those all-important race wins.

DIFFERENT GOALS, DIFFERENT SOLUTIONS

Racing is a highly specialized field, and its challenges often create unique engineering solutions. One has only to look at a modern Formula One or World Rally car to see all kinds of exotic materials and innovative techniques for shaving that extra tenth of a second off lap times. The same principles that apply to exotic, cutting-edge racing cars also apply to racing motorcycles, and the differences between the best bikes in different racing categories are far more vast than those between the smallest dirtbike and the fastest of road-racing motorcycles. Let's take a quick look at some of the various motorcycles racing categories, and how creative strategies and aftermarket solutions are used together to achieve results.

Land Speed Record and Drag Bikes

These two classes have more in common than some might think. A land speed record attempt, from the perspectives of the engine and the fuel management system, is simply a very, very long drag race. These bikes are run at or near full throttle nearly all the time. This makes it simple to handle fueling. There is only a single row on the load/speed table to be concerned with (full throttle), and there is little need to worry about delta alpha (changes in throttle position). Essentially, the drag racer has eliminated two of the biggest variables handled by EFI today.

Mechanical fuel injection has long been used on such machines. Fuel injection in general is much easier to set up for such bikes and the wide range between idle and top-speed power. Carburetors have the same problem on such bikes as they do on big V-twin sportbikes; they have difficulty delivering consistent idle without restricting full-throttle high-rpm airflow. FI is also much easier to set up for turbocharging and nitrous oxide injection, two common additions on both drag and land-speed-record bikes.

With the popularity of EFI driving the cost down, and the ease with which it can be tuned when compared to mechanical FI (which usually requires specially shaped, precision-ground cams in the fuel distributor to provide proper fuel delivery over a range of alpha, plus a mechanically driven fuel pump that is driven off the engine), people have been coming over to EFI for these machines. One of the most common solutions is to replace any stock fuel delivery hardware with either an adapted automotive system or a specialty aftermarket system (like the one from Hilborn mentioned in the previous chapter). The main goal here is to get injectors and a fuel pump in place that can deliver enough fuel for highly modified engines under full load at redline. Since only a small part of the total operating range of the engine is ever encountered, tuning is greatly simplified. Smooth/low-emissions cruise, emissions-controlled idle, and delta alpha are all ignored, as they are never encountered. This means that it is often fairly simple to adapt a system from an automobile, since the only things that really matter are the last row of the load/speed table (where load = 100%) and making the machine idle smoothly. Use of automotive-style manifolds can sometimes increase the maximum airflow into the intake ports, and custom manifolds are increasingly common on turbocharged applications in particular.

If a turbocharger is added to an existing motor, the whole game changes. As was mentioned in the history chapter, EFI is well-suited to turbocharging. This is because you can separate out almost any variable, measure almost any parameter, and design your tuning around the ones that are important. Adding a turbocharger changes the IAP in a way that does not necessarily correspond to engine speed or load, so it is extremely important when tuning a turbocharged engine to be able to make best power without having reliability issues. In this, EFI excels. In addition, things like water injection, air shifting, and nitrous triggering can be integrated with control of fueling. This will allow best use of the add-ons without risking costly engine damage.

EFI's ability to separate out individual sensor parameters and use them differently under different operating conditions allows for the kind of complex control that is often needed to make power reliably on multiple interactive power-generating and detonation-control systems. Some systems even have knock sensor that can take multi-stage action when detonation is detected, keeping an expensive engine from self-destructing before the finish line. In addition, wastegate control is offered on some systems, notably those from MoTeC. There is no need to keep the turbo spooled up at part load or closed throttle, as there is on World Rally cars. All we really need is to control maximum boost to avoid detonation with the fuel and combustion chamber shape we are using. This makes it relatively simple for us to do some testing and to determine whether electronic wastegate control would be helpful for our application.

Increasingly, machines that come with fuel injection as stock are being used for drag racing and land speed records. In some cases, the rules of the class disallow replacing the ECU, and sometimes even the injectors. Other solutions are then needed. These range from oversized injectors to adding a Power Commander or other programmable enrichment device. One big trick that is not often discussed is changing the pressure regulator and increasing the output of the stock fuel pump. Increasing the pressure in the fuel line has a similar effect to installing larger injectors and is a great trick to have up your sleeve if there is a requirement to retain all the stock EFI hardware. By raising the voltage to the fuel pump, it is possible to increase line pressure. This trick also has use when fitting larger injectors, since there must be sufficient flow rate from the pump to feed larger injectors and/or a greater fuel demand that might be used on a performance drag race application. RC Engineering, among others, offers testing of fuel pumps to determine flow rate and line pressure available from a pump based on voltage applied to that pump. Such testing will let you know in advance whether your pump will make the grade on your drag bike and allow you to tailor your pump voltage and pressure regulator to meet your needs. One of the important things about specialized applications is to eliminate as many variables as possible, so that you can focus on particular areas for more power or to solve issues and problems. Looking closely at things like the behavior of your injectors and fuel pump can be instrumental in getting the most from your machine with the least confusion and time investment on your part.

Road Racing

The other major venue where EFI has made its mark is road racing. Today's four-stroke GP bikes are all fuel-injected, and other classes are increasingly ending up with injected bikes being the only ones on the starting grid. Due to its great flexibility, ability to separate out different operating conditions and tune for each, and the speed at which such systems can be set up and tuned, there is very little to lose in switching to EFI. In fact, almost all the production bikes that are eligible for Superstock-class racing now come with EFI. Manufacturers realize that homologation with a good system in place will confer great advantages to race teams that are limited to using stock parts in their fuel delivery system.

Stock and Stock Replacement ECUs

An excellent example of a tunable stock ECU is the Denso system used on most Suzuki sportbikes. It has an inbuilt capacity for tuning to compensate for most aftermarket exhausts and air filters; this allows tuning for Supersport applications where intake and engine modifications are prohibited. By eliminating the need for an external add-on tuning box, there are many savings: weight, reduction of possible failure points (no extra connections on the wiring harness, less hardware and software to cause surprise problems when it really counts), and keeping all changes within the design of the stock system (remember what I said earlier about the add-on boxes, and how they sometimes would fight against the stock system's other priorities?).

Honda offers race boxes for the RC51 and other raceable sporting machines that replace the stock ECU. Honda's stock ECUs cannot be trimmed, but the replacement race ECUs have roughly the same internal trim capacity as the stock Denso units on Suzukis. Honda sells this as a kit with a lightweight wiring harness (although the stock harness can be adapted to work with the race ECU) and a programmer unit that is very similar in operation to the famed "Yosh box" for EFI Suzukis. As of this writing, Honda does not appear to offer a race ECU that can be tuned to the same degree as the Suzuki/Denso unit (when tuned with the TEKA SFI remapper tool).

Systems like the race-based Marelli systems used by Ducati and others also allow trackside fine-tuning of maps, and some even allow this to be saved for future use. Flashable maps, as found in the SAGEM ECUs, allow even more trackside tuning, at the expense of more knowledge and experience on the part of the tuner. The more you can adjust something, the worse you can make it when making mistakes.

Aftermarket Solutions

In some cases, unlimited modifications or custom construction is allowed. This is particularly true with GP bikes. Where performance, flexibility, and ease of use are essential (and this is especially true when major facets of your engine design can change in the course of a season), high-end systems with data-logging and excellent software become the choice of the day. And few offer better performance and usability than MoTeC. They've been serving the top levels of racing around the world for many years, and the world of motorcycle road racing is no different.

By allowing very specialized control of each cylinder, multiple injectors per cylinder, and almost any cylinder configuration you can imagine, MoTeC's offerings provide the kind of flexibility that allows mechanical designers to run wild, building engines with no holds barred. There is no restriction required to suit the EFI system already in use; the ECU can be easily and quickly reprogrammed to handle almost any change in design. Further, there's no need to retrain the tuning staff and engineers for a new system; problems and issues are greatly reduced, and there is much less risk of having a problem on race day that cannot be solved quickly and easily. The same hardware can be used on dozens of possible engine designs, helping keep costs down. And the staff of MoTeC offers

RACING

142

support in case the team hits a snag and needs quick answers. The technology of designing engines, intakes, and other components for no-holds-barred racing is light-years away from that found in production motorcycles. But the same basic priorities are in play with tuning them, even though they are weighted quite differently.

WHAT IS THE GOAL OF TUNING?

As noted earlier by Marc Salvisberg of Factory Pro Tuning, there are a wide variety of possible throttle response "feels" that one can develop with extremely minor alterations of fueling and ignition mapping. With extremely powerful bikes used in Formula Xtreme or AMA Superbike racing, for instance, it is often necessary to detune the performance of the bike in some areas to make it more controllable, especially on tight courses. Believe it or not, it is often possible to get around the track faster if there is less peak power, but the available power delivery is more controllable by the rider. Tunability (whether provided by add-on boxes, capabilities in the stock ECU, or replacement with an aftermarket ECU) is of tantamount importance when tuning a racing bike. If the rider can't handle the power delivery, nothing else matters; they will be slow around the track. Sometimes making the bike feel comfortable to the rider is the most important part of race tuning. If you need to make choices for race tuning purposes, remember that raw power is not all that is needed to win races. People don't race on the dyno; keeping your focus on getting your rider around the track faster is what it is all about. Remembering this will help you choose the right tools for the job and stay within the regulations for your class. It can be very educational to walk around the paddock and see what others are doing. Thinking about the choices they are making can help you further focus your own priorities and get you where you want to be: yourself or your rider on the box at the end of the day.

THE WHOLE PACKAGE

Racing is a complicated sport. There are thick rulebooks for each class that must be adhered to. At the same time, you are trying to find a way to gain an advantage without breaking the rules. Each type of racing has different needs, and each rider has a different mindset and approach. When choosing tools and hardware, as with anything else, it pays to be solidly oriented with the interaction of needs and limitations between rider, budget, time frame, and rulebook. Fortunately, EFI offers advantages in nearly any form of racing, although it does so very differently in different venues. Know your needs, research your products, and you can gain advantages that will help you and your team throughout the season, and in years to come.

Current EFI systems are designed to provide for the needs specified by the manufacturer (and sometimes by the government) at the lowest price possible, both in terms of development and dealer maintenance and repair. However, as technology improves, prices drop, and legislation marches ever forward, some of the advantages of unused technologies will become cost-effective for manufacturers. Some things done routinely in today's automobiles are yet to be pioneered in the world of motorcycles. Listed below are some of the more promising candidates for increasing future incorporation into computerized fuel injection and engine management for motorcycles.

ACOUSTIC KNOCK SENSING

This is the simplest form of knock sensing and is in common usage on cars today. Using a microphone attached to the engine block, the raw signal is heavily filtered to leave only frequencies that are characteristic of detonation (usually 5–8 kHz). This signal is then used to generate a "go/no-go" signal—a simple on-off signal to the ECU that signals that detonation is or is not occurring. The ECU is then programmed to retard ignition timing in increments until the detonation stops.

While ion-sensing is specific to the cylinder in which it is being measured, both pressure-sensing and acoustic forms of knock sensing tend to be less specific. Systems have been created that allow sensing of individual cylinders, but often pressure-sensing and acoustic types are used to control ignition timing across the board, as this not only reduces the required number of sensors, but the amount of necessary processing power as well.

Recent developments in integrated circuitry manufacturing have allowed the production of affordable high-speed standalone proces-

Motorcycles like Harley's new V-Rod show us the shape of things to come, with its sophisticated Delphi EFI system. Interconnected with a number of other electronic control systems on the motorcycle, it boasts a simple form of ion sensing to help prevent misfire and detonation. Future EFI systems will have even more advanced features, allowing us to make more power more reliably with fewer emissions than ever before. Motorcycle courtesy of San Diego Harley-Davidson

Wideband oxygen sensors allow much more useful data to be gathered than today's narrow-band units, allowing feedback to the ECU under a much wider variety of running conditions. Bosch GmbH

sors (ASICs) for use with acoustic and piezoelectric knock sensors, which allow more sensitive measurement of the start of knocking, and can also time the sound transmission and determine which cylinder is knocking. Individual cylinders can then be adjusted for optimal timing without knock. Note that this is a less expensive alternative to ion sensing, but without the other advantages. It is, however, much more likely to be widely available on production motorcycles over the next decade.

The older, lower-cost acoustic sensing designs are a good choice for low-cost applications and will probably be found in the nearer future on entry-level or economy motorcycles. Motorcycles that are more performance-oriented are already using individually triggered stick coils and will likely see the high-performance acoustic or piezoelectric knock sensing first, with an eventual move to ion sensing for its larger variety of gathered data. However, don't expect to see full ion sensing on most production motorcycles for quite some time.

CLOSED-LOOP INJECTION

While we have some bikes that are currently using a limited closed-loop system (to reduce emissions during part-throttle cruise), there is much room for expansion. Current OEM closed-loop systems are limited to usage for adjusting mixture to the narrow range that allows operation of a catalytic converter. This narrow range provides very poor power and slightly reduced fuel economy and can only be used during cruise conditions.

The possibility exists of using a wideband oxygen sensor (WBO_2) to act as a feedback loop, using the data from the sensor to trim the ECU and help it maintain fueling that was as close to ideal as possible under a much wider variety of conditions. WBO_2 sensors are very expensive, wear out quickly, and often are in short supply at present. Since residual oxygen at best power settings roughly follows the inverse of the torque curve (an engine makes its best possible power with more complete combustion when near its torque peak), such feedback is of limited use in maintaining

More and more of today's motorcycle ECUs are based on automotive designs, like this *Magneti Marelli* unit for on a *Ducati 998*. Compact and lightweight, they will also be more and more likely to offer sophisticated I/O features typically found only on automobiles today. ECU courtesy of GP Motorcycles

best power (i.e., you still need some kind of VE table to trim for best power based on feedback from a WBO_2 sensor). It is, however, of more utility in producing improvements in overall fuel efficiency. The biggest problem is that exhaust gases do not proceed smoothly and at a constant speed down the exhaust tract. What this means is that the signal has to be filtered a great deal to extract information that can be of real use to an ECU. The time delay involved in the actual motion of the gases, the stabilization of the exhaust mixture, and the filtering involved (which takes time and also removes some useful data on occasion) means that this would be a very slow method of providing the ECU with direct fueling feedback. Ultimately, that tends to consign such a design to use in situations where torque demands have a low delta, usually meaning steady-state running, or cruise.

WBO_2 sensors require support electronics to give a useful output signal, requiring increased cost and complexity above and beyond their basic manufacturing costs. In current use, there is also no need for the signal range of a WBO_2 sensor. It is likely that we will see increasing use of WBO_2 sensors as the price of manufacture drops, and as requirements for emissions data increases (in the current crop of passenger cars, for instance, some run in a lean-burn mode for emissions and economy, which requires a type of WBO_2 sensing for accurate cruise fueling; also, emissions regulations require passenger vehicles to sense when the

main O_2 sensor or catalyst is faulty, thus also requiring a WBO_2 sensor after the cat to check for problems). If emissions regulations tighten sufficiently, we may see similar arrangements appearing on motorcycles.

EMISSIONS CONTROL

Since the driving factor that developed EFI in the first place was emissions regulation for automobiles, and the technology we are using was largely taken straight from the automotive world, we shouldn't be surprised to see more emissions laws for motorcycles in the future, and more automotive components and ideas to show up on motorcycles as well.

For instance, cars now have a purge valve to control when and how much of the fuel vapors from the charcoal canister are burned by the engine, which helps to prevent an over-rich mixture. It is controlled by the ECU so that the vapors can be burned while in closed-loop mode where it will not heavily affect drivability and emissions can be controlled. Most motorcycles do not have this implemented yet, but as emissions requirements for motorcycles continue to increase, it will likely increase in popularity.

Another long-time automotive emissions control feature not seen on motorcycles is EGR (exhaust gas recirculation). EGR has two functions: It reduces NO_x emissions by slowing the combustion event, which cools the combustion gases, and it reduces pumping losses (power from the engine that is used up by pulling against the vacuum of a closed throttle at cruise), thus producing better economy. This is another useful cruise strategy, and one that may well find its way into motorcycles eventually.

Newer and more complex strategies, like GDI (gasoline direct injection), are on the horizon as well.

GASOLINE DIRECT INJECTION

Similar in concept to the two-stroke GDI system used by the Orbital-designed Aprilia system, a four-stroke system would offer even more advantages. Greatly reduced fuel consumption and emissions without a loss of power are certainly inviting goals, especially with tightening emissions regulations, and the limited effectiveness of catalytic converters over the operating range of most four-stroke engines. GDI offers the potential of reducing fuel consumption between 10 and 25% over the best current EFI designs, in addition to decreasing emissions in kind.

One current automotive system implemented by Bosch has six distinct operating configurations. Most of these are some combination of conventional (homogeneous) mixture and stratified-charge (as is used in the Aprilia two-stroke system). By having a variety of intermediate operating modes, the ECU can control transitions between operating modes very smoothly, as well as to perform special emissions control functions (such as purging excess sulphur from the NO_x storage catalyst). Since one mode gives best power, one gives best emissions, and one gives best fuel consumption, it is necessary to have a very complex ECU with many open- and closed-loop subsystems to allow determination of which operating mode would be best under given conditions.

In addition, to handle pollutants from a range of different operating conditions, the system requires two different kinds of catalytic converters, three different exhaust sensors (a standard and a wideband O_2 sensor plus an EGT [exhaust gas temperature] sensor), and a complex control system to process the inputs from those sensors and provide feedback to the main control systems. The system is actually complex enough, and has enough sensor data, to diagnose defective catalysts without external testing or measurements! The requirement for special modes to accommodate the needs of the catalysts, other emissions control elements, the variation in fuel pressure, and to drive the throttle and charge motion valve (manifold diverter) controls (it has a drive-by-wire throttle, necessitated by the stratified-charge operating mode) necessitates tremendous complexity in hardware and software design, and a tremendous amount of processing power. In addition, it is completely intolerant to even minor changes in combustion chamber and intake port design. The need for dual catalysts and multiple sensors, as well as the tremendous complexity of the software, make changes to exhaust and fueling nearly impossible, even in the aftermarket. Any such changes would inevitably make power, efficiency and emissions all worse.

Such a full-scale GDI system is still currently under technical development, and it is not a fully mature technology. In addition, the most advanced current GDI systems for four-stroke operation involve a high number of extra components, much higher fuel pressure, and approximately 4,000 times as much processing power as conventional port injection systems. The components necessary to drive the super-fast-response high-pressure injectors are also much more fragile than those used to drive port injectors, so the ECUs for sophisticated GDI systems tend to be more fragile and do not hold up as well to impacts or vibration. Thus, unless there are great leaps forward in fuel economy and emissions

legislation for motorcycles, the increased weight, complexity, cost and safety issues preclude its use in the motorcycle world in anything but simpler forms.

IMPROVED I/O

Most of the current-generation production motorcycle ECUs have little or no I/O capability. With the exception of the SAGEM, Delphi, and Bosch ECUs, the only I/O capabilities on current production bikes are storage and communication of trouble codes and limited remapping capabilities (Suzuki/Mitsubishi, and a number of race-only replacement boxes).

Cars currently have the OBD II system (on-board diagnostics), which is a standard designed for ensuring the proper operation of emissions control devices, and which allows sensors and trouble codes to be read in real time (as well as stored trouble codes) by using a scan tool or software. In addition, some manufacturers allow reading of sensors whose data are not required by the standard, as well as some adjustment of operating parameters (on certain models). It uses a universal connector and data protocol, with different software expressions by manufacturer. The end result is that a single box can be used to check sensors and wiring and read diagnostic codes for any currently available passenger automobile (with extra detail and utility from using the proper manufacturer-specific software), all by using just one diagnostic tool.

OBD II also has provisions that require that any emissions-related failure (such as misfire, a bad catalyst or O_2 sensor, or similar problem) be detected by the ECU and communicated via trouble codes. As emissions regulations for motorcycles tighten and the complexity of emissions control solutions increases, expect to see some sort of similar requirement in the future, regardless of the standard format at the time. The EPA is currently discussing plans to add motorcycles to the upcoming OBD III standard.

Because the OBD standards require all vehicles listed in them to conform to a particular communication protocol and have certain standardized commands and responses, it has become possible to create universal scan tools for automobiles. These tools can give basic diagnostic information about all OBD-compliant vehicles; they can also be loaded with specific data for a given manufacturer, which allows complete listings of trouble codes, and often access to extra stored data. In some cases, mapping modifications can even be uploaded to the ECU by using such devices.

Today, only Triumph uses the OBD II protocol in motorcycles. But when motorcycles are added to the OBD requirement, you will see all fuel-injected motorcycles popping up with such abilities.

Now that cellular telephones have fast, powerful processors, it is actually possible to write scan tool software that will run on a phone, rather than having to buy a scan tool! In the future, this may allow diagnosis of your engine management system on the side of the road (or from a mechanic's bench) simply by connecting the ECU to a cell phone with the proper diagnostic software loaded. Data can then be read from the ECU and sent back to a service center for analysis and diagnosis of the problem.

Bosch has also developed the CAN (Controller Area Network) system to allow a high-speed serial connection between multiple controllers, as well as sensors and even data logging devices. This has evolved into a set of standards, and an expanded version (CAN 2.0B) specifically designed for automotive systems. CAN allows asynchronous (not requiring a master clock to get all the components on the same page) data transmission between almost any sort of controller or smart sensor at up to 1 megabit

ABS sensors (as shown on this BMW police model's front wheel) have been used extensively on cars for integrated traction control. In the future, this may become an option on motorcycles as well.

per second. It is currently being used to share data and information between controllers in a variety of highly computerized passenger cars, where using a single processor for multiple functions is not practical. For instance, it can share sensor data and command information between ignition control, fuel injection, and ABS systems for dynamic skid control.

Some of the current generation of high-power embedded processors (which are the microcontroller core of most fuel injection systems) include a pair of CAN 2.0B controllers, each running on a separate data bus. This assists in allowing multiple processors to handle simultaneous separate tasks on a vehicle, as well as offering the possibility of having a separate CAN channel that could be used to connect to a personal computer or diagnostic device and allow the sharing of real-time running data. It can also allow the possibility of building a separate box for data-logging that you could simply plug into the CAN bus with a connector and which would save data use for later analysis (excellent for racing, diagnostics, and development work). Since the CAN protocol sends out tagged data and any CAN terminal can listen in and decide if the data is of interest, it is trivial to make data-logging applications, assuming that the relevant data is being sent out on a CAN channel.

CAN has already been specified as the core of the coming OBD III standard. The future will likely bring faster standards of universal data interchange for devices in motor vehicles.

ION SENSING

Ion sensing is a very useful method of gathering feedback data about what's going on inside the combustion chamber. Since differences in combustion pressure and temperature change the chemical reactions during a combustion cycle, those differences can be inferred and analyzed by gathering data using the spark plug as a sensor. When a spark plug is not being used to develop spark, a low-voltage sensing current is applied through the electrodes. This signal varies based on the content and density of the gases in the combustion chamber, as well as the condition of the spark plugs—a sufficiently advanced ion sensing system can tell you when they need replacing! Computing power is becoming available (and soon, affordable) to allow large amounts of this data to be analyzed in real time and used for feedback on the following fronts:

1) Closed-Loop Spark Timing. It has been found that the best peak combustion pressure on a given engine will always be within a range of a few crank degrees, regardless of engine rpm or throttle position. That makes it relatively easy to use ion-sensing data to continually optimize spark timing. By filtering out data about the timing of the peak pressure pulse (PPP), this can be compared to actual crank rotation, and spark can be adjusted by the spark control section (which is often a separate processor or an ASIC) so that the PPP moves toward the ideal point. It can even be used to compensate for changes in humidity (where increased humidity slows down combustion speed, requiring more spark advance). This has never before been possible!

Aside from the obvious increases in power and efficiency in the motor from using such a system, there is also less variation in power output between engine cycles when the PPP is kept close to optimal. This means improved smoothness of engine output, which not only means longer component and engine life, but better drivability and smoother throttle response as well. And since a system like this can use all available spark plugs as sensors, it can adjust individual cylinders separately for best power (or best emissions, or a compromise between the two), given sufficient processor speed. A full closed-loop ignition system requires a fairly high amount of computing power (usually a very fast dedicated processor), and is not considered cost-effective or feasible on production vehicles at this time. Some racing ECUs use this technology to a limited degree, and at least one do-it-yourself ECU is being developed that will allow closed-loop spark timing.

2) Engine Phase Sensing. While a cam sensor signal is necessary for initial starting of an engine, ion sensing is a potential method for redundancy in case of cam sensor failure. Since a cam position signal informs the ECU of which cylinder is in what phase (the crankshaft rotates twice for each cylinder's combustion event, making it useless for determining phase), running sequential spark or ignition requires some kind of cam/engine phase sensing. By keeping track of which cylinder has a combustion event through ion sensing, it is possible to generate a signal that indicates engine phase. This can be used to keep an engine running properly in the event of a cam sensor failure, or could even be used to replace the cam sensor entirely (by using batch-fire injection and waste-fire ignition during starting, to the point in time where the ion-sensing processor has enough information to generate an engine phase signal).

3) Detonation Control. With emissions regulations requiring leaner and leaner mixtures (especially where catalytic converters are mandated), spark advance becomes more and more limited by detonation. Higher compression engines often increase the risk of detonation, especially when run on lower-octane fuels. These changes often mean a requirement to retard ignition timing when poor quality fuel or high ambient temperatures are encountered. Ion sensing can be used to retard timing if using an open-loop spark map when necessary to prevent detonation. Obviously, this would be incorporated with other ignition functions in the implementation of full closed-loop spark control, but detonation control alone will require a great deal less processing power than full closed-loop control. This means it is cheaper and easier to implement. Some Harley-Davidson and BMW motorcycles, and many cars, take advantage of this capability today.

4) Misfire/Lean Mixture Control. Since catalytic converters require fairly lean mixtures, and cruise in general is a good place to save on fuel, we are seeing leaner and leaner cruise mixtures. However, if you end up with too lean a mixture, there will be a misfire—a lack of a combustion event, leaving extra fuel and air in the exhaust. This can then burn in the exhaust, especially in a hot catalyst, damaging the catalyst or O_2 sensor. In addition, there are obvious reductions in power and fuel economy, not to mention drivability, associated with lean misfire.

Since ion sensing can easily detect misfire, it can be used to send a signal to the main ECU informing it that the mixture has been leaned too far and to compensate; thus it can allow an ECU to run right at the edge of lean misfire without a loss of economy, or damage to the catalytic converter. By itself, this would be a relatively low computing power addition, and it is used on a number of production cars today (mainly to allow low emissions without damage to the vehicle or drivability problems). It is one of the primary advantages of ion sensing, from the standpoint of using technology to meet emissions regulations (the OBD II specifies a method for recording and, ideally, preventing misfires; prior to ion sensing, a fairly crude system of reading changes in crank angle speed and analyzing it with a high-speed dedicated chip has been used; it results in a lot of false misfire detections, which can then result in a lot of "Check Engine" lights with no actual fault in the injection or ignition system). Harley-Davidson has already incorporated this development on its Delphi ECU-equipped models.

PRESSURE KNOCK SENSING

This is a more direct but less data-rich method of knock measurement than what you can obtain by using ion sensing. Pressure sensing uses a piezoelectric device (the principles of which were discussed in the chapter on sensor design—the very thin, round speakers found in many small electronic devices operate under the piezoelectric principle) pinched between a cylinder head bolt and the cylinder head, or a spark plug and the cylinder head. These are much smaller and lighter than current piezoelectric knock sensors and tend to be even more sensitive to knock.

Such devices can be used to measure intensity and timing of the peak pressure pulse (PPP) in a similar manner to ion sensing, or it can be mounted elsewhere and used in the same manner as acoustic sensing (this is the less-favored method). It is limited in scope when compared to ion sensing in that it cannot determine combustion temperature, but it is excellent at determining overall burn times. It is substantially less expensive to implement than ion sensing and can be used for detonation sensing, less-precise closed-loop ignition timing, and in some cases, lean mixture control and engine phase sensing. It is more sensible and less complicated to use it in situations where only detonation

sensing is desired. Multiplexing allows a single dedicated processor setup to evaluate sensors on multiple cylinders (as opposed to having a separate processor for each cylinder), but this requires increased processing speed (since the amount of time available for processing gets divided by the number of sensors when multiplexed).

SMART SENSORS

Many cars are beginning to implement smart sensors; these are not just raw sensor components, but ones that also have support hardware onboard. An example is an aftermarket MAF sensor, which, instead of outputting a logarithmic voltage, processes the signal and outputs either a digital PWM signal (which is then read by the ECU via timing the length of the pulse), a linearly corrected analog voltage (so that a voltage reading is exactly proportional to changes in airflow), or even a CAN signal. Not only do such sensors make it far easier to design and implement an ECU (you don't have to write special code or build extra onboard hardware for a particular sensor's output characteristics), but eventually, there will be the ability to create an ECU that can plug into a CAN bus with little if any other wiring to the vehicle. The modularity would make it far easier to create and modify fuel injection and vehicle management systems, as well as reducing the size and weight of the wiring harness. However, CAN has a design that makes it so universal in its application that it would delay some time-critical sensor data; in addition, the cost of most sensors would go up several thousandfold if made smart using today's componentry. This means we will probably not see much implementation of smart sensors until well into the future. As the technology comes farther down in price, and new communication standards are developed, this concept will likely become a solid reality.

The biggest application might be in using smart components, like starter motors or alternators. Such applications are less time-sensitive, and can use a data bus for activating signals, or to change their operating mode depending on the anticipation of demand as signaled by an ECU. There are also many automotive sensors that use standard analog signals, but pre-process sensor data onboard to reduce the complexity of the ECU and aid in standardization.

TRACTION CONTROL

One of the main enemies of the motorcycle rider is loss of traction. Even worse would be losing it and then regaining it suddenly, which can result in a highside crash. With ABS being fitted to more and more motorcycles, it would be trivial to compare the signals between the two wheels and, say, retard ignition timing to reduce power smoothly when the ECU detects rear wheel spin. By gently reducing torque through retarding ignition timing, a traction control system would be able to prevent most highsides, and many lowsides. Of course, one would program the system to ignore situations where the front wheel was not turning, to allow dyno runs, wheelies, and smoky burnouts.

VARIABLE VALVE TIMING

Several different forms of variable valve timing are in use on cars today, and it has been tried (with limited success) on motorcycles as well. The principle is in changing either cam overlap or actual lobe profile to help optimize VE for both low-speed and high-speed engine operation, as well as improving the thermal efficiency of the engine (how much potential heat energy from the fuel gets turned into useful work).

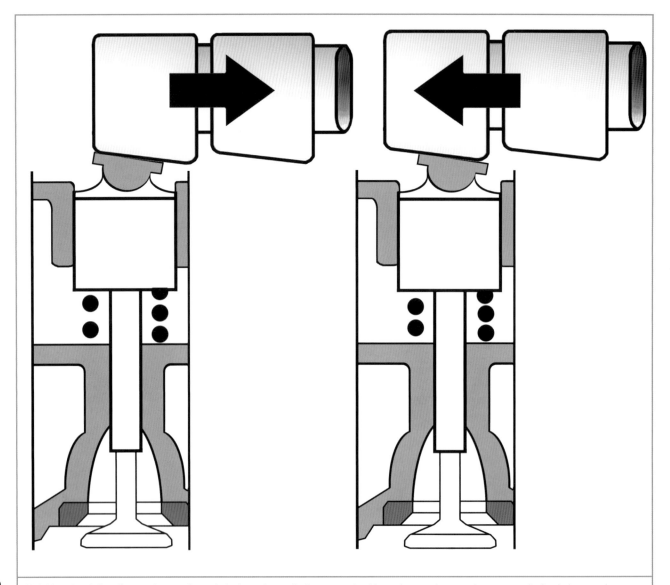

Variable valve timing allows valve opening and closing to be much closer to optimal for a given engine speed over an engine's whole operating range. The system shown here is similar to the Bosch Valvetronic system, in that it allows almost infinitely variable and progressive alterations of intake and exhaust valve timing. Maya Culbertson

The simplest systems use increases in oil pressure based on engine rpm to either open a second intake valve or change cam lobe or lifter profile. These systems are mechanically the simplest, and have two discrete settings. This leads to a somewhat abrupt change in engine behavior at the switchover engine speed. It also tends to result in increased engine height and extra difficulty in setting valve clearances, and thus has limited use in the motorcycle world.

More complex systems use electrohydraulic or electropneumatic actuators controlled by a microprocessor. The advantage here is that they can change valve lift, timing, and duration by a combination of altering cam advance and changing lifter or cam lobe height. The disadvantages here are extra weight, height of the engine, and the requirement for second microcontroller to run the VVT hardware. BMW's Valvetronic system, developed by Bosch (which has infinitely variable control of both the intake and exhaust cams), actually has as much processing power in its controller alone as some of the highest-performance racing ECUs for Formula 1 automobile use.

VVT's disadvantages in weight, size, and cost outweigh any advantages in most motorcycles on which it would be terribly useful; and the more useful the system is, the heavier, more complicated, larger, and more expensive it tends to be. So far it has been limited to being a technological showpiece on very small engines and sport-touring bikes. However, faster and cheaper dedicated processors, as well as shrinking actuators, will drop the cost and complexity of such systems and handle some of the space issues. Watch for it to appear first on larger bikes, like touring motorcycles, and then work its way in both directions on the performance and price spectrum as time goes on.

As an ECU's mapping strategy becomes more complicated, and tends toward integrating more and more priorities under a greater variety of operating conditions, it will become more difficult to adapt OEM systems to end-user goals, such as racing. In the automotive world, the obvious answer was replacement ECUs, and the situation is very much the same for motorcycles as well. Here we see the prototype of a MoTeC drop-in ECU replacement for a Suzuki GSX-1300R Hayabusa. Note the RS232 data connector at the top center. The two units on the upper left are Bosch igniter units for producing spark; the spark triggering hardware is attached to the bottom of the M4 ECU. System courtesy of MoTeC Systems USA

REPLACEMENT ECUS

As we have seen in the early chapters of the book, ECUs are designed and tuned to meet a wide variety of needs and desires under a wide range of operating conditions. Most of these adaptations are designed directly into the mapping strategy and how the approach to mapping changes under various operating conditions. This means that the final approach is rarely able to meet a different set of needs without replacing the ECU. In racing, for instance, we only care about maximum power and drivability (generally at half or more throttle), and emissions control is not a great concern for us. Further, we may wish to be able to push the motorcycle to the finish, even if it is overheating. Clearly, stock ECUs cannot be readily adapted to these desires, even with add-on boxes or remapping. The best solution is to replace the stock ECU with one that is either extremely flexible in its operation, or one designed specifically with an intended end use in mind.

This has already begun in the world of Harley-Davidson motorcycles, where installation of a bigger cam can render useless the stock ECUs measuring strategies for manifold pressure. Replacement ECUs that are alpha-n based are available from a number of manufacturers already. At the time of publication, Daytona Twin Tec offers the most comprehensive system in terms of ease of tuning and quick adaptability. (14-06)

MoTeC Systems USA has begun developing a drop-in ECU replacement for the Suzuki GSX-1300R Hayabusa and plans to expand availability to the rest of the Suzuki sportbike line as well.

Using their M4 ECU, the kit will come with all components and hardware and will be pre-calibrated to use the stock sensors on the bike. With the wide range of options and tunability that are available in all MoTeC ECUs, this should be a great lower-cost alternative to designing a MoTeC system from scratch for racers, while still allowing any engine modifications one could imagine. If you converted your Hayabusa to a turbocharged system with nitrous, a few extra sensors and some alterations in mapping and mapping strategy would allow you to continue using the same ECU and most of the old sensors. This would, of course, greatly lower the cost of adapting the engine management controls to future modifications.

CONCLUSION

The future holds many directions for controlling fuel and air in the motorcycle world. Many of those directions are dependent on cheap, plentiful computing power. A very large number of microcontrollers are currently available that offer a variety of functions and utility, at a variety of costs—and the list grows almost daily. Even the microcontrollers used in current OEM ECUs often have more available utility than is actually used. In the future, more and more of that capability will be used, in a variety of ways. The addition of custom, high-speed application-specific subprocessors (ASICs) is taking off as we speak. ECU chips will continue to become even more flexible, faster, and cheaper, allowing economical applications that are only available today through expensive aftermarket solutions.

APPENDIX A: ABBREVIATIONS AND ACRONYMS

1D:	One-Dimensional		**CO:**	Carbon Monoxide
2D:	Two-Dimensional		**CO$_2$:**	Carbon Dioxide
3D:	Three-Dimensional		**CPS:**	Crank Position Sensor
AAP:	Ambient (or Atmospheric) Air Pressure (sensor)		**CT:**	Coolant Temperature (sensor)
AAT:	Ambient (or Atmospheric) Air Temperature (sensor)		**CV:**	Constant Velocity (or Vacuum) (carburetor design)
ABS:	Antilock Braking System		**DC:**	Direct Current
AC:	Alternating Current		**DDFI:**	Dynamic Digital Fuel Injection (Buell)
A/D:	Analog to Digital		**D.F.I.:**	Digital Fuel Injection (Kawasaki)
ADL:	Advanced Data Logger		**DIP:**	Dual Inline Package
AFR:	Air/Fuel Ratio		**DIY:**	Do-It-Yourself
ALU:	Arithmetic Logic Unit		**DMA:**	Direct Memory Access
AMA:	American Motorcycle Association		**ECU:**	Electronic Control Unit
ASIC:	Application-Specific Integrated Circuit		**EEPROM:**	Electronically Erasable Programmable Read-Only Memory
BDC:	Bottom Dead Center		**EFI:**	Electronic Fuel Injection
bhp:	Brake Horsepower		**EGR:**	Exhaust Gas Recirculation
BSFC:	Brake Specific Fuel Consumption		**EGT:**	Exhaust Gas Temperature
C:	Celsius (temperature scale)		**EPA:**	Environmental Protection Agency
CAN:	Controller Area Network		**EPROM:**	Erasable Programmable Read-Only Memory
CART:	Championship Auto Racing Teams		**ET:**	Engine Temperature (sensor)
cc:	Cubic Centimeters		**EXUP:**	Exhaust Ultimate Power (Yamaha trademark)
CDI:	Capacitor Discharge Ignition		**F:**	Fahrenheit (temperature scale)
C.F.I.:	Computerized Fuel Injection (Honda)		**FI:**	Fuel Injection
CHT:	Cylinder Head Temperature (sensor)		**FN:**	Fuel Nanny
CNC:	Computerized Numeric Control (milling machine)		**GDI:**	Gasoline Direct Injection

GM:	General Motors
GP:	Grand Prix
HC:	Hydrocarbons
hr.:	Hour(s)
IAC:	Idle Air Control (solenoid)
IAT:	Intake (or Inlet) Air Temperature (sensor)
I/O:	Input/Output
KB:	KiloBytes (thousands of 8-bit bytes)
kHz:	KiloHertz (thousands of cycles per second)
lb:	Pound(s)
LC:	Inductor/Capacitor (circuit)
LCD:	Liquid Crystal Display
LED:	Light-Emitting Diode
LUT:	Look-Up Table
MAF:	Mass Air Flow (sensor)
MAP:	Manifold Air Pressure (sensor)
MB:	MegaBytes (millions of 8-bit bytes)
MCU:	Microcontroller Unit
MEGO:	My Eyes Glaze Over
MHz:	MegaHertz (millions of cycles per second)
min.:	Minute(s)
n:	Engine Speed
N_2:	Nitrogen (molecular)
NO_x:	Nitrogen Oxides
NTC:	Negative Temperature Coefficient
O_2:	Oxygen
OBD:	On-Board Diagnostics

OE:	Original Equipment (manufacturer)
OEM:	Original Equipment Manufacturer
P&H:	Peak and Hold (injector driver)
PC:	Power Commander, or Personal Computer
PGM-FI:	Programmed Fuel Injection (Honda)
Ph.D.:	Doctor of Philosophy
PLM:	Professional Lambda Meter
PPP:	Peak Pressure Pulse
PROM:	Programmable Read-Only Memory
PSI:	Pounds per Square Inch
PWM:	Pulse-Width Modulation
RAM:	Random Access Memory
RF:	Radio Frequency
RFI:	Radio Frequency Interference
ROM:	Read-Only Memory
rpm:	Revolutions Per Minute
sat.:	Saturated (injector driver)
TDC:	Top Dead Center
TIP:	Throttle Inlet Pressure (sensor)
TPS:	Throttle Position Sensor
v:	Volts or Voltage
VAF:	Volumetric Air Flow (sensor)
VE:	Volumetric Efficiency
VVT:	Variable Valve Timing
WBO_2:	Wideband O_2 (sensor)
WEGO:	Wideband Exhaust Gas Oxygen sensor

Alpha is a measure of throttle angle. Alpha-n mapping methodology uses a 2D table with engine speed on one axis and throttle position on the other. Delta alpha is a measure of the rate of change of throttle position and can be used for a variety of **ECU** functions, including adding extra fuel to compensate for the sudden addition of air by rapidly opening the throttle.

An **ASIC** is an application-specific integrated circuit. This is a custom-designed chip with one purpose only. By creating a custom, streamlined solution for the problems at hand, an ASIC can take a great deal of load off of the **MCU** and can even add new features not available from the MCU. They are essentially standard on almost all **ECU**s today.

Burn rate is the speed at which the mixture burns. It is affected by density and charge temperature, as well as **lambda**. Choosing the best time to make a spark requires us to know both the engine speed and the burn rate.

CAN is short for controller area network. It is a standardized data protocol that allows smart **sensors**, ECUs, and actuators to communicate with each other throughout the vehicles. MoTeC uses CAN on its new generation of **ECU**s, as well as on its data-logging dashboard. As technology marches forward, individual wires will likely be eliminated in favor of a "spinal cord" that links everything together in a single data bus.

A **catalytic converter** is a device that uses various metals bonded to a ceramic honeycomb. Now most catalytic converters are three-way; in such converters, the metals catalyze (or facilitate the combustion of) the unburned oxygen, nitrous oxides, unburned hydrocarbons, and carbon monoxide into carbon dioxide, water, and molecular nitrogen.

Compression ratio is the comparison of combustion chamber volume between **top dead center** and bottom dead center. A higher compression ratio will turn more of the available chemical energy into useful work, but raising the compression ratio will increase the temperature of the mixture, and can cause **detonation** unless higher octane fuel is used.

CV carburetors are found on most non-EFI motorcycles built since the late 1970s. They can be identified by their vacuum-operated slides. They work very well at delivering good power, smooth throttle response, and acceptable fuel economy.

Detonation occurs when ignition occurs too early, or the **burn rate** is too high. Pressure rises very quickly, which raises the pressure (and thus temperature) in the remaining mixture. When the temperature reaches a critical point, all the rest of the mixture burns at once. Detonation will burn holes in pistons, and can even damage engine bearings.

Dwell angle is the number of crank degrees during which current is allowed to flow through the primary side of an ignition coil. It is typically measured in degrees of crank angle because it needs to be added to the advance angle to calculate when this switching needs to take place. At higher engine speeds, a greater number of degrees of crank angle are covered in the same period of time. Since it takes the ignition coil the same amount of time to saturate regardless of engine speed, the dwell must increase as engine speed increases.

An **ECU** is the electronic control unit that correlates all the **sensor** data, retrieves values from various **maps**, and then specifies the length and timing of injection and spark events. A typical **ECU** will have an **MCU**, one or more types of memory, and drive electronics to activate injectors and ignition coils. Many have extra features and hardware that can be used for better control or improved integration.

EEPROM: See PROM.

EFI is electronic fuel injection. An electronic controller unit (**ECU**) reads information from **sensors** and uses **maps** to determine the length of time each **injector** should be open, as well as when to trigger spark for each cylinder.

Engine phase is an indication of which half of the combustion cycle the engine is actually on. Since it takes two full revolutions of the crankshaft to complete a full combustion cycle, some method is needed to determine which phase a given cylinder is in. Typically, a cam position **sensor** is used for this purpose (since cams turn at half the speed of the crankshaft).

EPROM: See PROM.

Fuel injectors are **solenoids** that meter fuel delivery to the engine. There are two main types: peak and hold injectors (which

can open and close very rapidly, but require heavy-duty circuitry that creates a fair amount of heat in the **ECU**) and saturated injectors (which are slower to open, but require none of the costly and heat-generating electronics needed for peak and hold injectors). They can be mounted at the top of the **velocity stacks** (commonly know as shower injection), or in the intake manifolds (known as port injection).
\

GDI is short for gasoline direct injection. Borrowing some technology from diesel engines, GDI allows fuel to be injected directly into the cylinder at high pressures. This gives an extended period of time for fuel delivery, and uses heat from the piston to vaporize fuel during the entire intake stroke, as well as during compression. This technology is starting to gain widespread use in the automotive world, and already has an entrant from the world of motorcycles.

Homogenous mixtures are thoroughly mixed. Achieving the most homogeneous mixture in a motorcycle engine is important due to the relatively narrow range of mixture compositions that will support combustion.

Idle air control is seen primarily on large-displacement two-cylinder motorcycles. It is sometimes the case at idle (especially when cold, or during cranking) that the engine cannot draw in enough air to sustain combustion and idle. In such cases, a **solenoid** is often used to bleed extra air into the intake manifold(s), thus allowing the machine to idle until it has warmed up.

Inertia is the property of matter that, once in motion, it will stay in motion unless a force is applied to it. Inertia can work for or against us, depending on the design of the intake and exhaust systems.

Ion sensing is a method for determining the quality and temperature of the burn in the combustion chamber. By applying a small voltage to the spark plug after the end of the spark event, it is possible to watch the changes in conductivity. Misfire, lean mixture, rich mixture, and even detonation can be detected by this method. However, it is costly to implement, and the more complex it is made (to allow measurement of more and more different conditions), the more expensive it becomes.

Lambda is another name for the **stoichiometric ratio**. When lambda = 1, there is exactly enough oxygen in the mixture to burn all the available fuel. Rich mixtures have a lambda greater than one; lean mixtures, less than one. For pump gasoline, lambda =1 is 14.7 parts air to one part gasoline by mass. Since fuel is much denser than air, it takes large volumes of air to burn small volumes of fuel.

Limp-home modes are used in the case of **sensor** failure. If there is a backup system that can be used (like alpha-n in the case of failure of the MAP **sensor**), the **ECU** will use it. In the event that there is no acceptable substitute, a default value from the PROM is substituted for **sensor** data. In many cases, this will allow the bike to run well enough to get yourself home, where you can better deal with the failure.

Maps are tables of values stored in the memory of the **ECU**. The **ECU** reads input from the **sensors**, sometimes doing some calculations with those values, and looks up the corresponding data from one cell of the map, to help determine what it should do, and when to do it.

An **MCU** is a microcontroller unit. It is a microprocessor with onboard flash **EEPROM**, and sometimes some other circuitry as well. It is the middle ground between a simple central processing unit and an entire **ECU**.

n is a representation of engine speed. It is the "n" in "**alpha**-n."

OBD, or on-board diagnostics. This is a standard that allows fault codes to be read out from storage, as well as viewing current ones. Most OBD-compliant vehicles will also allow observation of various **sensor** values while the vehicle is running. OBD was developed to ensure that there was a standardized way of detecting and recording emissions-related problems with the fuel injection system. Cars have been required to be OBD-compliant for almost a decade now; motorcycles will be as well in the near future. Now, only the SAGEM **ECU**s are capable of utilizing the OBD interface.

An **oxygen sensor** is a device that can measure the ratio of oxygen to other gases in the exhaust stream. There are a number of different types of oxygen **sensors**, each with its own potential uses. They are commonly used on vehicles with emissions controls to ensure a **stoichiometric** mixture that will allow a **catalytic converter** to completely combust unburned fuel and air as they leave the combustion chamber.

Peak pressure pulse is the point at which combustion chamber pressure is at its highest. Cylinder pressure increases from burning fuel, but decreases because the piston is going down, increasing combustion chamber volume. By working to ensure the PPP occurs at or near a given crank angle, we can avoid detonation while getting the best possible **thermal efficiency**.

Plasma is a fourth state of matter (the other three being liquid, solid, and gas), created when a great deal of electrical energy ionizes the matter between two electrodes, creating a superheated stream of ions. This is what we commonly refer to as a spark, and the formation and maintenance of that plasma stream are the key to understanding how ignition timing needs to change to get acceptable performance, good emissions, and even prevent engine damage.

The **plenum** is essentially an air reservoir that has enough volume to avoid huge changes in air pressure after an intake cycle on one cylinder. By keeping this reservoir of air, the engine can make more power more smoothly. Cars have their plenum between the **throttle body** and intake runners; motorcycles have theirs before the **throttle bodies**. This makes motorcycles much more responsive to changes in throttle opening.

PROM stands for programmable read-only memory. It can be programmed permanently with instructions and maps to be used by the **ECU**. Many older PROMs are socketed, meaning they can be removed and replaced with alternate units with different maps. Some can be erased with ultraviolet light and reused; these are EPROMs (erasable programmable read-only memory). Some can be erased via an electrical signal and reprogrammed in place; these are EEPROMs (electronically erasable read-only memory), otherwise known as flashable or flash memory.

Pumping losses are a measure of the energy needed to pull the piston down against the inertia of the intake charge, as well as the low pressure created by a partially or fully closed throttle plate.

PWM stands for pulse width modulation. It can be used in another form of peak and hold injector drive. By switching current on and off many times a second, it has the equivalent effect on the **fuel injector** as a regular peak and hold setup, but without the high heat generation. The downside is increased radio frequency noise.

RAM is random-access memory. It can be easily written to and read back, which makes it useful as a scratch pad. It can also be read much more quickly than any type of **PROM**, but it needs to have power applied to it constantly or it will lose its data.

Ram air is a system where the forward motion of the motorcycle forces air into the intake, and raises the pressure inside the airbox. This increases **volumetric efficiency** when compared against atmospheric pressure and can be used to generate more power when traveling at high speed.

Resonant frequency: See standing waves.

Saturation is the state of an inductor where the maximum possible magnetic field is being generated. Saturation plays a part in both **fuel injectors** and **ignition coils**, as they are both electromagnetically driven devices.

Scavenging is using low pressure in the exhaust, high pressure in the intake, or both to help remove the last of the exhaust gases from the combustion chamber in the moments before the exhaust valve closes.

Sensors are devices that change discrete measurements into electrical signals. Among the things they can measure are temperature, pressure, position, and speed.

A **servomotor** is an electric motor combined with a potentiometer as a feedback mechanism. It allows for precise positioning anywhere in its range of motion. Servomotors are used in Mikuni dual-butterfly throttle bodies, and can occasionally be found in idle air bypass solutions.

A **solenoid** is an electromagnet that creates mechanical motion. Some are used as switches, like a starter solenoid. **Fuel injectors** are solenoids as well, but instead of acting as an electrical switch, they open a pathway for fuel between the fuel rail and the intake manifold.

Speed density mapping uses engine speed and manifold air pressure to calculate how much air is being ingested by the engine. By recording ambient air temperature and pressure, the density of the air can be calculated; by measuring the velocity of the air via the manifold air pressure **sensor**, the **ECU** can calculate ingested air mass.

Standing waves are generated when the wavelength of the energy (for our purposes, a pulse of gases) is the same as the length of the tube in which the energy is traveling. The energy in each cycle of the wave is additive, building a more and more powerful pulse as it bounces back and forth within the tube. It is the key concept for tuning intake and exhaust systems. The frequency at which a given tube will generate standing waves is known as its **resonant frequency**.

Stoichiometric ratio: See lambda.

Thermal efficiency is the amount of useful work generated from burning fuel, as opposed to how much is wasted (through the exhaust, air, metal of the engine, and coolant). It is impossible to get 100% thermal efficiency, because it would cause the engine components to melt.

Throttle bodies are devices that can be restricted (or throttled) to decrease the amount of air entering the engine, thus modulating power development. Most motorcycles use a butterfly-style throttle, which is a round plate that rotates on a shaft inside of the throttle body itself. Some have multiple throttle plates to feed multiple cylinders, and others two throttles (one controlled by the **ECU**) per throttle body, but most only contain a single throttle plate.

Top dead center is the point where the piston is the closest to the top of the combustion chamber. It occurs twice per engine cycle; once just after ignition by spark, and once at the end of the exhaust stroke.

Vaporization is the change of a substance's state from liquid to gas via the addition of heat. Vaporization of gasoline helps promote a **homogeneous** mixture, leading to a more efficient burn.

Velocity stacks are extensions to the airbox side of the **throttle bodies**. They help the air to flow in a less turbulent fashion, as well as helping tune the length of the intake tract. Changing velocity stacks can increase power in one engine speed range, but this is often at the cost of lost power elsewhere in the rev range.

Volumetric efficiency is a measure of how much air mass is trapped within the combustion chamber when the intake valve closes. As an example, we'll use a cylinder that has an internal volume of 250cc. One hundred percent volumetric efficiency is achieved when the air trapped in the cylinder has the same mass as 250cc of air at atmospheric pressure and the current ambient temperature. If the cylinder traps less air, it is operating below 100% VE; if it traps more (as may be the case with intake tuning, ram air, or turbocharging), then it has greater than 100% VE.

INDEX

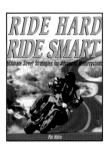